·BRITAIN AND INDIA

LIBRARY OF POLITICS AND SOCIETY

General Editor Michael Hurst

Church Embattled: Religious Controversy in Mid-Victorian England by M. A. Crowther

New French Imperialism 1880–1910: The Third Republic and Colonial Expansion by James J. Cooke

The New Internationalism: Allied Policy and the European Peace 1939–1945 by F. P. King

The Peelites and the Party System 1846–1852 by J. B. Conacher

Political Change and Continuity 1760–1885: A Buckinghamshire Study by Richard Davis

The Politics of Government Growth by William C. Lubenow

Unionists Divided: Arthur Balfour, Joseph Chamberlain and the Unionist Free Traders by Richard A. Rempel

BRITAIN AND INDIA: THE INTERACTION OF TWO PEOPLES

M. E. Chamberlain

DAVID & CHARLES : *Newton Abbot*
ARCHON BOOKS : *Hamden, Connecticut*
1974

This edition first published in 1974 in Great Britain by
David & Charles (Holdings) Limited, Newton Abbot, Devon,
and in the United States of America by Archon Books, Hamden,
Connecticut 06514

0 7153 6406 5 (Great Britain)
0–208–01423–3 (United States)

Set in eleven on thirteen point Imprint
and printed in Great Britain
by Latimer Trend & Company Ltd Plymouth

Contents

Acknowledgements

The author would like to thank the authorities of the India Office Library; the Public Record Office (Carnarvon and Cromer Papers); the Manuscript Room of the British Museum (Ripon Papers); National Library of Scotland (Minto Papers); Dr John Mason and his staff of Christ Church College, Oxford (Salisbury Papers, the property of the Salisbury Trustees) and the National Trust (Disraeli Papers at Hughenden Manor) for their many kindnesses in facilitating the use of their collections: and also the BBC for the quotation from Lord Shinwell's broadcast of 9 December 1971.

I would like to thank my colleague, Dr Richard Newman of the Economic History Department, University College, Swansea, and my former colleague, Dr John Davies, now of University College, Aberystwyth, for their kindness in reading and commenting on the manuscript; also Mrs Betty Nicholas and Miss Anne Jones for typing the manuscript and my father for indexing it.

Introduction

IF THE British empire is dead, it has an unquiet ghost. The problems which have arisen in the empire's successor states, in Nigeria, Rhodesia, Uganda, India, Pakistan and Bangla Desh, remain daily news. The empire and its dissolution is thus still a matter of politics as well as of history. Slogans about 'imperialism' have too often been a substitute for knowledge. Seventy years ago the fashionable dogma was a right-wing one. It was the duty and destiny of the advanced nations of Europe to govern and educate the backward nations of Asia and Africa. Today the fashionable dogma is more often a left-wing one. The relationship between Europe and the rest of the world was one of calculated selfishness and exploitation. Both are the slogans of political debate. The historical truth is always a great deal more complex.

Direct trading and cultural relations between Britain and India have existed for less than four centuries. For about half that period Britain ruled large parts of India. Tudor England, which established the first contacts with the India of the great Mogul emperor, Akbar, was different economically, politically, and intellectually from the late Victorian Britain which ruled so confidently (to outward appearances at least) over her huge Asian dependency. It would be absurd to suppose that one set of assumptions about the relationship can cover the whole period. Equally, neither 'Britain' nor 'India' was a single monolithic entity. Within Britain there were always antagonistic economic groups and rival political philosophies. India resembled the continent of Europe, rather than a single nation, in its diversity. A continual debate went on within Britain—often, admittedly, within a small circle of interested parties, and only very occasion-

7

ally involving the nation as a whole—as to whether the connection with India was good or not, and what form it should take. Indian reactions to British influence and pressures varied enormously and, at different times, Britain found herself with very different enemies and very different allies in India. To take a single example, in 1857 the most westernised Indians were generally on the British side against the so-called 'mutineers', but by the twentieth century it was the westernised Indians, Lord Salisbury's 'formidable array of seditious article writers', who were the strongest opponents of British rule.

Halfway through the period under consideration, in the second half of the eighteenth century, came the industrial revolution in Britain, the forerunner of similar developments in other 'western' countries, including the United States. For the latter part of the period, then, one is considering a dual problem: not just the impact of a particular country, Britain, on India, but the impact of a civilisation which had undergone a full-scale industrial revolution on one which (despite some degree of commercial and industrial development in India) had not. This merges into a yet larger problem. The twentieth century has seen the creation of something like a universal civilisation, aided by the unprecedented development of communications, and predominantly western in form. It is not easy to disentangle the specific influence of Britain on India from the participation of both countries in the emergence of this modern civilisation. Even in an earlier period Britain did not exist in isolation but was part of the general civilisation of Europe; and important elements in the French political philosophy of the eighteenth century were mediated to India through the Utilitarians in the early nineteenth century.

Experts in Indian or African history are nowadays understandably concerned to present the continuity of the indigenous history of those continents in which the period of European colonialism appears as a temporary intrusion. In Africa the colonial period was very short. An octogenarian could well have seen his territory absorbed into a European colony and lived to see it regain its independence. The time scale in India was different. The British were an important element there for six or seven generations. In the long view, they only added one more layer, and a comparatively thin one, to the long history of conquests of India, but it covered a period of exceptional change.

Britain was a maritime and trading power. She became an imperial one and it was essentially her Indian empire which made her so. From the sixteenth century onwards Britain participated with other European powers in the planting of colonies of her own people in what were regarded (however erroneously) as uninhabited areas, but it was India which made her the ruler of millions of people of alien stock. Britain's own previous experience, both domestic and colonial, was influential in the decisions she took in India, and it is for this reason that the 'British empire' remains a meaningful unit for historical studies, however irrelevant it may have become to the political and economic groupings of the contemporary world. Between the two World Wars enthusiasts for the empire, both scholars and politicians, congratulated themselves that it was an organic growth, not an artificial creation like the League of Nations. Its structure, like the English common law, had evolved largely by precedent. Decisions taken in one part of the empire could be applied elsewhere. 'Responsible government', in effect internal self-government, accorded to Canada in the 1840s, could be extended to Australia or South Africa, and eventually to India. Control of tariff policy, granted to Canada in 1859, could similarly be extended to other colonies in time. India was eventually to follow the path marked out by Britain's older dominions and in turn the African colonies were to tread the route pioneered by India. African leaders were very aware of this. The Nigerian, Chief Awolowo, wrote in his *The Path to Nigerian Freedom*: 'India is the hero of the subject countries. Her struggles for self-government are keenly and sympathetically watched by colonial peoples.' In South Africa an 'African Congress Party' was founded on the model of the Indian National Congress.

Britain became the greatest colonial power in the world in the late nineteenth century, ruling a quarter of the world's population.

It was, therefore, of global significance that she transferred to
other parts of the world the philosophy of empire which she had
worked out in ruling India. It was largely a pragmatic philosophy,
hammered out in the face of immediate problems, but Britain
had been compelled to face most of the major questions with
which colonial powers were confronted: how far a metropolitan
power should try to assimilate its new subjects; how far leave
them to their own government and culture; whether it should risk
the creation of an educated élite; how far it was responsible for
the 'progress' of its dependencies; how far coercion was either
possible or desirable; how far it must rely upon the co-operation
of important forces in the subject nations and how that was to be
achieved. English answers to these questions were distinctive,
differing in many particulars from those given by other nineteenth-
century colonisers, such as the French, Germans and Russians.
To take only the most obvious example, the British never
attempted an assimilation policy comparable to those of either
France or Russia. Their disinclination to try to assimilate the
empire, even when imperial ties were at their strongest in the late
nineteenth century, owed something to ingrained British pre-
judices but also much to the great debate between 'conservatives'
and 'westernisers' on the government of India earlier in the
century.

The one constant theme in Anglo-Indian relations was trade.
It was trade which originally took Englishmen to the East, however much the desire for trade was reinforced by the urge for
adventure or the romantic lure of distant civilisations. The
relationship remained a trading one for generations and Englishmen did not hesitate to drive hard bargains when they got the
chance, knowing that the same treatment would be extended to
them. There is no doubt that when they were in a position of
political power in India the British continued to drive some hard
bargains, particularly on questions such as military expenditure.
It was a matter almost of dogma to the British treasury that
overseas dependencies must be self-supporting and in no way a
charge on the British tax-payer. It was inevitable that British

manufacturers would be in a position to bring some influence to bear on the British government to manage the Indian economy in such a way that it brought benefit to them. What is remarkable is not that Britain sometimes exploited India but that the process was checked by the emergence of such a powerful sense of responsibility. Today, in the latter half of the twentieth century, many people can be found in Britain to protest against the enforcement of apartheid policies in South Africa. The protesters are not themselves black South Africans nor are they personally affected by the policy; yet they find it curiously easy to believe that such altruism is peculiar to their generation. It is not. At least from the time of Edmund Burke there have been those in government and official positions, as well as those in opposition, who have held high views of responsibility and the universal nature of justice. The British government, as distinct from individual Britons, was drawn into Indian affairs in the late eighteenth century at least partly by the scandals of what liberal historians have called the period of 'power without responsibility'. As a quasi-permanent Indian government, the British were compelled to take a long view of the welfare and development of India. Their attitude was bound to be different from that of mere 'get rich quick' speculators. When the British finally quit India in 1947 a number of eminent Englishmen tried to draw up balance sheets of the profit and loss on both sides. They themselves thought the attempt premature and it may always prove impossible because there are too many imponderables and one cannot assess what would have happened if Britain had not ruled India. But a quarter of a century after the dissolution of most of the European colonial empires it has become clear that neo-colonialism, when economic exploitation is not checked by official participation, can be worse than colonialism.

The British claimed too much for themselves, especially in the late Victorian period, when they felt unprecedented confidence both in their ability to control, at least in the long run, natural as well as social forces, and in their superiority to their non-British subjects. As a result they came to be blamed for many things, including the slow development and continuing poverty of India which, as events since independence have demonstrated, are almost beyond the wit of man to cure.

A longer perspective does not make it possible to draw up a balance sheet but it does make it possible to view the Anglo-Indian connection as a matter of history, created in part by individuals, both English and Indian, but also by events well beyond the control of individual men, in both Europe and India, at a particular epoch when Europe was technologically much more advanced and so stronger than the rest of the world.

Chapter 1 DID THE BRITISH INTEND TO CONQUER INDIA?

IN APRIL 1579 a Jesuit priest, Father Thomas Stephens, sailed from Lisbon for Goa. He is the first Englishman definitely known to have visited India.[1] It was ironic in view of later history that Stephens was not a trader and that he went under the auspices of a foreign power. The fact that, as a missionary, he went with the intention of changing Indian society makes him even more untypical of the hundreds of Englishmen who followed him during the next two centuries.

Europeans at first regarded the Orient, which like Columbus they confused with the Americas, with caution, respect, even awe. To the Elizabethans it was a place of fabulous wealth and powerful rulers. Edmund Spenser, wishing to describe riches almost beyond human dreams, wrote in *The Faerie Queene* (III, iv, 23):

> Shortly upon that shore there heaped was,
> Exceeding riches and all pretious things,
> The spoyle of all the world, that it did pas
> The wealth of th'East, and pompe of *Persian* kings;
> Gold, amber, yuorie, perles, owches, rings,
> And all that else was pretious and deare . . .

Shakespeare too uses the East almost as a synonym for wealth. Mortimer, praising the generosity of his father-in-law, Owen Glendower, says he is 'as bountiful as mines of India'. (*1 Henry IV*, III, i) The Duke of Norfolk, describing the Field of the Cloth of Gold, tells the Duke of Buckingham:

> Today, the French,
> All clinquant, all in gold, like heathen gods,
> Shone down the English; and, tomorrow, they
> Made Britain, India: every man that stood
> Show'd like a mine.
>
> (*Henry VIII*, I, i)

It was, however, Christopher Marlowe in his *Tamburlaine the Great*, who first brought an Asiatic hero to an English stage. The themes of oriental wealth and power run together throughout the play. Tamburlaine holds sway over lands 'from the bounds of Afric to the banks of Ganges'. He can promise his future bride, Zenocrate,

> A hundred Tartars shall attend on thee,
> Mounted on steeds swifter than Pegasus;
> Thy garments shall be made of Median silk,
> Enchas'd with precious jewels of mine own.
>
> (*1*, I, ii)

He is about to meet a thousand horsemen in battle whose equipment is described thus:

> Their plumed helms are wrought with beaten gold,
> Their swords enamell'd, and about their necks
> Hang massy chains of gold down to the waist;
> In every part exceeding brave and rich.
>
> (*1*, V, i)

The cumulative effect of prodigious wealth piled on prodigious wealth is continued throughout the play. Some no doubt stemmed entirely from Marlowe's powerful imagination but much, particularly the details, sprang from stories then circulating in England. Even the geographical confusion still apparently prevalent in the public mind in the 1580s is reflected in the lines in which Tamburlaine dreams of extending his power 'from the East unto the furthest West' and commanding the seas,

> Until the Persian fleet and men-of-war,
> Sailing along the oriental sea,

Have fetch'd about the Indian continent,
Even from Persepolis to Mexico,
And thence unto the Straits of Jubalter.

(*1*, III, iii)

But however faulty their information may have been in certain particulars, the Elizabethans clearly did not doubt that they were in touch with great and powerful civilisations, at least as ancient as their own, and possibly more skilled and sophisticated. Trading contacts between East and West reach far back into prehistory. In classical times Roman grandees coveted the luxuries of the East, especially the silks and spices, and experienced the same 'balance of payments' difficulties as their seventeenth- and eighteenth-century successors because there were comparatively few European goods that the Indians or Chinese wanted in return. Pliny complained that the eastern trade drained 55 million silver sesterces (worth perhaps £500,000 in modern money) from Rome every year. Throughout the European middle ages the trade between Europe and the East was carried on through Moslem intermediaries. Only in 1498 did the Portuguese, Vasco da Gama, open up a direct route to India round the Cape of Good Hope. Constantinople had fallen some forty-five years earlier and the Turkish advance had seriously obstructed, if not closed, many of the old routes. Shipping eastern goods directly to Europe therefore seemed likely to prove an immensely profitable undertaking. Silks and jewels were luxuries always in demand, increasingly so with the rising standard of taste and opulence associated with the Renaissance. Spices such as peppers, cloves and mace were necessities rather than luxuries when, because of the lack of winter fodder, most cattle had to be killed each autumn and the population subsisted throughout the winter on dried and badly preserved meat.

Trade, then, was the first and dominant reason for the new direct contact between Europe and the East. There were others. The Portuguese were strongly influenced by their desire to out-flank their ancient Islamic enemy.[2] The voyages to the East were a method of carrying on the crusades by other means. This in

itself was only one manifestation of a wider movement. Until the
sixteenth century Europe had been on the defensive. Now it was
ready to counter-attack. It was an extrovert society buoyed up
by the new spirit of inquiry stemming from the Renaissance.
Even the fact that it was torn by religious dissension was a sign
of vigour rather than dissolution. Europeans were supremely
self-confident, and this confidence allowed them to destroy the
ancient civilisations of the Americas in an incredibly short time.

Asian societies proved tougher. India, geographically about
half the size of the continent of Europe, but with a population
in the sixteenth century probably about equal to that of Europe—
in the region of 100 millions, was a complex and delicately balanced civilisation. All the major races of mankind were represented
there. Among the earliest inhabitants was a negroid element which
survived in the negritos such as the Andaman Islanders. There
were traces of Australoid stock in the south and centre and a
marked Mongoloid element in the north. There was a complex
admixture of Caucasoid stock, especially of the Mediterranean
type, descendants of a people who probably entered India during
neolithic times and brought an important megalithic culture
with them. They were to be associated with the Dravidian culture
of southern India. In the second millennium BC there came
another great invasion, this time of a Nordic people, the 'Aryans'
—tall, fair meat-eaters from the steppes of Central Asia—who
became dominant in northern India. Many centuries before the
modern Europeans arrived, Indian society had been formed like
a palimpsest by layer after layer of successful, and partially
successful, invasions. These groups merged but never totally
melted into one another. There was a tendency for the men of
southern India to be darker than those of northern India and, as
Indian scholars themselves point out, colour-consciousness in
Indian literature long ante-dated the coming of the Europeans.[3]

In the nineteenth century British administrators, anxious to
prove that Indian nationalism was an exotic product, stressed
these differences and were fond of asserting that India, like
Metternich's Italy, had never been more than a 'geographical

expression'. Like Metternich they were only partly right. Modern commentators have tended to emphasise rather the underlying unity of Indian civilisation. Ethnic differences certainly existed, but they were often overlaid by religious and linguistic loyalties. Language was a particularly complex case. Censi conducted during the British period revealed over two hundred Indian languages—and this too was used as an argument for the fragmentary nature of Indian society. But this was essentially misleading. Most of the two hundred were variants of the ten major languages spoken by the vast majority of the inhabitants of the sub-continent. In the south the two main Dravidian languages, Telegu and Tamil, were widely understood, as was Western Hindi in the north. Another Aryan language, Bengali, which was to play a crucial role in the development of modern Indian vernacular literature, was also understood by millions. Gujerati, although spoken by a much smaller group of people, was the *lingua franca* of commerce over wide areas of western India. Given that many people, at least in the towns and among the commercial classes, could speak more than one language, it seems doubtful whether diversity of language, although certainly a problem, was a greater barrier to communication than a similar diversity of language in contemporary Europe.[4]

The real binding force in the sub-continent was, however, the all-pervasive influence of Hinduism. Hinduism has frequently been compared to a great sponge which absorbs endlessly. In the early centuries of the Christian era it almost totally absorbed Buddhism. Even today Moslem and Christian converts from Hinduism sometimes retain enough of their old customs to seek their marriage partners only within their original sub-caste.[5] To European observers the most obvious manifestation of Hinduism was the caste system. It was also the most puzzling. No one has ever succeeded in giving either a completely convincing explanation of the origins of the caste system—although it must be connected with the invasion patterns and the emergence of dominant groups in prehistory—or even a wholly satisfactory description of the relationship of the 3,000 odd castes that exist.

B

The four classic castes of the Hindu scriptures, the Brahman (priest), the Kshatriya (warrior), the Vaishya (trader) and the Sudra (cultivator or artisan), have constantly proliferated. Sometimes sub-castes are linked with occupation but often they are not. 'It suggests,' said one commentator, 'a division of the inhabitants of England into families of Norman descent, Clerks in Holy Orders, positivists, ironmongers, vegetarians, communists, and Scotchmen.'[6] The best working description is probably the often quoted one of Guy Wint, 'A caste is a group of families whose members can marry with each other and eat in each other's company without believing themselves polluted.'[7] Avoiding pollution or undergoing ritual purification when pollution had occurred was (and is) a complicated and time-consuming business for the orthodox Hindu. The caste system also created the Untouchables and the even more depressed 'Unseeables' whose touch or even appearance was polluting to other castes. It may be that the caste system made for stability and reduced tensions in a plural society, since everyone knew his place and could not greatly change it. By its sanctification of tradition it may also have provided some safeguard against arbitrary authority. But the impression that it made on Europeans (and later on westernised Indians) was of a society confined in a strait-jacket.

The rigidity of the caste system provoked reactions in India long before there was any western influence. In part Buddhism itself, originating in northern India in the sixth century BC, was such a reaction. But a thousand years later, although it had by then spread to other parts of Asia, it had virtually disappeared in India itself. Only in very recent times has there again been an increase in professing Buddhists in India, significantly a high proportion of them converts from the former 'Untouchable' castes.[8] Even older than Buddhism was Jainism, which some scholars have seen as a survival of the original prehistoric opposition to the imposition of Brahmanical control. Jainism had a good deal in common with Buddhism but laid even greater stress on the virtues of asceticism and on the sanctity of all forms of life. It was the Jains who wore muslin masks over the lower parts of their faces so that they might not accidentally swallow a fly. For the student of modern India much of the interest of Jainism derives from the fact that Mahatma Gandhi, with his willingness to criticise the caste system, came from a partly Jain background.

Although Hinduism has a theology, it tends to appear to the outsider as a distinctive solution to particular social problems rather than as a set of beliefs. As a philosophy, unlike Buddhism, it has never seemed suitable for export from India. This, however, is not to say, as some nineteenth-century historians did, that India has always been introverted or that Indian learning and thought have not played an important role in the world. Hegel was nearer the truth when he wrote: 'India as a land of Desire formed an essential element in general history. From the most ancient times downwards, all nations have directed their wishes and longings to gaining access to the treasures of this land of marvels . . . The way by which these treasures have passed to the West has at all times been a matter of world historical importance bound up with the fate of nations.'[9] Hegel makes it clear that he means not only 'treasures of nature', jewels, perfumes and the rest, but also 'treasures of wisdom'. It is not surprising that this emphasis on India's 'treasures of wisdom' should come from a German philosopher, for no nation showed more interest in disentangling the complex heritage of Indian thought in the nineteenth century than did the Germans. In three particular fields, mathematics, astronomy and medicine, the Indians made remarkable advances in human knowledge. It was a long time before the West realised that the numerals known to them as 'Arabic' were in fact Indian in origin, the symbols 1 to 9 being derived from the initial letters of the Sanskrit names and the zero or 'o' from the initial letter of the Sanskrit word for 'empty'. It was in part their advanced knowledge of mathematics which enabled a remarkable line of Indian astronomers to arise who both learnt from and taught the Greeks in the last three centuries BC. In the early centuries of the Christian era Indian medicine was far ahead of that of the West in its knowledge of both anatomy and pharmacology. Indian surgeons were famous and even ventured into the field of plastic surgery. As in mathematics, some of this knowledge was eventually transmitted to the West by the Arabs. But in the eighth century Indian medicine began to decline, its decline apparently connected with the extinction of Buddhism and the resurgence of a strictly orthodox Hinduism which held contact with blood or dead bodies to be polluting.[10]

But while Indian learning spread abroad, India herself suffered periodic invasions in historic times, as she had done in prehistoric times, usually through the traditional gateway of the north-west frontier. In 326 BC came the invasion by Alexander the Great. It may have been the reaction to Alexander's invasion that enabled Chandragupta Maurya (Sandracottos of the Greek historians) to take power to found the first of the great empires that tried to bring India under one sway—although Professor Basham, among others, has counselled caution in accepting too easily the view that it was European stimuli that brought about great events in India.[11] Chandragupta's empire reached its greatest extent under his grandson, Asoka, in the middle of the third century BC. It provided Indians of later centuries with the one example of an indigenous empire to which they could look back. The attempt of the Gupta dynasty in the fourth century AD to revive the Mauryan empire failed, shattered in part by the invasions of the Huns.

The first wave of Moslem invasion, that of the Arabs in the seventh century AD, penetrated only a short distance into India with the temporary conquest of Sind in the eighth century. Much more important was the invasion of Muhammad of Ghor (Shahab-ud-din) who overran much of the Gangetic plain in the late twelfth century. The Sultanate of Delhi was founded in 1206 and at the end of the thirteenth century under Ala-ud-din, Shah of Delhi, Moslem influence began to penetrate into the south of the continent, into the Deccan. Late in the fourteenth century came the devastating incursions of the Mongol Tamerlane, Marlowe's Tamburlaine. In the second decade of the sixteenth century Babur, descended on his father's side from Tamerlane, and on his mother's from that other great and terrible Mongol leader, Jenghiz Khan, founded the Mogul empire in northern India. Despite his Mongol forbears, Babur regarded himself as a Turk and, like his descendants, spoke Turkish in private. His new empire almost fell to pieces on his death in 1530, but was firmly re-established by his grandson, Akbar, in 1556.[12]

By any standard of comparison Akbar was one of the world's great rulers. In bodily vigour he invites comparison with Peter the Great of Russia but he was a better-tempered and better-balanced man than Peter. His empire extended over the whole of northern India as far as the Vindhya Hills. It was an empire with a deep division within it: most of his subjects were Hindus; Akbar and his immediate followers were Moslems. Nineteenth-century English historians were fond of comparing the relationship, *mutatis mutandis*, with that existing between the Normans and the Saxons. It was a comparison with some flavour of truth in it. Akbar showed his statesmanship by the way in which he dealt with this difficult situation. He conciliated his Hindu subjects by giving defeated Rajput (ie warrior) princes military commands and Brahmans high administrative office. His finance minister was a Hindu, Todar Mal. He instituted a large measure of religious toleration—a man of an intensely inquiring mind, he was not a very orthodox Moslem himself—and abolished the discriminatory poll tax on non-Moslems. The official language of Akbar's court was Persian which, it has been suggested, was more acceptable to his Hindu subjects than Turkish or even Arabic, which were associated with earlier phases of Moslem conquest, would have been. With the Persian language came a very high culture, notably in poetry and architecture. But it was not an indigenous culture and Dr Spear is probably right in calling it 'an abortive aristocratic civilization' which did not take deep enough root in India to withstand future storms.[13]

Despite Akbar's conciliatory gestures towards the Hindus, the Moslem conquerors remained the governing class. The ranks of Islam were, however, reinforced during the centuries of Moslem political predominance by converts of very different social origins. Some became converts from fear—although in general the Moslems in India never tried to enforce mass conversions as they had done in some parts of the world; some converted for obvious career reasons; a significant number came, as they did later to Christianity, from the most depressed classes of Hindus, above all from the Untouchables, who had little to hope for in their existing society. By the time the modern Europeans arrived Islam had spread, although in some places spread very thinly, all over India. The Moslems were no longer a homogenous social or ethnic group, still less a geographical one. Hence some of the later problems of 'partition'.

Akbar's tolerant policy was, in general, carried on by his son, Jehangir, and by his grandson, Shah Jehan, although the latter, the builder of the Taj Mahal, reverted to a stricter observance of the precepts of Islam than his grandfather. But in 1658 Shah Jehan was deposed by his son, Aurungzabe. Aurungzabe was a strong man. He embarked on conquests which, for the first time, extended the Mogul empire from Kabul, the modern capital of Afghanistan, in the north, to Cape Comorin, the southernmost tip of India. But Aurungzabe's critics have generally agreed that this spectacular extension of empire overstrained and so weakened the whole structure. At the same time Aurungzabe abandoned Akbar's wise policy of conciliating the Hindu majority among his subjects and began to discriminate against non-Moslems. Nevertheless Aurungzabe reigned for nearly half a century, until his death in 1707, and the Mogul empire still appeared as one of the world's great monarchies.

When Europeans first made contact with India in the sixteenth century, India was not then in a state of political decline. On the contrary the Mogul empire was just rising to its greatest height. The Moguls had not yet, however, subdued the south, and the Portuguese made common cause with some of the Hindu rulers there, notably with the king of the potentially powerful state of Vijayanagar. The Portuguese plunged into Indian politics from the beginning in a way which their successors, the British and the Dutch, tried to avoid. They became involved in fierce warfare, partly trading battles, partly a religious crusade, against the

Arab traders who had previously dominated the sea-borne commerce of western India. They tried actively to secure converts to Christianity and, especially during the captain-generalcy of Alfonso de Albuquerque (1509–15), they initiated a deliberate policy of intermarriage between Portuguese and Indians which resulted in the establishment of a considerable mixed community round the Portuguese base of Goa.[14]

The British made their first contacts with India when Elizabeth I reigned in England and Akbar in India. Thomas Stephens may have been a Jesuit priest who had left his country for conscience's sake, but his father was a leading London merchant. Thomas wrote telling his father of the new country in which he found himself. His letter was passed from hand to hand and aroused great interest among the London merchants. In 1583 four Englishmen, John Newbery, Ralph Fitch, William Leedes and James Storie, set out for India, travelling overland from Aleppo.[15] Storie died. Newbery became a shopkeeper in Goa, having received some protection from Thomas Stephens. Leedes entered the service of the Mogul. Fitch alone returned to England in 1591 after many adventures and wide travels in the East. His accounts set off a new wave of enthusiasm. England was confident after the defeat of the Armada in 1588. A number of Portuguese carracks (large merchantmen) had been captured during the hostilities of the previous few years and had opened English eyes to the richness of the eastern trade. Some had also yielded valuable maps and charts. As early as 1582 Edward Fenton, accompanied by men who had sailed round the world with Drake in 1577–80, had set out from Southampton, hoping to trade directly with the eastern spice islands, but Fenton never reached the Indian Ocean. In 1591 another expedition set sail under George Raymond. One ship of this expedition, commanded by James Lancaster, reached India and the Malayan archipelago and returned home with a profitable cargo but at a terrible cost in human lives. Only 25 of the 198 men who sailed with Lancaster returned.

Men hungry for profit were not, however, easily deterred. Previously England had obtained her share of eastern goods through the Levant Company, a group of English merchants who traded with the eastern Mediterranean. But the 1590s saw a serious slump in the Levant trade. The final straw seems to have come in 1599, when the Dutch merchants raised the asking price of pepper from 3s to 6s or even 8s a pound. Eighty London merchants, including Ralph Fitch, met at Founders' Hall on 22 September 1599 with the Lord Mayor in the chair and agreed to form an association to trade directly with the East. Government consent was not at first easy to obtain—Elizabeth was trying to secure a *détente* with the Spaniards, who had controlled Portugal and so the Portuguese trade with the East since 1580. But on 31 December 1600 the English East India Company was incorporated by royal charter under the title 'The Governor and Company of Merchants of London trading to the East Indies'. It had 125 shareholders and, initially, capital of £70,000.

The prize was not India. It was the 'Spice Islands', roughly the modern Indonesia. Java and Sumatra were the main sources of pepper, and the Moluccas, Amboina and the Banda Islands at the eastern end of the chain supplied the still more valuable spices such as cloves, nutmeg and mace. Valuable metals also came from the islands, as well as from the Malay peninsula. From the British point of view their main competitors were not the Portuguese who, despite the Pope's decree of 1492 giving them a monopoly of eastern trade, were already beginning to decline in importance and influence, but the Dutch. The Dutch had arrived in the East at about the same time as the British. In fact the first Dutch trading voyages to the Spice Islands dated from 1595, some four years after the Raymond-Lancaster expedition, but during the next few years the Dutch rapidly went ahead. Between 1595 and 1601 fifteen Dutch fleets sailed for the East. In 1602 the Dutch East India Company was incorporated with strong government backing and capital of over £500,000. It began to establish bases both in the Spice Islands (Batavia in Java was founded in 1619) and on the east coast of India. The Dutch company had much the better of the contest in the Spice Islands and, after the torture and murder of the British traders at Amboina in the Moluccas in 1623—an event long remembered in England, the British retreated from the field.

This, however, was still in the future when the newly formed East India Company sent out its first voyage, under James Lancaster, in 1601. Both the first and the second voyages were destined for the Spice Islands and India was not even mentioned. The third voyage, which sailed in 1607, had the opening up of trade with the west coast of India as a very secondary objective. The second-in-command of that voyage, William Hawkins, an old Levant merchant, made his way to the Mogul capital and impressed the emperor, Jehangir, by his knowledge of Turkish, still the family language of the Moguls. But the Portuguese intrigued long and skilfully against Hawkins and Jehangir's favour did not last long. Hawkins lost the concession he had just secured permitting the British to establish a 'factory', that is a trading base, at the main Mogul port of Surat. In 1612, however, a British fleet defeated a strong Portuguese squadron at Swally Roads, the anchorage near Surat. The battle was watched with interest by Mogul officials who had begun to feel the need for naval auxiliaries in the disorderly trade war which was being waged on their western coasts. The Mogul empire had no desire to become a naval power itself and began to show favour towards the British. In 1613 the British were allowed to establish their factory at Surat.

This success encouraged the East India Company to persuade James I to send out at the company's expense Sir Thomas Roe, a man who had already made his mark in American ventures, to negotiate a commercial treaty with the Mogul emperor. Roe's mission was a landmark in Anglo-Indian relations. It marked the first opening of formal diplomatic relations between the governments of England and India. The strange position of an ambassador, accredited by a government, but paid for by a commercial company, symbolised the complicated relationship between the British government and the East India Company which was to endure for over two hundred years. Roe's careful reports for the first time gave Englishmen some real understanding of the India

of the Moguls and replaced the strange travellers' tales which had
formed the basis of Christopher Marlowe's knowledge.[16]

Roe landed at Surat on 26 September 1615. He complained
that he was inconvenienced by the customs and that, generally, he
was not accorded the treatment due to an ambassador of a foreign
power. The Indians, however, were sceptical of his credentials
and suspected 'that I might be an Imposture as well as the rest'.
They were plainly already very wary of the European merchants
invading their shores. Roe proceeded to the court of Jehangir
where he was treated courteously enough. His object, however,
was to secure a commercial treaty. Such an idea was entirely
foreign to Jehangir. The emperor granted, and withdrew,
privileges to certain traders at his discretion. So did his officials,
as a natural part of their perquisites of office. To suggest that he
should bind himself permanently by an agreement with a handful
of representatives of a distant and probably barbarous kingdom
seemed slightly ludicrous to Jehangir. A similar divergence
between western and eastern concepts of how to conduct international relations was to bedevil Anglo-Chinese relations until
well into the nineteenth century. In the Chinese case the British
cut the Gordian knot by resorting to force in 1839. But, in the
seventeenth century, Europeans did not yet regard their own
conventions as necessarily the norm for the whole world. Roe had
to content himself with a general permission for British merchants
to continue to trade in India.

Almost as useful as this was the information which Roe was
able to supply. Like earlier travellers he was impressed by the
ostentatious wealth of the court, but he saw further into the
political and administrative structure of the empire and into the
arbitrary nature of the emperor's authority. He wrote to James I,
'Fame hath done much for the Glory of this place. Yet it cannot
be denied that this King is one of the mightyest Princes in Asia,
as well in the extent of territory as in revenew; equall to the
Turke, far exceeding the Persian. But the Gouerment so
vncertayne, without written law, without Policye, the Customes
mingled with barbarisme, religions infinite . . .' Perhaps Roe

did not deem it wise to dwell too much on criticisms of arbitrary authority in a letter to the king, but he wrote more freely to the Archbishop of Canterbury: 'Lawes they haue none written. The Kyngs judgement byndes, who sitts and giues sentence with much patience, once weakly, both in Capitall and Criminall causes; wher sometymes he sees the execution done by his Eliphants, with two much delight in blood. His Gouernors of Prouinces rule by his *Firmanes*, which is a breefe lettre authorising them. They take life and goodes at pleasure . . .' Roe also realised, although without altogether understanding the situation, that the Moguls were newcomers. 'In generall,' he wrote to Lord Carew, 'all the old Cities are beaten down, by what policie I vnderstand not; but the King seeketh the ruine of anything not begunne by his Ancestors, so that all the Land hath not a house fit for a Cottager, but in such Cities as hee fauoreth.'[17]

Roe and his successors aroused widespread interest in the Mogul empire in England. It seems likely that Roe knew John Milton in his later years. Milton was unusually well informed about India[18] and his description of Satan, 'High on a throne of royal state, which far/Outshone the wealth of Ormuz and of Ind', may be a direct echo of Roe's description of the Mogul emperor sitting 'high on a gallery, with a canopy over him and a carpet before him . . . in great and barbarous state'. A generation later Dryden was to write a verse drama on the last of the great Mogul emperors, *Aurungzeb* (1675). Other men after Roe extended British knowledge, notably the Frenchman, François Bernier, who visited India several times between 1640 and 1666. Roe had noted that private property, at least landed property, did not exist as it did in the West. The emperor was the ultimate owner of all. 'He is,' wrote Roe, 'euery mans heire when he dyeth, which maketh him rich, and the Country so euill builded. The great men about him are not borne Noble, but Fauorites raised . . .'[19] This theme was seized upon by French writers who wished to make oblique comments about absolute monarchy in France.[20] By the late seventeenth century, then, India had already thoroughly entered into European consciousness both as a subject of literature and also as a theme for social comment.

The main link between India and the West, however, was still, as it always had been, trade. The English East India Company sent out twelve voyages between 1601 and 1612. All, except the fourth, were profitable. These, the so-called 'separate voyages', were conducted on a kind of rudimentary joint stock principle. Members of the company were free to subscribe to each voyage or not, as they wished, but once they had subscribed to a particular voyage all investments were treated as part of a single capital. After 1612 all voyages were conducted on joint stock account. From the beginning the company's business methods were relatively sophisticated and it has been suggested that this was due to its early connection with merchants who had traded in the Levant and were familiar with advanced Mediterranean methods.[21] It soon established itself as one of the most important of English companies, closely connected willynilly with the government. There were two sides to this. On the one hand the company, whose charter was subject to periodical renewal, wished for obvious reasons to be on the side of the government of the day. On the other, the government soon began to find the company a useful source of financial support. The company on the whole sailed successfully through the stormy waters of English seventeenth-century politics. The outbreak of the Civil War found it on rather bad terms with Charles I and it survived the Commonwealth. Indeed, financial stringency compelled Oliver Cromwell to grant it a new charter in 1657. Charles II was prepared to confirm the essentials in this charter in 1661 in return for a large loan. The company was, however, caught unprepared by the fall of James II in 1688 and its many enemies, who resented its monopoly of eastern trade, saw their chance. In 1698 a 'New' Company, the 'General Society trading to the East Indies', was incorporated. Whether or not John Evelyn was correct when he noted in his Diary, 'the old East India Company lost their business against the new Company by 10 votes in Parliament; so many of their friends being absent, going to see a tiger baited by dogs',[22] the old company had certainly temporarily lost its political grip. Neither company could, however, completely worst the other and in 1709, as a result of a compromise arranged by Sidney Godolphin the previous year, the two joined forces as the 'United Company of Merchants of England trading to the East Indies'.

During the long period of Whig ascendancy, following the death of Queen Anne in 1715, the United Company steadily consolidated its position. Its activities, together with those of that other great corporation, the Bank of England, helped to make London one of the great money markets of the world. Its stock was the nearest contemporary equivalent to 'gilt-edged' and one of the few investments which ranked with land in terms of security. As a result it attracted a significant amount of money from abroad, especially from Holland. It played a key role in public finance. When the government wanted loans its usual method was to approach certain individuals behind whom stood important interests. The company was such an interest. Even in 1709 it was 'one of the major creditors of the State in the new system of funded debts that had grown up since the Revolution'[23] and this role continued throughout the century.

The company was deeply embedded in the whole structure of British politics at this time. Its influence was less than that of the sometimes rival West India interest, but it commanded an impressive range of patronage at the disposal of the twenty-four directors of the company. This patronage, although it was one of the most valued perquisites of the directors, was rarely used crudely for immediate financial advantage but more often to obtain political support. The company was also linked with a web of connected economic interests. There were the bankers and brokers who supplied it with silver bullion for export. There were the diamond merchants who bought the precious stones it imported—diamonds because of their small bulk and high value soon established themselves as one of the most satisfactory methods of transferring profits home from the East.[24] There were even the clothiers who supplied it with wool exports. The market in the East for these last was not good, but political considerations dictated that the company should ship them out even at a loss. Finally, there was the powerful shipping interest. In the seventeenth century the company had given up owning its own ships and instead had begun to hire the specialised merchantmen it needed from wealthy managing owners, the 'ships' husbands', who came to form a close-knit group, with interests sometimes passing from father to son.

Despite, or because of, its powerful position, the company was under constant attack from many directions. It was an oligarchy. All stockholders holding £500 worth of stock were members of the Court of Proprietors. They elected the twenty-four members of the Court of Directors, each of whom must hold at least £2,000 worth of stock. The charter of the United Company contained a provision that no director should serve for more than four consecutive years, but as an attempt to prevent the creation of a self-perpetuating oligarchy this was ineffective. Directors simply stood down for a year and were then promptly re-elected. The company was not only an oligarchy. It was also a monopoly, with exclusive rights of trade between Britain and the East—although not of the 'country trade', that is, trade between different centres in the East. Almost from the beginning its monopoly had been challenged by other groups of merchants in London who wanted similar privileges. The 'New' Company of 1698 had merely been the most important and successful of such challenges. In the East freelance 'interlopers' constantly encroached on the company's business, sometimes with the help of foreign East India Companies.[25]

Some criticised the company for the damage it was inflicting on British industry. It is a little ironic, in view of later Indian nationalists' charges that England ruined India's industries, to recall that in the seventeenth century Englishmen were equally convinced that India had ruined England's industry. In the seventeenth and eighteenth centuries India's main export to Britain was no longer spices but textiles, both cheap cottons and luxury goods, silks and muslins. These were seen as a great threat by English cloth-makers. In 1677 Parliament, in a despairing gesture, forbade the use of any but woollen goods in winter and twenty years later, in 1797, the Spitalfield weavers staged a great demonstration. A vigorous pamphlet war was waged in the early eighteenth century in which writers of the stature of Richard Steele participated. *Aqua fortis* (nitric acid) was thrown at the weavers of Indian calicoes. Heavy duties and even prohibitions were tried first against printed, and then against white, calicoes. Demonstrations, Acts of Parliament, literary eloquence were all in vain. Fashion continued to demand Indian textiles and the demand was met.

The most persistent charge made against the company was that it was draining the country of bullion, mainly in the form of silver coins, to pay for eastern goods. This put it at the centre of the whole mercantilist and bullionist controversy. The old problem still remained, namely that, although there was a small demand in India for European manufactures, especially novelties, Europeans were generally much more eager to acquire Indian goods than the Indians to acquire European ones. The balance had to be made up in silver. The company's first voyage, that of 1601, carried manufactured goods worth £6,860 but silver coin to the value of £28,742. This was anathema to the orthodox mercantilists of the time. As early as 1601 Gerard de Malynes wrote *A Treatise of the Canker of England's Commonwealth*, complaining that his countrymen were 'as simple as West Indian savages in exchanging precious metals for luxuries and trifles'. An anonymous writer 'J.R.' wrote a widely read pamphlet *The Trade's Increase* in 1615—the title was an ironic reference to the company's new flagship of that name lost on her maiden voyage to the East—claiming that the trade brought far more loss than profit to the English economy. Other writers replied on the company's behalf, among them Sir Dudley Digges in his *The Defence of Trade* (1615) and Thomas Mun in his *A Discourse of Trade from England into the East Indies* (1621). Modern economists have shown scant sympathy for these mercantilist arguments, pointing out that there was in fact no shortage of silver in Europe at this time—on the contrary there was a superfluity of American silver—and no good reason why it should not be exported in exchange for other goods. But these bullionist arguments, which persisted well into the eighteenth century, carried much weight with contemporaries and the East India Company sought to reduce silver exports by any means at its disposal, including plunging deeper into the Asian trade of which India formed only one component part.

Asian trade had flourished before the coming of the Europeans although, apart from certain metals, it tended to be a trade in luxuries rather than in staple commodities in which most Asian countries were self-sufficient. China exported silks, porcelain, lacquer work, sandalwood and zinc; Malaya provided gold and tin; Indonesia, spices and gold; India, precious stones, pepper, textiles and opium. In 1557 the Portuguese managed to secure permission from reluctant Chinese authorities to establish a small base at Macao. By the eighteenth century the China trade was regarded as the great prize in Asia, as the Spice Islands trade once had been. To the older commodities like silk and porcelain a new one had now been added: tea, mainly produced in Fukien province, for which the British public was acquiring an inordinate taste. To some extent the British paid for this in silver but a more complicated trading pattern had begun to emerge. The British bought raw cotton and cotton textiles in eastern India and transported these to China. For a short time this had a significant effect on the development of the Indian textile industry. But a more profitable alternative now presented itself to the traders. India grew excellent opium and there was a large potential market for it in China. By the early nineteenth century opium had replaced cotton as the staple commodity in the trade between India and China, now in European hands. The consequences of this belong perhaps more to Chinese than to Indian history—the Chinese objections to the trade on economic as well as moral grounds, the so-called Opium War of 1839–42 (which was not only concerned with opium) and the forcible opening of China to western trade—but they afford one illustration of the dynamic results of western intervention in Asia. Unless the Europeans were prepared to withdraw altogether, which they were not, they were bound to become more and more deeply involved and their mere presence began movements the consequences of which they hardly foresaw.[26]

This was true in India itself. To William Hawkins or Sir Thomas Roe the idea that the English East India Company might one day rule India would have seemed simply ludicrous. As Professor Harlow puts it, 'they were foreign merchants, admitted on sufferance because they were useful,' and they no more expected to be concerned with the high politics of the Mogul empire than the Muscovy Company expected to rule the Russias.[27] They hoped that law and order and security of trade would be provided by the local rulers. The attraction of Surat as a base was largely that it was within the immediate protection of the Moguls. For well over a century the directors in London set their faces against the acquisition of the type of fortified base favoured by the Portuguese and the Dutch. No one counselled this more forcibly than did Roe. 'A warr and trafique are incompatible,' he wrote to the company in 1616. 'It is the beggering of the Portugall, notwithstanding his many rich residences and territoryes, that hee keepes souldiers that spendes it . . . He neuer Profited by the Indyes, since hee defended them. Observe this well. It hath also been the error of the Dutch, who seeke Plantation heere by the Swoord. They turne a wonderfull stocke, they proule in all Places, they Posses some of the best; yet ther dead Payes consume all the gayne.' Roe's advice was based on expediency, not morality. He had no objection to sea warfare and he made it clear that his objection to land warfare was because of its unpredictable outcome. 'One disaster would eyther discreditt you, or interest you in a warr of extreame Chardge and doubtful euent.'[28] The last was to prove a true prophecy.

In practice the directors' determination to avoid entanglements sometimes wavered from the beginning. They established bases which were not under effective Mogul protection, notably at Masulipatnam on the east coast from which they could export cotton piece goods to other parts of Asia. The Dutch harassed them. The British then moved south, partly to avoid the Dutch, partly because they could obtain better supplies of goods there. In 1639 an Englishman, Francis Day, obtained a grant from the local ruler, the Rajah of the Carnatic. This grant was subsequently confirmed by the Rajah's overlord, the King of Golcanda, a Moslem ruler who had carved a territory for himself out of the old Hindu empire of Vijayanagar. The grant permitted Day to build a small fortified station, Fort St George, around which grew up the town of Madras. It was a momentous decision. Day himself was not thanked; but the company accepted the position. In 1658 Madras became the headquarters of all the company's activities on the east coast.

The potentially rich trade of Bengal also attracted the English. They had tried to participate in this trade from the Mogul capital of Agra, but without success. In 1633 an expedition from Masulipatnam, with the permission of the King of Golcanda, opened up a small trade with the coast of Orissa. The following year the company obtained rather grudging consent from the Mogul emperor to trade with Bengal itself, and in 1650 it established a trading base on the Hugli river which was eventually to give rise to the great city of Calcutta. Calcutta was entirely the product of western trade, the site originally being occupied by a few villages.

Calcutta and Madras were later to be two of the three 'Presidency' towns of British India. The third was Bombay, whose history was somewhat different from that of the other two. The island of Bombay had been ceded to the Portuguese in 1534. In 1661 it passed to Charles II of England as part of Catherine of Braganza's dowry. Seven years later he transferred it to the company in return for a nominal rent and a large loan. It was not at first highly regarded even by the company, mainly because it was regarded as exceptionally unhealthy. Of the 500 British soldiers sent to take possession of it in 1665, only 100 survived. It was not until 1687 that it superseded Surat as the headquarters of British trade on the west coast.

By the beginning of the eighteenth century these three places in India were already beginning to bear a British stamp. An

English merchant, Charles Lockyer, described the new town of
Madras in 1710:

> The prospect it gives is most delightful; nor appears it less
> magnificent by Land; the great Variety of fine Buildings that
> gracefully overlook its Walls, affording an inexpressible Satis-
> faction to a curious Eye . . . The Publick Buildings are the Town
> Hall, St. Mary's Church, The College, New House and Hospital,
> with Governor's Lodgings in the inner Fort . . . The Governor,
> during the Hot Winds, retires to the Company's new Garden for
> Refreshment, which he has made a very delightful Place of a
> barren one. The costly Gates, lovely Bowling Green, spacious
> Walks, Teal-pond and Curiosities preserved in several Divisions
> are worthy to be admired.

The English population of Madras was very small at this time,
perhaps 400 in all, of whom 114 were civilians (including 19
women) and the rest European soldiers. Round it had grown up
a flourishing Indian city, the so-called 'Black Town'. Estimates
of its population vary between 250,000 and 400,000.

Bombay was not flourishing at the beginning of the eighteenth
century. It had been in a better state twenty years earlier when
the chaplain, Thomas Ovington, wrote of it:

> The island lies in about Nineteen Degrees North, in which is a
> Fort, which is the Defence of it, flanked and lined according to the
> Rules of Art, and secured with many Pieces of Ordinance, which
> command the Harbours and the parts adjoining. In this one of the
> Company's Factors always resides . . . The Island is likewise
> beautiful with several elegant Dwellings of the English and neat
> Apartments of the Portuguese.

But Bombay's reputation for being unhealthy continued. Captain
Alexander Hamilton, an 'interloper', that is to say not an employee
of the company, wrote: 'In the Mornings there is generally seen
a thick Fog among those Trees that affects both the Brains and
Lungs of Europeans and breeds Consumptions, Fevers and
Fluxes.' Bombay had gone through troublous times. In 1683
the garrison had refused to accept the authority of the company

and had appointed Captain Keigwen, the commander of the troops, as governor, declaring that the island had reverted to the Crown. The rebellion lasted a year until the rebels gave in gracefully at the express command of Charles II. More serious than internal dissension, however, were threats of Maratha raids as the authority of the Mogul empire weakened. Surat itself, hitherto inviolate, was raided in 1664. Worst of all was the war with the Moguls themselves in which the company briefly became involved in 1687. The European population of Bombay is said to have sunk from 700 to 60 and the Indian population from 40,000 or more to 16,000.

Calcutta was still very new at the beginning of the eighteenth century but Alexander Hamilton was impressed by it, although deploring the unnecessarily unhealthy site which had been chosen for it. 'The Governor's house in the Fort,' he wrote, 'is the most regular Piece of architecture that I ever saw in India. And there are many convenient Lodgings for Factors and Writers within the Fort and some storehouses for the Company's Goods and the Magazines for their Ammunition. The Company has a pretty good Hospital at Calcutta, where many go in to undergo the Penance of Physick but few come out to give account of its Operation. The Company has also a pretty good garden that furnishes the Governor's Table with Herbage and Fruits; and some Fish-ponds to serve his kitchen with good Carp, Calkrop and Mullet.' The rest of the town had grown up in a haphazard fashion, each building where the owner chose, 'everyone taking in what Ground most pleased them for Gardening so that in most houses you must pass through a Garden into the House, the English building near the River's side and the Natives within Land'.[29]

In one sense then the English had clearly arrived in India by the early eighteenth century, establishing their settlements with their characteristic buildings and gardens; but these bases might well have remained, in Professor Harlow's words, 'self-reliant enclaves with a recognised status, capable of defending themselves against neighbouring war lords, and vested with a local revenue to support the military charges'—have become, in fact, like 'medieval Calais under the Merchants of Staple'.[30] Why did they not do so?

To liberal English historians, from T. B. Macaulay to Ramsay Muir, it was a matter almost of dogma that the English conquest of India was unpremeditated. Macaulay wrote in 1841 that it was only the 'encroaching policy' of Dupleix that 'transformed the servants of the East India Company against their will into diplomatists and generals'. Ramsay Muir, writing in the 1920s, held the same view. His book *The Making of British India* is still in print after fifty years, and is still used as a textbook in some universities in the sub-continent. 'Never was an Empire less the result of design than the British Empire of India,' wrote Muir. 'The most astonishing and paradoxical thing of all in regard to this Empire is that the traders who made it never at any time planned it or wanted it. They struggled against it. They regarded it as a burden to be avoided, a distraction from their true business of buying and selling.'[31] He believed that they were dragged unwillingly into the maelstrom of Indian politics during the breakdown of the Mogul empire, compelled to ally with those princes and rulers who would offer them some protection and tempted eventually to help their friends and plan the downfall of their opponents. Jawaharlal Nehru, rather against his will, almost felt compelled to agree with him. 'Looking back,' he wrote, 'it almost seems that the British succeeded in dominating India by a succession of fortuitous circumstances and lucky flukes. With remarkably little effort, considering the glittering prize, they won a great empire and enormous wealth which helped to make them the leading power in the world. It seems easy for a slight turn in events to have taken place which would have dashed their hopes and ended their ambitions.'[32]

Other writers have held that the authorities in London, whether government or company, remained opposed to entanglements but that they were dragged into them by ambitious men in India, by Robert Clive and his ilk. Other historians have questioned even this modified acquittal of official British involvement.

R. P. Masani for example concludes that, although it was private enterprise that established the British empire in India, it was only able to do so 'through its power to purchase the consent of the Government in London'. It built 'on the foundations already and purposefully laid in London'.[33]

At first sight there seems to be a good deal in favour of the view of Ramsay Muir, that the assumption of political power was not only insidious and accidental but regretted even by the actors immediately involved in the drama. The Mogul empire did steadily disintegrate after the death of Aurungzabe in 1707, although this decline was at first hidden from the outside world. The empire had always been a loose construction and its authority far from firmly established in the south. The Moguls had set up an elaborate administrative structure, a good deal of which was later taken over by the British. At the height of their power they had ruled their various provinces through *subadars*, governors or viceroys who represented the emperor. These had originally been paid officials, removable at the will of the emperor. As the power of the centre weakened, however, the provincial officials became stronger. They began to regard their office as their property, possibly to be made hereditary in their family. Strong men competed for office with scant regard for the will of the emperor. Foreign threats to the empire emerged. The Persians, under Nadir Shah, sacked Delhi in 1739 and, amid other booty, carried off the famous peacock throne of the Moguls. The Afghans tried to repeat the triumphs of Muhammad of Ghor six centuries earlier. But the greatest threat of all to the Moguls came from the Marathas.

The Maratha homeland was in the Western Ghats, the range of mountains which, running south from the Vindhya Hills, separates the narrow western coastal plain from the upland plateau of peninsula India. The Marathas first rose to prominence under one great leader, Sivaji, who lived from 1627 to 1680. They kept Britain's west coast bases, Surat and Bombay, in a constant state of alarm. In 1677 Gerald Aungier, who was both president of the Surat factory and Governor of Bombay, spelt out the problem to the directors in London in the clearest possible terms. British commerce was no longer secure and their protests carried no weight. 'Our complaints, remonstrances, paper protests, and threatenings are laughed at,' he said. He told the directors, 'The times now require you to manage your general commerce with your sword in your hand.' The original response of the directors was orthodox enough. They would have none of this. Sir Josiah Child, who became governor of the company in 1681, pronounced soon after his appointment, 'All war is so contrary to our constitution as well as to our interest that we cannot too often inculcate to you our aversion thereunto.'[34]

Six years later Child had changed his mind. Relations in Bengal had become very strained. The British refused to pay what they regarded as unreasonable extra exactions by subordinate Mogul officials. Some Englishmen were subjected to minor indignities such as being compelled to walk barefoot through the town of Patna. The English in Bengal found a militantly minded leader in Job Charnock who set about organising a military defence. Josiah Child supported him. In contrast with his earlier pronouncements, Child now declared that the company 'must establish such a politie of civil and military power, and create and secure such a large revenue to maintain both . . . as may be the foundation of a large, well-grounded, sure English dominion for all time to come'. Child meant only in a small area of Bengal, but this was a sufficiently startling change from his earlier attitudes; and his actions were as vigorous as his words. He sent out six companies of infantry and ten armed vessels to make war on the Mogul empire, although only two ships and about 300 soldiers actually reached the Hugli river. The expedition was not helped by Child's geographical confusion which led him to dispatch the expedition to capture Chittagong on the Karnaphuli river 200 miles away, under the impression that it lay on the Ganges. The troops were not in fact able to do much more than assist Charnock to make a fighting withdrawal to Madras. The campaign was marked by picturesque incidents long remembered on both the British and the Indian sides. Charnock, when he had safely boarded his ship in the Hugli river, used a powerful magnifying glass to concentrate the sun's rays and start a devastating fire on shore. When the enemy stretched a heavy chain across the river to prevent his escape, Charnock severed it with a blow from his sword. Charnock became a legend, but memories of his robust personality could not disguise the fact that when the company first tried military conclusions with the Mogul empire it was totally unsuccessful. The directors, however, rightly calculated that the company had become too valuable to the empire as a link in its Asian trade to be left permanently in disgrace and, in fact, in 1690 when the company had paid a heavy fine and promised to be of good behaviour, Charnock was allowed to return to Bengal.[35]

It had been made clear in the 1680s that the empire was still the master and the company dependent on its favour, but events in Bengal would also seem to show that there was not so much unwillingness to resort to force on the part of the company as has sometimes been suggested. The temptation was obviously greater in the eighteenth century. There was another factor too, Anglo-French rivalry. J. A. Hobson, speaking mainly of the late nineteenth century, regarded the existence of a number of competing empires as one of the characteristics of modern, as distinct from classical, imperialism, and this was equally true in eighteenth-century India.[36] From the time of the appearance of the first Europeans in India, the conflicts of European powers, primarily concerned with European issues, were introduced into Indian politics. In the early days the conflicts of Portuguese, Dutch and English largely manifested themselves as struggles for the favour of Indian rulers. By the eighteenth century they could take more forceful action for themselves. The main protagonists were now England and France. The French East India Company, the *Compagnie des Indes Orientales*, had been founded in 1664. It had challenged the British position on both the west and the east coasts but, fifty years later, its only really important base was Pondicherry in the Carnatic.

European squabbles were not always immediately transferred to India. During the War of the Spanish Succession (1702–14)

Britain and France observed neutrality in India. At the beginning of the War of the Austrian Succession in 1741 both the English and the French traders were prepared to continue this policy. A British fleet which appeared off Pondicherry was persuaded to leave on the grounds that the Nawab of the Carnatic would preserve the neutrality of his dominions. This, however, failed to prevent a French fleet under Admiral La Bourdonnais from seizing Madras in 1746. Although Madras was restored to the English by the Treaty of Aix-la-Chapelle in 1748 and its temporary loss attracted little attention in England, its capture in the course of a European quarrel opened a new era in relations between the West and India.[37]

Although Britain and France were at peace in Europe after 1748 their representatives in India began to exploit the weaknesses in Indian politics to over-reach their rivals. There was plenty of opportunity. Two potentially powerful states were emerging in the south. In 1724 Nizam-ul-mulk had converted the viceroyalty of the south into the hereditary kingdom of Hyderabad. Nizam-ul-mulk was strong enough to secure order in Hyderabad although even he could not prevent a contest for power in the subordinate state of the Carnatic. After Nizam-ul-mulk's death in 1748, Hyderabad too became a prize for warring factions. The other emergent state was Mysore. It had originally been a small state subordinate to the Hindu empire of Vijayanagar but, as that empire declined under Moslem attacks, Mysore rapidly increased in extent and asserted its independence. In 1763 effective power was seized in this still predominantly Hindu state by Hyder Ali, the son of a Moslem officer.

It is difficult to deny, without a deliberate distortion of history to make it fit a theoretical pattern, the critical importance of individuals in the rise of European power in India, comparable to the role of individuals in the establishment of the Mogul empire. One man, Joseph François Dupleix, who became director-general of the French company in 1741, supplied much of the driving force for French activities in India until his recall in 1754.[38] The extent of his ambitions is controversial. Some have

seen him as an 'imperialist' in the mode of Cecil Rhodes who
dreamt of a great French empire in India and set out to create it.
Others have attributed to him only the more limited ambition of
over-reaching the English. There is no denying the vigour of his
policy. He gave his backing to Muzaffar Jang, the grandson of
Nizam-ul-mulk, in his bid for the Nizamship of Hyderabad and
to his ally Chanda Sahib in his attempt to become Nawab of the
Carnatic. Four hundred French troops helped Chanda Sahib to
defeat the reigning Nawab, Anwar-ud-Din Khan at the battle of
Ambur in August 1749. This, combined with an earlier engage-
ment in 1746 when 200 Frenchmen and 700 Indians had
defeated Anwar-ud-Din's son and a force alleged to number
10,000, convinced Indian rulers that European auxiliaries were
well worth having. They welcomed them as allies and classically
minded Englishmen looking back a hundred years later had no
difficulty in seeing the parallels with the Roman empire in decline
welcoming the *foederati* who were to destroy it.

The British were alarmed by the completeness of the French
success and gave their support to Anwar-ud-Din's son, Muhammad Ali, and to the existing Nizam of Hyderabad, Nasir Jang,
Nizam-ul-mulk's son. Initially the British were unsuccessful.
Nasir Jang was killed. So was Muzaffar Jang but a new French
puppet, Salabat Jang, was made Nizam and accepted the great
French soldier, Charles Castelnau de Bussy, as his adviser. Two
major figures were, however, emerging on the British side:
Stringer Lawrence, who became commander of the company's
forces in India, and Robert Clive.[39] The latter had arrived in
India as a clerk aged eighteen in the service of the East India
Company and had served as a soldier during the War of the
Austrian Succession. In 1751 he effected the spectacular capture
of Arcot, the capital of the Carnatic, and the following year
brought about the defeat of Chanda Sahib and the succession of
the British candidate, Muhammad Ali. The recall of the great
Dupleix in 1754 has often been looked upon as an act of the
grossest folly by the French government but more recent writers
have tended to take the view that, in the circumstances of the

time, it must have looked like sensible retrenchment. The French company, unlike the English, had never been a financial success. Whereas the English company lent large sums of money to the government, the French company was a drain on the government. In 1754 the situation in the Carnatic was a drawn battle and the French had too many problems in Europe to extend themselves in India.

Two years later the Seven Years' War broke out. This saw the final expulsion of the French as a political force from India although they retained their base at Pondicherry until after Indian independence in 1947. The French defeat was partly due to better generalship on the English side, partly to the continued divisions in French counsels on the priority to be given to their position in Europe and their position overseas. The French concentration on Europe was subsequently to be regretted by some Frenchmen who would gladly have seen the verdict of the Seven Years' War reversed during the War of American Independence or the Napoleonic Wars.

The British had been more single-minded in their concentration on maritime and commercial affairs and they had triumphed. This must be seen in its proper perspective. From one point of view the Seven Years' War was important. The British had finally ousted any likely European rival from India. This produced a sense of euphoria in some quarters in England. Combined with their simultaneous triumph in North America it made Englishmen feel for the first time like 'an imperial people'. This was new. When Tudor statesmen talked of the 'empire of England', they meant to assert only that England was a sovereign state, not subject to the Pope or any other European power. They did not mean that Englishmen had rights over other peoples. Now some Englishmen began to see England as a world power and for the first time to make those comparisons between the British empire and the Roman empire which were to become a platitude in the next century. But at the same time British success in the Seven Years' War was very limited in Indian terms. They had worsted the French in the Carnatic. Simultaneously, and largely coincidentally, they had become the strongest single power in Bengal. They had now become a 'participating element' in Indian politics, one of the many successor powers to the Mogul empire, but they were still very far indeed from being the dominant power in India.

The situation in Bengal was somewhat different from that in the Carnatic. It had always been more directly under the control of the Mogul emperors than had the south. But the Nawab of Bengal, like other imperial officials, had been tempted by the weakness of the empire to assert his independence. From 1742 until 1756 the Nawab of Bengal was Aliverdi Khan, himself an Afghan adventurer. He was a staunch Moslem and his relations with his Hindu subjects were not of the happiest. He was also intensely suspicious of the foreign traders, especially the British, in his dominions. Shortly before his death he is said to have advised his grandson and successor, Siraj-ud-daula, 'Keep in view the power the European nations have in this country. This fear I would also have freed you from if God had lengthened my days. The work, my son, must now be yours. Their wars and politicks in the [South] should keep you waking. On pretence of private contests between their kings they have seized and divided the country of the King [Mogul emperor] and the goods of his people between them . . . The power of the English is great . . . reduce them first; the others will give you little trouble, when you have reduced them. Suffer them not, my son, to have fortifications or soldiers: if you do, the country is not yours.'⁴⁰

Aliverdi's assessment of the situation was shrewd. Whether or not Siraj-ud-daula was directly influenced by it, he quickly acted. He had good reason to complain about British activities in Bengal. The emperor had granted them exemption from normal excise and transit dues in respect of goods for export. The exemption had never been intended to cover trade within Bengal. From the beginning, however, the company's servants and, still more, Indian hangers-on of the company, had put their own very liberal interpretation on their privileges.⁴¹ The company had deplored the abuse but had never been able to stop it. In June 1756, two months after Aliverdi's death, Siraj-ud-daula marched on Calcutta. Calcutta was totally unprepared. Some, including the governor, hastily sought refuge on ships in the river but a handful, led by John Holwell, held out in the fort for a short time. They were captured on 20 June. That night they were placed in the guardroom, the famous Black Hole.[42] It was a room only 15ft by 18ft and of the 146 confined there in the evening only 23 were alive in the morning. The rest had suffocated. There seems to have been no deliberate cruelty on the Indian side. They wanted to keep their prisoners safe, not to murder them. But the Black Hole lived on in English folk memory, the first in a long series of incidents which were to have totally different meanings for the two sides. Siraj-ud-daula was not present and was not personally responsible for the disaster but he showed no particular revulsion when he heard of it. He was neither the monster of English legend nor the hero of some later Indian nationalist propaganda. He was simply one of the tough men concerned in the battle for the succession.

The English were determined to avenge the Black Hole and to regain their position in Calcutta. In October Clive set sail from Madras. By this time there were many forces operating in Bengal politics. Aliverdi Khan had been a strong ruler but his family had no special claim to the viceroyalty. Other Moslem nobles, notably Mir Jafar, who was eventually to throw in his lot with the English, felt that their claims were at least as good. Pannikar contends that the Hindus also saw their chance of regaining power from the Moslems. Previously political power had been based on land and on the military aristocracy. But, by now, Bengal had been subjected for a century to the influence of a commercial economy based on oceanic trade. A new merchant class, the Marwari merchants, had emerged and had many interests in common with the European traders. They would in any case have been unhappy to see them expelled, since their own prosperity depended on the sea-borne commerce carried on by the Europeans. But personal factors were added too. The leading Bengal merchant, Jaga Seth, had been insulted by Siraj-ud-daula and he took the lead in allying with the East India Company.

It has long been accepted that the famous battle of Plassey of June 1757, which laid the foundations of the British dominance in Bengal, was not much of a battle. Pannikar goes so far as to say, 'Plassey was a transaction, not a battle, a transaction by which the *compradors* [capitalists] of Bengal, led by Jaga Seth, sold the Nawab to the East India Company.'[43] Certainly there were plenty of conspirators against Siraj-ud-daula in the ranks of his own army, while Mir Jafar, supposedly commanding part of his forces, held off until he saw which side was likely to win. Mir Jafar became Nawab in Siraj-ud-daula's place. Mir Jafar, however, was plainly the puppet of the company. He was to be deposed in 1760 in favour of his son-in-law, Mir Kasim, who was to be deposed himself a few years later in favour of a restored Mir Jafar and subsequently the youthful Najm-ud-daula.

This was the period which was to appear in liberal textbooks as that of 'power without responsibility', the worst of all forms of government. The situation was aggravated in 1765 when the emperor granted the company the *diwani* of Bengal. Under the Moguls the *diwan* of an area was nominally responsible for the collection of revenue and for administration including justice. By the 1765 agreement, however, the company was not responsible for the collection of the revenue but only for the receipt of a lump sum, from which they had to pay specified amounts to the emperor and the Nawab, the latter for administrative purposes. The company expected a fat profit from the transaction. Looked at from one point of view it was simply the heir of the inequitable taxation system of the Moguls which had something in common with the tax farming system of France under the *ancien régime*, that is to say, the government contracted with a powerful group to provide a certain revenue. How it reimbursed itself and how much profit it obtained was largely a matter for the company. It was at best a wasteful, and at worst a severely oppressive system because the amount wrung from the peasantry always greatly exceeded that required or received by the government. The company proposed to put the expected profit to a new use, namely to balance its books in India by using it to purchase goods for export. These hopes were disappointed, as new military commitments swallowed up the profits.

The results were even more unhappy for the inhabitants of Bengal. In May 1769 Richard Becher, himself an employee of the company, wrote home 'since the accession of the Company to the *diwani*, the condition of the people in this country has been worse than it was before . . . this fine country which flourished under the most despotic and arbitrary Government is verging towards its ruin'. Becher had political reasons for his denunciations but criticisms of this kind began to arouse serious misgivings in Britain.[44]

The first large-scale British venture into Indian government had not been propitious for either party. Did the British by their entanglement with Indian affairs as the Mogul empire collapsed also prevent the emergence of a satisfactory indigenous government? Indian nationalists later, very naturally, claimed that they did. The argument, however, is not an easy one to sustain. The only serious indigenous contenders for power were the Marathas. They were a remarkable group which rose from obscurity within one generation. They have not had a good press from western historians who have seen them essentially as marauders. Even an historian as sympathetic to the Indian point of view as Dr Spear concludes that, having failed to defeat the Mogul empire under Aurungzabe, they lost their sense of direction and became 'toughened raiders notorious for their rapacity and ruthlessness as much as for their daring',[45] too much hated by their fellow Indians to be accepted as national leaders. In the last resort the Marathas did not show enough cohesion to overcome the great obstacles before them. Some communist historians have suggested that this was because of their social divisions, the unbridgeable gap between the small dominant Brahman class and the majority of Sudras or cultivators.[46]

Most historians, however, have laid more emphasis on the divisions between the Maratha leaders after the death of Sivaji in 1680. By the middle of the eighteenth century there were five separate centres of Maratha power, the Peshwa, nominally the

chief minister of the Maratha confederation at Poona, the Gaekwar of Baroda, the Bhonsla of Nagpur and two northern chiefs,
Holkhar at Indore and Sindia at Gwalior. They lost their one
great chance to seize the empire when the emperor called upon
them to assist him against the Afghans in 1761; the Marathas
were defeated by the Afghans at the battle of Panipat and after
that the confederation began to fall to pieces. Nevertheless some
Hindu nationalists have seen them not only as the authentic
continuation of Hindu resistance to the spread of the Mogul
empire in the seventeenth and early eighteenth centuries but
also as the driving force behind resistance to the English up to the
'Mutiny' of 1857.[47] These views received some support from an
earlier generation of Englishmen. The Duke of Wellington, who
fought them, praised their 'patriotism'. Sir William Hunter, the
great nineteenth-century historian of India, says categorically
that the British won India from the Hindus, meaning the
Marathas, not from the Moguls.[48]

However unintentional British involvement in the government
of India may have been in an earlier period, the same cannot be
said of the era of the Revolutionary and Napoleonic Wars.
Deliberate British expansion reached its height when Wellington's
brother, Marquis Wellesley, was Governor-General from 1798
to 1803. The reason was simple and obvious. The British feared,
with reason, that the French would make common cause with
their enemies in India and try to reverse the results of the Seven
Years' War. Hyderabad and Mysore were regarded as being at
risk. The aged Nizam of Hyderabad was persuaded to dismiss
the French troops he had employed as a defence against the
Marathas and replace them with troops under British officers.
Tipu Sultan of Mysore was made of sterner stuff. He hated the
British—his cherished model of a clockwork tiger eating an
Englishman is well known to visitors to the Victoria and Albert
Museum—and he refused to sever his connections with the
French. He had miscalculated his strength. Wellesley marched
against him and Tipu Sultan died fighting in the defence of his
capital, Seringapatam. Part of Mysore was annexed and the

British had a new power base in southern India. But the most formidable Indian fighting force, even if now disorganised, was still the Marathas. The future Duke of Wellington defeated them in the hard-fought battle of Assaye in 1803. Political doubts in London prevented him from completing his plans for crushing the Marathas and their final defeat in the field was postponed until 1818. Victorian textbooks had no hesitation in choosing 1818 as the date when the British finally came to control India. They were well aware that much of India, the princely states, never came under direct British rule and that a Mogul emperor lived on, a pensioner in Delhi, until 1858; but after 1818 there seemed to be no power left which could seriously challenge the British in India.

The story was an extraordinary one. A small offshore island in the Atlantic, which at the beginning of the story was still fighting for its life against stronger continental powers, had come to rule a sub-continent with a population the size of Europe, 10,000 miles away by sea at the other side of the world. Thoughtful Englishmen never ceased to be amazed at it. Macaulay called it the 'strangest of all political anomalies'. Ramsay Muir, nearly one hundred years later, considered 'there is nothing that can be compared with it in the whole history of the world'. Was it indeed unpremeditated? On the face of it Sir Thomas Roe would have considered the idea absurd—and yet, the Spaniards had done equally extraordinary things in South America. The conquistador tradition was already there in European experience. Modern inhibitions simply did not apply. Ideas of self-determination were not part of the mental furniture of the eighteenth century. Even in Europe territories still changed hands for purely dynastic reasons. Nothing that was done in India was morally worse than the partitions of Poland or the Prussian seizure of Silesia.

It is true that the British government never gave the state backing to the company that the Portuguese, Dutch and French companies received. From the beginning there were Englishmen who said that these overseas ventures were costly and not really productive of the national good. The directors themselves

C

officially frowned on political commitments. Yet this policy of
minimum commitment was not always upheld. When European
complications intervened, as in the wars with France, the government would back the company, even force action upon it. The
mere presence of European traders in India was itself transform-
ing society, whether the Europeans wished to change Indian
society or not. After the Seven Years' War the British seem to
have emerged with a new self-confidence, a willingness to take
on almost any responsibility. This expansive mood was soon to
be shaken in the American War of Independence. But the loss of
the American colonies itself only served to confirm a tendency
which Professor Harlow believes to have been present for a
generation before the war, namely a loss of interest in colonies of
settlement which were troublesome to govern and did not fit
comfortably into prevailing mercantilist theories, and a swing of
interest to the East where profits were believed to be high and
administrative costs low.[49] If Professor Harlow's theory is
correct, what resulted was one of the great ironies of history.
What the British committed themselves to in the East was not
profitable trade instead of expensive dominion but a much more
complex form of dominion, not over people of their own stock
and traditions, but over alien peoples.

It was in India that the British first faced the problem of
governing alien peoples on any significant scale. They were later
to acquire dominion over another 70 million people of non-
European stock, mainly in Africa. The decisions they took and
the traditions they established in India were therefore to have
worldwide significance. They did not reach those decisions in an
intellectual vacuum. They brought to them their previous experience of governing colonies, however remote these might at first
sight appear to be from Indian experience. The development of
the British empire was a single process and the conventional
separation of India from the rest of the story has led to many
misunderstandings and lost insights. Britain also had strongly
developed constitutional traditions of her own. The development
of India was profoundly affected by the fact that it was Britain

and not any other European power which established itself as the successor of the Moguls. At the time that Britain assumed responsibility for the administration of India, however, Britain itself was undergoing profound changes from a predominantly agrarian, oligarchical state to a predominantly industrial, more democratic state. Britain was also part of Europe and the eighteenth and nineteenth centuries saw bewilderingly rapid changes in European political philosophy. They saw both the apparent triumph of *realpolitik* and the dawn of a new, and more universal, humanitarianism. All these factors affected British thinking about India and, in turn, the need to solve Indian problems affected the development of British political thinking and practice.

Notes to Chapter 1 will be found on pages 236–8.

Chapter 2 THE BRITISH REACTION TO INDIA

THERE WAS no cult of India as there was of China in the eighteenth century. No great philosopher exalted her as Voltaire and Quesney did China—or at least a highly abstract ideal of China—as a rational society which might serve as a model for contemporary Europe. Indian art was not so influential as Chinese art. But neither was there yet the patronising attitude to all things Indian which was to become widespread in the following century. There was curiosity about India, part of the general eighteenth-century curiosity about the world in which they lived which caused scholarly men to make serious researches into Indian history and culture. There was a growing recognition that India was a land of contrasts and extremes, particularly of wealth and poverty. Like China, although in a different way, India became a symbol for some European thinkers—a useful illustration for western reformers of the stultifying effects of eastern despotism. As India became increasingly involved with British politics, doctrines of 'trusteeship' began to evolve. As the British eventually faced the fact that they were *ipso facto* the rulers of India, the conflict became manifest between the 'conservatives' who, for a variety of reasons, desired to interfere as little as possible with Indian society, and the 'westernisers' who wanted to reform India and make it over in a western image.

The late eighteenth century produced a number of men who made a serious study of Indian philosophy and culture. Pre-eminent among these was Sir William Jones, the son of another William Jones who had been a distinguished mathematician and member of the Royal Society.[1] The younger William Jones who

was a remarkable linguist—he was reputed to know twenty-eight
languages—went out to India in 1783 as a judge in the Calcutta
Supreme Court. He went, partly for career reasons because he had
failed to obtain the appointments he sought at home, but also to
pursue his genuine interest in oriental learning. In particular he
had in mind to compile a complete code of Hindu law. In Bengal
he found a small group of men, of whom Charles Wilkins was the
most important, already interested in Indian studies. With
Wilkins's help he learnt Sanskrit. Jones was one of the very few
men with sufficient scholarly background, scientific, legal and
linguistic, to be able to attempt a serious evaluation of Indian
civilisation. He already had a high regard for Indian powers of
literary imagination and he was impressed, as he expected to be,
by Indian poetry. He was more surprised to find himself
impressed by Indian philosophy and science, concluding that
the Indians had come very near to anticipating Newton's theory
of gravity.

Jones was convinced that the Indian classics should be given to
the West in good translations. His friend Wilkins was the pioneer
in this field, producing a translation in 1784 of the *Bhagavad Gita*,
perhaps the most famous Sanskrit ethical text which, set in the
form of a dramatic poem, argued the need for every man to do his
duty in his own place in society. Three years later Wilkins
translated the *Hitopadesia*, a collection of pious maxims. Wilkins
and Jones won the support of the Governor-General, Warren
Hastings, for their work and Hastings himself contributed a very
interesting preface to Wilkins's *Bhagavad Gita*. Rather surprisingly, he took it for granted that until recently his fellow countrymen had regarded the Indians as 'creatures scarce elevated above
the degree of savage life' and considered that this prejudice had
been abated but not eradicated. He thought that 'these [ie Indian
writings and western appreciation of them] will survive when the
British dominion in India shall have long ceased to exist, and when
the forces which it once wielded of wealth and power are lost to
remembrance'. Jones himself, although he translated some legal
texts, concentrated mainly on literary works. He translated

Kalidasa's comedy, *Sakuntala*, which was immediately popular in England and led some critics to compare Kalidasa with Shakespeare.

Although the translations were important in introducing Indian thought to the West, Jones's foundation of the Asiatic Society of Bengal (later to be the Royal Asiatic Society of Bengal) in 1784, soon after his arrival in India, was to be even more significant. The society was deliberately modelled on the Royal Society with the specific object of studying Indian culture and history. It enjoyed official patronage—Warren Hastings was a staunch supporter. It was initially a European society and Indians were not admitted to membership until 1829 but from the beginning Indian scholars contributed to its published proceedings which soon established themselves as a major scholarly publication. It was to play a crucial role in the revival of interest in Indian history not only among westerners but among the Indians themselves. In one sense history was omnipresent in Hindu society but in another, in the sense of critical inquiry, it had never been prominent in Hindu scholarship. Too much had been overlaid by superstition.[2] Indian nationalists were later to draw deep at the well of newly discovered knowledge about their past. Gandhi himself, who was much influenced by the classical texts, especially the *Bhagavad Gita*, admitted that he had been enabled to return to his own roots partly through the work of foreign scholars.[3]

This scholarly tradition was never entirely lost in the European approach to India.[4] Sir William Jones was followed in India by Henry Colebrooke and Horace Hayman Wilson, who later became the first professor of Sanskrit at Oxford. Interest sprang up in Europe too. The Royal Asiatic Society was founded in London in 1821. In the course of the nineteenth century English scholars extended their interest from literary sources to archaeology. The pioneer of Indian archaeology was Alexander Cunningham (later General Sir Alexander Cunningham), a Royal Engineers' officer, whose work extended from 1831 to 1885. The great patron of Indian archaeology in the early twentieth century was Lord Curzon who, as viceroy, reformed the Indian Archaeological

Survey which worked under a great series of directors from Sir John Marshall to Sir Mortimer Wheeler.

The British, however, allowed the initiative in linguistic, although not in archaeological, studies to pass to continental scholars. The French began to take a serious interest during the Napoleonic Wars but it was the Germans who made the field peculiarly their own. A Bavarian, Franz Bopp, virtually established the science of comparative philology by taking up the tentative suggestions of William Jones as to the striking similarities between Sanskrit and the classical languages of Europe, to try to reconstruct a primitive original. Max Müller, German by birth, although married to an Englishwoman and holding the post of professor of comparative philology at Oxford, spent thirty years producing a translation of the Vedic Hymns, the *Rig Veda*. Müller was conscious of the impact his work was likely to have in India as well as in Europe. Although the *Rig Veda* was regarded as the most sacred of all the Hindu scriptures, in Sanskrit it was inaccessible to all but Brahmanical scholars. In translation, Müller believed, it would have as much impact as the printing of the Bible had in Europe. He also wrote a *History of Sanskrit Literature* and edited a massive series of translations, *The Sacred Books of the East*, which included a number of Indian texts.

This scholarly tradition of inquiry, however, was only one of a number of European approaches to India. Even in the late eighteenth century there were Englishmen who had concluded that the Indians were 'benighted heathen' who must be saved from themselves. Prominent among these was Charles Grant the elder. Grant was a servant of the East India Company who had served in India. He was one of the great Evangelical group who became known as the Clapham Sect and were foremost in a number of reform movements, including that for the abolition of slavery. Grant's motives were of the best but he had no doubt about his views on Indians. 'Upon the whole,' he wrote, 'we cannot avoid recognising in the people of Hindostan, a race of men lamentably degenerate and base; retaining but a feeble sense of moral obligation; yet obstinate in their disregard of what they know to be right,

governed by malevolent and licentious passions, strongly exem-
plifying the effects produced on society by a great and general
corruption of manners, and sunk in misery by their vices, in a
country peculiarly calculated by its natural advantages, to promote
the prosperity of its inhabitants.'[5]

In the eyes of most Englishmen in the late eighteenth century,
however, a more pressing problem than the salvation of Indians
was the impact of Indian wealth upon British society and British
politics. In their early days in India, the British merchants who
established themselves at Surat, Madras, Bombay or Calcutta give
the impression of very ordinary men who adapted themselves,
more or less, to what one contemporary described as a life 'more
like unto a College, Monastery, or a house under Religious Orders
than any other'.[6] They dined each day in a common mess and, at
least in theory, attended the services of the established church
every day and observed a curfew every evening. A few took to
drink. Some acquired Indian mistresses. The climate, and perhaps
the constant threat of ill-health and an early death, frayed the
tempers of others. There were occasional scandals and even rare
resorts to violence but the general impression is one of the sober
pursuit of routine business.

The picture appears to change spectacularly in the eighteenth
century when new opportunities for amassing great wealth suddenly opened up. Men felt no inhibitions about seizing these
opportunities. Their salaries from the company had always been
very small. 'Writers', the most junior grade, were expected to
serve for five years at £10 per annum, having given a bond of £500
for good behaviour when they were first employed. Even chiefs
of factories were paid only £40 per annum plus board and
lodgings.[7] It is hardly surprising that the young men often found
themselves seriously in debt. But a man was not only permitted,
but expected, to supplement his salary for himself. Even in
England the perquisites of an office were regarded as an important
aspect of a man's remuneration. In India the company's servants
were not so much salaried employees in the modern sense as men
paid a retaining fee to perform certain duties for the company and

free to trade on their own account for the rest. When Robert Clive told a parliamentary committee of inquiry a little later that, far from being ashamed of the fortune he had acquired, he 'stood astonished at his own moderation', it was a completely honest answer and one that most of his contemporaries in India would have thoroughly endorsed.

The first effect the British public noticed was the return of the 'nabobs', men grown suddenly rich on Indian profits. The *nouveaux riches* are always resented and satirical pieces appeared in contemporary periodicals about the 'Mushroom family' seen through the eyes of John Homespun.[8] Macaulay said later that they raised the price of everything in their neighbourhood 'from fresh eggs to rotten boroughs',[9] in other words they were a seriously disturbing element in English society. It was not just dislike of the *nouveaux riches*. Men began to fear that this new wealth would destroy the delicate balance of the constitution. The 'balance' of the constitution was a fundamental principle to men of the eighteenth century. It was a system which later reformers condemned as 'corrupt', with its placemen and its rotten boroughs, but contemporaries—at least the political and governing classes— saw it as a balance of interests which preserved the 'liberties' of Englishmen far better than contemporary continental despotisms preserved the rights of their nationals.

The 'East India' interest had always played its part in this balance, less powerful than the West India interest, but important in its place. The sudden accretion of new wealth on this scale could not easily be fitted in to the system. More specifically, men feared that this immensely valuable source of patronage might fall into one set of hands, perhaps those of the government. George III had become king in 1760. Very probably his ambition was to become, as Professor Namier has said, 'the first among the borough-mongering, electioneering gentlemen of England', rather than to revive the absolute prerogatives of the Stuarts. But contemporary fears were summed up in Dunning's famous resolution: 'The power of the Crown has increased, is increasing, and ought to be diminished.'

The first British Acts of Parliament dealing with India, North's Regulating Act of 1773 and Pitt's Act of 1784, were generated by the needs and fears of British politics but this did not prevent them from having important effects in India. The 1773 Act was intended as an interim measure until the company's charter came up for renewal in 1780. It made some alterations in the constitution of the Courts of Directors and Proprietors in London. More important, it raised the governor of Bengal to the status of governor-general with, unfortunately ill-defined, authority over Madras and Bombay, and set up a council of four in Bengal to share decision-making with the governor-general. It established a Supreme Court at Calcutta with four judges to try cases involving 'British subjects'. It restricted the right of company servants to engage in private trade and made provision for them to be prosecuted in England for certain offences committed in India. Some of the most important effects of the Act were not anticipated. The Supreme Court of Calcutta introduced a new element of anglicisation into India because the law it enforced was English law. The British settlements in India had been allowed to enforce their own law locally before—not always in an enlightened fashion: a man was burnt at the stake for witchcraft at Bombay in 1671.[10] But this was on a different scale and 'British subjects' for this purpose was frequently held to include Indians acting in some capacity for the company. More immediately apparent, however, were the drawbacks inherent in the divided authority of the governor-general and his council which opened the way for the bitter quarrels of Warren Hastings and Philip Francis.

It was not until 1784 that the British government assumed any direct responsibility for the management of Indian affairs. Fox's India Bill of 1783 passed the Commons but was thrown out by the Lords who feared that it placed too much patronage in the hands of Fox's friends. Pitt's India Act of the following year was similar in many ways to that proposed by Fox but left patronage in the hands of the company. It began the cumbersome system of dual control by the government and the company which was to last until 1858. The Court of Directors remained in London but now to superintend its activities there was the 'Board of Control' consisting of six privy councillors, presided over by a secretary of state. Direct British government responsibility for Indian affairs therefore began long before 1858. But it was a curious system in which a great trading company was also an important organ of government. The company's charter came up for renewal at intervals, usually every twenty years. In 1813 it lost its monopoly of trade with India (although not with China). In 1833 it ceased to trade.

This element of government participation focused the attention of Englishmen upon what their fellow countrymen were doing in India. It is true that the reactions of many men, including Edmund Burke himself, were significantly influenced by domestic political considerations but it would be superficial to suppose that that was the only factor at work. The eighteenth century saw a great advance in ideals of humanitarianism and reform, however brutal life remained for the majority.[11] The growing feeling that the Atlantic slave trade was no longer tolerable was one manifestation of this. The British also had an 'image' of themselves—to use twentieth-century jargon—as a constitutional people. A little later even the conservative Lord Castlereagh was to lecture his fellow European diplomats on the merits of the glorious revolution of 1688. In all their colonies of settlement the colonists took their rights as British subjects with them, their civil rights and their rights under English common law. The situation the British were facing in India was a totally new one and no one supposed that old solutions could simply be transferred there, but they were influenced by their previous experience and their general framework of political ideas. As Professor Stokes puts it: 'The transformation of the Englishman from nabob to sahib was . . . fundamentally an English and not an Indian transformation.'[12]

The first important man to be challenged was Robert Clive himself. In 1759 the Mogul emperor had granted him a *jaghir* or military fief in the form of a large allotment of land near Calcutta, nominally sufficient to keep up 6,000 foot and 5,000 horse. This had been questioned even before his return to Britain. When he did return for the last time in 1767 he lived ostentatiously. He bought Claremont in Surrey from the Duchess of Newcastle, leased Lord Chatham's house in Bath, employed the famous landscape gardener, Capability Brown, to lay out his pleasure gardens in Shropshire and, according to the custom of the time, returned seven MPs to Parliament. His private enemies at India House pursued him and in 1772 a parliamentary select committee —of which Clive was a member—was set up to inquire into the affairs of the company. The following year another committee— the secret committee—was appointed by the Prime Minister, Lord North. Serious charges of financial misconduct were brought against Clive but the final vote of the House was ambiguous. They voted on 22 May 1773 by 155 votes to 95 that, as a matter of fact, on Mir Jafar's accession to the Nawabship of Bengal and subsequently Clive did enrich himself to the value of £234,000, but 'Lord Clive did at the same time render great and meritorious services to his country'.[13]

The great debate was to concern Warren Hastings and it is significant that the charges brought against Hastings were less of personal gain and more of public misconduct. Hastings was not perhaps altogether innocent of some of the charges brought against him[14] but against that must be weighed the fact that they were brought by personal and ambitious enemies and that Hastings had himself fought hard against corruption and improper practices. Hastings first went out to India in 1750 as a writer in the service of the East India Company. He served under Clive and returned to England in 1764, one of the few prominent men in this period not to return with a great personal fortune. He went back to India in 1768 and, in 1772, became president of the council in Bengal. The following year he was named as Governor-General under North's Regulating Act. North's Act had effectively divided authority between the governor-general and the four members of his council. Hastings found himself faced by three enemies on the council, led by Philip Francis. Relations deteriorated so far that, in 1780, Hastings and Francis fought a duel in which the latter was seriously wounded. Ultimate authority, however, lay in London. In 1785 Hastings was recalled.

The following year proceedings were started against him in Parliament. The formal motion of impeachment was accepted by the Commons in 1787 and the trial before the Lords dragged on until 1791. At the end of it Hastings was acquitted. Before the end, the trial which had been one of the sights of London had come to be regarded as a monumental bore and public sympathy had veered towards Hastings and away from his great accuser, Edmund Burke.

The impeachment was not a clash between two rival Indian policies. On the contrary there was remarkable agreement between Hastings and Burke on essential principles. Both agreed, not only that the welfare of the inhabitants of India ought to be taken into account, but that it ought to be the first consideration of policy. Both expressed considerable respect for Indian traditions and agreed that they should never be interfered with lightly. Hastings indeed had rejected Clive's so-called 'dual system' of sharing governmental responsibility between Englishmen and Indians and had tried to make his government as Indian as possible. The Hastings trial did not inaugurate a great era of debate about Indian affairs. On the contrary, the boredom it ultimately engendered made India an unfashionable subject.[15] But despite this it may still remain 'one of the most spectacular crises of conscience through which an imperial power has ever passed'.

In his eloquent attacks upon Hastings, Burke formulated principles for the proper rule of alien people. This is not to say either that Burke's own motives were wholly disinterested or that the principles he proclaimed were consistently acted upon thereafter. But they were there on record; they could be appealed to by critics at home and in India. The British had rejected a purely cynical view of their relations with India and had proclaimed to the world that they had moral responsibilities in India and indeed that the legitimacy of their position there depended upon the fulfilment of those responsibilities. It was a bold claim and the acquittal of Hastings did not affect it. Hastings had not rejected the concept of responsibility but had claimed, successfully, that he had not sinned against it.

Burke did not disguise the fact that his anxiety about India sprang in part from his concern for the British situation. He dreaded, he said, the letting loose of 'all the corrupt wealth of India, acquired by the oppression of that country, for the corruption of all the liberties of this . . . Today, the Commons of Great Britain prosecute the delinquents of India—Tomorrow the delinquents of India may be the Commons of Great Britain.'[16] But this was entirely consistent with his view that justice was indivisible and one could not apply different standards to oneself and to other people without disaster. He had proclaimed earlier, when Fox's India Bill was before the House, 'The rights of *men*, that is to say, the natural rights of mankind are indeed sacred things . . .' He rejected Hastings's defence that he had sometimes been compelled to act in India in ways that would have been judged reprehensible in Europe. 'My Lords,' said Burke, 'We positively deny that principle . . . the laws of morality are the same everywhere; and . . . there is no action, which would pass for an act of extortion, of peculation, of bribery, and oppression in England, that is not an act of extortion, of peculation, of bribery, and oppression in Europe, Asia, Africa, and all the world over.'[17]

Central to Burke's argument was his belief that all authority is a trust. 'Every species of political dominion, and every description of commercial privilege,' he once proclaimed in the Commons, 'are in the strictest sense a trust.'[18] He did not argue that Britain should withdraw from responsibility in India. On the contrary he came close to saying that she had acquired a kind of divine right and obligation there. 'There we are placed by the Sovereign Disposer; and we must do the best we can in our situation. The situation of man is the preceptor of his duty.' What he did believe was that empire should be benevolent and not exploitative. Contemporaneously Adam Smith had condemned the old empires of Spain and Portugal for being empires of exploitation and argued that this was sterilising and restrictive and did not even make good economic sense.[19] Burke saw no reason why the economic connection between Britain and India, properly and responsibly maintained, should not be mutually beneficial.

Burke's concept of the proper relationship between Britain and her dependencies was at the root of two centuries of Britain's justification of her imperial role. Even after World War I Lord Lugard could write his *The Dual Mandate in British Tropical Africa*, arguing that the roles of colonisers and indigenous inhabitants were complementary, and economically and otherwise beneficial to both. The doctrine of 'trusteeship' permeated the Anglo-Indian relationship, above all through the Indian Civil Service. It spread beyond India in the work of men like Lord Cromer in Egypt who could claim that he had 'regenerated' a people.[20] It lay behind Rudyard Kipling's much misunderstood poem, *The Recessional*, in which, exasperated by the extravagances of the Jubilee celebrations of 1897, he prophesied that England's power could be 'one with Nineveh and Tyre' if she forgot her humble obligations to duty. It finds expression in Woodruff's study of *The Men who Ruled India* in which he compares the men of the ICS with the 'Guardians' in Plato's ideal state, and suggests that this may have been the unconscious model they had in their own minds.[21]

Platonic guardians, of course, had their drawbacks. They had, by definition, to be separate from the people whom they ruled. It is possible to exaggerate the freedom and equality of intercourse between Indians and Englishmen in the eighteenth century. There was much social exclusiveness on both sides even then.[22] But it did differ from the remarkable, indeed unique, experiment which was the Indian Civil Service. Out of the condemnation of the corruption of the eighteenth century grew what was admitted even by its enemies to be one of the least corruptible bodies in the world. A century and a half later another Englishman, Sir Eric Drummond, created the first international secretariat for the League of Nations. It was unprecedented but it quickly became the norm—so much so that men ceased to think that there was anything exceptional about it. In its day the Indian Civil Service was the same. It was far in advance in recruitment and training of the civil service at home. In 1793 Cornwallis as Governor-General, to save himself from embarrassing claims for patronage at home, laid down that ordinary vacancies in the company's service must be filled by those already in the company's service, in order of seniority. Promotion by seniority lasted until 1861 and, far from being stultifying, it seems to have been very important in saving the service from place-seeking and in creating a uniquely independent body in which men never hesitated to criticise their superiors or the government.[23] Haileybury College was founded in 1806 to provide preliminary training in England. As early as 1832 Macaulay argued for recruitment by open competition and this was finally accepted in 1853.

There was never any shortage of recruits. Until after World War I the ICS remained the prestige service of the empire. They were normally middle-class men with their careers to make, assured of good salaries and pensions but with no expectation of lush pickings. Often they were earnest Victorians, strongly imbued with fashionable evangelical sentiment. The *esprit de corps* of the service was remarkable. It saw itself as an instrument for justice and humanitarianism. Individuals identified closely with the people among whom they worked. Sometimes officials wrote to the central government more like MPs representing their constituents than like bureaucrats reporting to their superiors. Perceptive Indians, however, did not fail to see the dangers of this identification. Indian civil servants too readily became committed to defending 'their' India, often the India of the peasants and the simple people, not only against the iniquities of the British government but also against other elements in Indian society.[24] But it would be wrong to see the ICS as predominantly a conservative force. On the contrary it supplied a dynamic force. It had been suggested that social and other reforms in nineteenth-century Britain only gained momentum when early reforms had generated a bureaucracy with the interest and expertise to suggest further changes in society.[25] A not dissimilar process happened in India, sometimes associated with the same men who were the reformers in England.

This was an ironic result of the attacks upon Warren Hastings. Nothing was further from the mind of Edmund Burke than to suggest radical reforms in India. Burke was numbered among those who, like William Jones, respected Indian civilisation. He told the House of Commons: 'This multitude of men does not consist of an abject and barbarous populace . . . but a people for ages civilized and cultivated: cultivated by all the arts of polished life, whilst we were yet in the woods.' He reminded his hearers that there were to be found in India, 'a multitude of cities, not exceeded in population and trade by those of the first class in Europe; merchants and bankers, individual houses of whom have once vied in capital with the Bank of England . . .'.[26] But Burke's objections to rash interference in India went even deeper. He was already committed to that view of society which he worked out more fully in his opposition to the French Revolution. Society was not an artificial structure which could be rebuilt as each succeeding generation chose. It was a living organism which had developed slowly and, sometimes painfully, from the wisdom and experience of the past. Any man who wished to change it should approach his task cautiously, even reverently. In practical terms, if a particular community had created a particular form of society and lived successfully in it, it was strong evidence that it was well adapted to their needs. Only urgent necessity could dictate radical changes. Burke's views lived on. In his study of the influence of the Utilitarians in India, Professor Stokes concludes, 'The resistance which liberalism encountered in India was not the inertia of the existing order. It encountered what in a more intellectualised tradition would be called a rival political philosophy. It encountered the spirit of Burke.'[27]

This respect for the natural development of India found expression in widely read historians like William Robertson. It was shared by some senior officials of the Board of Control such as James Cumming who deplored the tendency of young English officials to think that they knew how to run the affairs of India better than the Indians did.[28] Some of the most important Englishmen in India, including Robert Clive and above all Warren Hastings himself, had shared this 'conservative' attitude to India. Clive had wished to interfere as little as was practicable with Indian administration and revenue collection; hence the cumbersome and inefficient 'dual government' in Bengal after 1765. Hastings had elevated what for Clive had only been an expedient into a principle of policy and had added to it a real interest in, and sympathy with, Indian civilisation.

'Conservatism' was soon to come into conflict with its opposite, 'westernisation'. Early examples of 'westernisation' or 'anglicisation' in India were limited and often accidental. For example, North's Regulating Act, by setting up the Calcutta Supreme Court, introduced English law into Bengal on a significant scale for the first time but this was not its primary intention. The first governor-general to pursue anything like a westernising policy was Cornwallis (1786–93) and he was no doctrinaire, quite the contrary. Ramsay Muir probably described him justly when he wrote, 'A man of the highest integrity and the most genuine public spirit, he was lacking in imagination, and could never escape from a sort of national and class complacency, which led him to believe that English institutions and customs represented the summit of human achievement, and that the English governing class of large landowners embodied all that was most excellent in English life.'[29] The most pressing problem with which Cornwallis had to deal was the revenue system in Bengal. He continually misled himself by looking for English parallels and precedents. He separated the civil jurisdiction from the revenue administration—a major departure from Mogul practice—and brought criminal jurisdiction under British control. The revenue was now the responsibility of the 'collector' in each district. Other matters came within the jurisdiction of the 'magistrate'. Cornwallis's model for the magistrate was that most English of institutions, the justice of the peace, who traditionally had much wider powers and responsibilities than merely the dispensing of justice. So far his reforms (which had been foreshadowed by Hastings) had a good deal to commend them. He was on more dubious ground when he insisted upon seeing the *zemindar*, the Bengal tax-farmer, as a landowner in the English sense. This represented a total misunderstanding of Indian systems of land tenure and of the rights of the peasant cultivators. But Cornwallis, in a laudable attempt to regularise the tax system so that men might know in advance what their tax burdens were, fastened the 'Permanent Settlement' upon Bengal in 1793. The settlement gave the *zemindars* inalienable rights over their districts which Cornwallis thought of as estates in the English sense. Cornwallis's chief adviser and successor, John Shore (Lord Teignmouth), begged him to limit the settlement to ten years but Cornwallis held that only permanency would give the *zemindar* sufficient security to encourage him to cultivate his 'estates'.[30]

The Permanent Settlement of Bengal represented a major breach with Indian traditions but it was, like the Calcutta Supreme Court, an accidental result. The next generation saw a much more serious and deliberate attack upon Indian forms of government and society. Two groups had few inhibitions about the introduction of western concepts, the Evangelicals and the Utilitarians. Among the Evangelicals the belief, so eloquently expressed by Charles Grant the elder in 1797, that the Indians were simply benighted heathen who needed rescuing, remained strong. Even Reginald Heber, the Bishop of Calcutta (1822–6), who travelled extensively in India and was, in many ways, sympathetic and appreciative of Indian life, was also the author of that most popular of missionary hymns, 'From Greenland's icy mountains', which runs in part:

> What though the spicy breezes
> Blow soft o'er Ceylon's isle,
> Though every prospect pleases
> And only man is vile,
> In vain with lavish kindness
> The gifts of God are strewn,
> The heathen in his blindness
> Bows down to wood and stone.
>
> Can we, whose souls are lighted
> With wisdom from on high,
> Can we to men benighted
> The lamp of life deny?

The clause forbidding missionary activity was finally removed from the East India Company charter in 1813. Its removal was preceded by a campaign in which petitions signed by half a million people were presented to Parliament. The campaign was organised by the Clapham Sect, that extremely effective Evangelical pressure group, and supported by William Wilberforce. The campaign had involved convincing the British people that Indian society was riddled with abuses which were intolerable in any civilised society. Practices like female infanticide and *sati*, the custom by which a Hindu widow was compelled to burn herself to death on her husband's funeral pyre, were undoubtedly abominations, which Hindu scholars themselves came in time to condemn. Other aspects of Hindu religion like the Juggernath processions (particularly condemned by westerners because they sometimes led to ecstatic suicides), which seemed pure superstition to missionaries, may well have had religious and social significance hidden from them.

The missionaries were eager to bring western learning as well as Christianity. The Baptist William Carey, for example, who had worked in India with a Danish mission before the company's charter was relaxed in 1813, was as indefatigable in translation as William Jones, but he was engaged in translating major western books into Indian languages. Some of his translations had a very practical intent, for Carey was convinced that only the introduction of western methods of agriculture would begin to solve the problems of poverty and famine in India.

Even more important than the Evangelicals were the Utilitarians.[31] The two philosophies were utterly different, even antagonistic, but in India as in Britain, they interacted to bring about major changes and reforms in the first half of the nineteenth century. The first Utilitarian to interest himself in India was James Mill who published his great *History of India* in 1818. In part it was a deliberate reply to what Mill regarded as the 'romantic' school of William Jones but, in his wholesale condemnation of the 'medieval' nature of Indian society, Mill was also voicing his condemnation of medieval and non-rational survivals anywhere,

in Europe as well as in India. The Utilitarians were at the opposite
pole from Edmund Burke. They had little reverence for the past
and no inhibitions about fundamentally changing societies, their
own or anyone else's. They believed like the French philosophers
of the eighteenth century—with whom their founder Jeremy
Bentham had been closely associated—that it was possible by
rational inquiry to establish the nature of the 'laws' which ought
to govern society and that these 'laws' were of universal application,
as appropriate for India as for Europe. There was a strongly
authoritarian streak in the Utilitarians and they did not share the
usual liberal distrust of executive action. Everything encouraged
the Utilitarians to use India, where vested interests were less able
to influence the government than in Britain, as their 'private
laboratory'. They were singularly well placed to do so. In 1819, as
a direct result of the publication of his book, James Mill was offered
a post as an assistant examiner at the India Office. From 1830 until
his death in 1836 he was the Examiner, in effect Permanent Under
Secretary. His son, John Stuart Mill, entered the India Office in
1832, became the Examiner in 1856 and held that post until it was
abolished in 1858. Within the office the Mills had the support of
other sympathisers such as Edward Strachey and Edward Thornton.

The men who actually administered India were not of course
generally committed to any particular political doctrine. Most
were, by both necessity and inclination, pragmatists, dealing
with practical issues as they arose, relying on their own experience
and taking ideas piecemeal from the theorists. Yet they were
building up a common stock of experience, identifying the problems and discussing possible solutions among themselves and
with friends in London. One of the most prominent among them
was Mountstuart Elphinstone, the son of an aristocratic Scottish
family which had long had connections with the East India
Company. He went to India in 1795 and divided his time between
administration and diplomacy. In 1808 he was the British envoy
in Kabul and later published his *Account of the Kingdom of Cabaul*
which was still very much in the William Jones tradition of

interested comment on an alien but not necessarily inferior
society. Yet he corresponded with Edward Thornton and Edward
Strachey and read Bentham's *Principles of Morals and Legislation*
with close attention. While he was Governor of Bombay from 1819
to 1827 he promulgated a legal code, famous in its day, yet at the
same time he wrote to Edward Strachey, 'I doubt whether anybody could tell me what was good for the Mahrattas. I was certain
that I could not, and I therefore wanted to be taught by time.[32]

Thomas Munro, who went to India in 1780, was another Scots-
man (there was truth in the old quip that Scotland had only two
exports—her cattle to Smithfield and her sons to India). He came
from a different background from Elphinstone, the son of a
merchant family in Glasgow, but the two men were friends.
Munro, like Elphinstone, was cautious. He read widely in Indian
literature and believed that many of the evils which the missionaries
condemned in Indian society were of recent origin and directly
attributable to the wars and disturbances of the immediate past.
He counselled leaving most of them alone. Yet in his own career
(he was Governor of Madras, 1820–7) he too introduced western
concepts into India. He disliked Cornwallis's exaltation of the
zemindars. Munro's sympathies lay with the peasants, the *ryots*,
whom he wished to see owning their own smallholdings. In later
years fierce battle was joined between the advocates of Cornwallis's *zemindari* system and Munro's *ryotwari* system. But
Munro's policy of turning the *ryots* into peasant proprietors was
itself almost as great a breach with the traditional system, which
had never been based on the principle of private ownership, as
was Cornwallis's.[33]

In 1828 Lord William Bentinck became Governor-General.
Bentinck had much sympathy with the Utilitarian position and the
1830s were in India, as in Britain itself, to be the heyday of
Utilitarian-inspired reform. Central to such reform was the question of education. The Utilitarians had a great belief in the power
of education to change the world. They interpreted education in
a very wide sense to include political education (usually in the
form of the press and actual participation in democratic processes)

and technical education (in practice usually associated with industrialisation) as well as formal education. The question of Indian education was already an old one by the 1830s. The Charter Act of 1813 had recognised an English obligation on the subject. It was part of the general concept of trusteeship. It was also linked with the still prevalent idea that the connection between Britain and India was an unnatural one which was unlikely to last long. It was in Britain's interest as well as India's that India should be well prepared for the separation. Nothing better illustrated the liberal hope that true altruism and true self-interest coincided.[34]

A long succession of British officials and politicians expressed the same views. Elphinstone acknowledged that Indian education was likely to be Britain's 'high road back to Europe' but he held, 'It is for our interest to have an early separation from a civilised people, rather than a violent rupture with a barbarous nation, in which it is probable that all our settlers and even our commerce would perish along with all the institutions we had introduced into the country.'[35] Macaulay proclaimed the same doctrine in ringing terms during the debate on the Charter Act of 1833:

> It may be that the public mind of India may expand under our system till it has outgrown that system . . . that, having become instructed in European knowledge, they may in some future age, demand European institutions. Whether such a day will ever come I know not. But never will I attempt to avert or retard it. Whenever it comes, it will be the proudest day in English history . . . The sceptre may pass away from us . . . Victory may be inconstant to our arms. But there are triumphs which are followed by no reverse. There is an empire exempt from all natural causes of decay. Those triumphs are the pacific triumphs of reason over barbarism; that empire is the imperishable empire of our arts and our morals, our literature and our laws.[36]

He assured the Commons in the same debate that to 'civilise' India was 'on the most selfish view of the case' a wise policy, for it would create a wealthy and orderly society linked commercially with Britain. Macaulay's younger brother-in-law, Charles Trevelyan, was even blunter in his *The Education of the People of India* (1838). He wrote:

> The existing connection between two such distant countries as England and India, cannot, in the nature of things be permanent: no effort of policy can prevent the natives from ultimately regaining their independence. But there are two ways of arriving at this point. One of these is through the medium of revolution; the other, through that of reform.[37]

If a wise course were followed, 'a precarious and temporary relation will almost imperceptibly pass into another far more durable and beneficial'. An alliance between 'the first manufacturing and the first producing country in the world' could only benefit both.

The British never seriously considered trying to keep their Indian subjects as helots who would supply British needs ignorant of any alternative. No one thought such a course either practical or defensible. But plenty of practical questions remained to be resolved. Should the education offered to the Indians be Indian or western in character? Should they aim at the education of an élite who might act as the leaven in the lump, or should they try to provide a thin coverage of elementary education for all? These questions were far more thoroughly discussed than comparable issues in contemporary English education.

The previous generation, the Munros and Elphinstones, had been pragmatists in this as in other matters. Munro thought that education had declined as the result of the conquest and to remedy this schools should be established in each 'collectorate', conducted partly in English and partly in the vernaculars, with translations of western books available and a concentration on what was 'useful'. In Bombay Elphinstone suggested village schools where the learning would be in the vernacular, leading to a Hindi college at Poona and an English college in the city of Bombay. James Mill favoured the use of the vernacular in instruction on practical grounds. The over-riding aim should be to teach what was 'useful' and to this end they should retain 'everything which was useful in Hindoo or Mohomedan literature'.[38] It was left to

Macaulay to deliver the most sweeping indictment of oriental learning ever to emanate from a responsible statesman in his famous Education Minute of 1835. About half the committee considering the question favoured using Sanskrit or Arabic as the *lingua franca* of Indian education. Macaulay would have none of this. He wrote that, after consulting men learned in oriental studies,

> I have never found one among them who could deny that a single shelf of a good European library was worth the whole native literature of India and Arabia . . . The question now before us is simply whether, when it is in our power to teach this language [English], we shall teach languages in which by universal confession there are no books on any subject which deserve to be compared with our own; whether when we can teach European science, we shall teach systems which by universal confession whenever they differ from those of Europe differ for the worse; and whether, when we can patronise sound philosophy and true history, we shall countenance at the public expense medical doctrines which would disgrace an English farrier, astronomy which would move laughter in girls at an English boarding-school, history abounding with kings thirty feet high and reigns 30,000 years long, and geography made up of seas of treacle and seas of butter.[39]

Macaulay's views prevailed. It was accepted that government-supported education in India was to be western education. It followed that only a minority could be so educated. Indeed, even if the decision had gone the other way, it would have been quite beyond the resources of the British government in India to have provided anything approaching universal education—which, of course, Britain itself did not enjoy at this time.

These decisions had far-reaching consequences in India, some foreseen, some not foreseen, by their authors. Apart from the content of the education it seems likely that, as a later pro-consul, Lord Cromer, realised, thinking in English helped to alter the whole cast of Indian thought. Cromer, in discussing 'assimilation' in the British empire (he was comparing it with the Roman), recognised that language was of critical importance and that a man who thought in English did not think precisely like a man who

thought in, say, French.[40] Western education clearly created a
minority—an élite in later jargon—who had to some extent
stepped outside their own society. Sometimes they identified with
the new rulers—as many of them did at the time of the 'Mutiny'—
but they also demanded a place in the new scheme of things. What
complicated matters further was that they were not drawn entirely,
or even mainly, from the old governing classes. This was to be the
constant problem in the British empire, in Africa as well as in
India. In India the old governing classes, the Moslems, at first
fought shy of western education. They had a highly developed
system of their own and they disliked the secular character of
western learning. The Hindus were less reluctant. The result was
the proliferation of the *babu*—which was not at first a term of
disrespect but simply a description of an educated Hindu. Soon,
however, the Bengal *babu* (a high proportion came from the
intellectually lively province of Bengal) was a stock figure of fun
to the English and an irritation to the Moslems. Attempts were
made as late as 1868 to try to redress the balance by offering
scholarships for education in Britain not 'upon the principle of
open competition' but with a bias towards 'the sons of Native
gentlemen of rank and position'.[41]

Apart from education the question of the rationalisation and
codification of the law was one very dear to the hearts of the
Utilitarians from Bentham onwards. In India it had come to seem
an urgent necessity. Many different systems of law co-existed,
although under the Mogul empire only Moslem law had been
officially recognised in the imperial courts. The coming of the
British and other Europeans had added elements of European law,
initially recognised by the Moguls under various privileges of
extra-territoriality. The British had no particular prejudice in
favour of Moslem law and recognised Hindu and other legal
systems where the Moguls had not. The result was chaos.
Macaulay spoke in the debate on the Charter Act of 1833 of
'Hindoo Law, Mahometan law, Parsee Law, and English law
perpetually mingling with each other and disturbing each other;
varying with the person, varying with the place'. British courts

had been compelled to administer 'a kind of rude and capricious equity'. The object of the reforms proposed in the new Act was to secure 'uniformity where you can have it, diversity where you must find it, but in all cases certainty'.[42] Macaulay went out to India himself in 1834 as the law member of the governor-general's council to carry out the proposed reforms. Macaulay was not himself strictly a Utilitarian but the great codification of Indian laws which he set in motion was essentially a Utilitarian project. It took a generation to carry out. Not until 1859 was a code of civil procedure enacted, followed two years later by the more famous code of criminal procedure. They were criticised—not least by some thorough-going Benthamites who did not think they went far enough—but their importance was recognised by British and Indian alike. Pannikar has compared them to the codes of Justinian and Napoleon and concludes: 'The legal system under which India has lived for a hundred years and within whose steel frame her social, political, and economic development has taken place is the work of Macaulay.' He does not hesitate to see this as an advance on what went before, above all in the establishment of the principle of equality before the law in a country where previously 'under Hindu law, a Brahmin could not be punished on the evidence of a Sudra, and, under Moslem law, the evidence of a non-Moslem could not be accepted against a Moslem'.[43] This equality extended to the treatment of Indians and Englishmen. Except that it provided for the exile of British delinquents— hardly appropriate in the case of an Indian—the penal code laid down exactly the same treatment for the two races. This attitude was also manifest in Macaulay's so-called Black Act of 1836. This made Europeans resident outside Calcutta subject to the company's courts in civil cases and deprived them of their right of appeal to the Supreme Court. This raised an outcry from some Europeans because Indian judges sat in the company's courts but not, at this time, in the Supreme Court. Their protests fore-shadowed the more famous agitation against the Ilbert Bill in the 1880s (see pp 165–7) and they forced some concessions but Macaulay, supported by John Stuart Mill and other liberals such as J. C. Hobhouse (Lord Broughton), now president of the Board of Control, fought manfully to maintain the principle of complete equality before the law.

English objections to the Black Act and subsequently to the Ilbert Bill were sometimes placed on the rather rarefied grounds that Magna Carta guaranteed trial by one's peers and that Indians were not an Englishman's peers. The self-interest in such an argument was obvious but it also reflected the real belief among Englishmen of the time that they took their rights and liberties as Englishmen with them to any part of the world under English control. This extended to freedom of speech. Englishmen resident in India were often highly critical of the company's government and demanded that they should be allowed to publish their views. Charles Metcalfe, the acting Governor-General, on Macaulay's advice, conceded this in 1835. A press developed in India subject only to the checks that governed the press in Britain itself, namely that an editor or publisher could be sued after the event for libel or subversion but that there was no pre-publication censorship. The right had been demanded by Britons and, in intention, it was conceded to them, but no one at this time made any serious attempt to prevent Indians from exercising the same right. An important English-language and vernacular press grew up. Without it, and the informal political education it provided, the path of the later Indian nationalist movement would have been much more difficult.[44]

Some Englishmen in India in the 1830s demanded not only a free press but also representative government. The hallmark of English colonies in the western hemisphere in the eighteenth century, in contrast to the colonies of other European powers, had been their possession of representative assemblies. Even the American War of Independence had not undermined the British belief in the expediency of establishing representative government in all but military outposts. India, however, represented a new problem. A decision of critical importance had to be taken. Should these Englishmen be given what they demanded as their inalienable right? Should this right be extended to the vast Indian majority? The Indians were not at this time British subjects, which provided a technical loophole for disregarding their claims. It was more difficult to refuse some form of representation to British subjects, but it was refused. Britain thereby avoided creating a settler parliament in India of the type subsequently created in, say, Rhodesia. The guardianship principle could continue.

Representative government apart, however, the problem of the role of the Indian in the government of an India now politically dominated by Britain had to be considered. The 1833 Charter Act specifically laid down that no distinctions were to be made on grounds of race or colour. It was, in a later phrase, 'colour blind'. The mere enunciation of the principle was important. Britain never committed herself, or wished to commit herself, to any principle of apartheid in India. In the long run the significance of this can hardly be over-estimated but there was an enormous gap between principle and practice. Subordinate administration always remained in Indian hands. It has even been said that one of the best things about the British raj was that many Indians never saw a white man.[45] But entry into the higher echelons of the Indian Civil Service, whether under the old system of patronage or the newer system of competitive examination, was for an Indian like the proverbial camel passing through the eye of a needle.

This displacement from any real role in the government of their own country was at the root of Indian discontent throughout the period of the British raj. But there were other factors too. The reforms of the 1830s and the missionary activities of the Evangelicals were disturbing to Indian life and society in a way in which the mere imposition of a new suzerain in the place of the Mogul empire was not. The reforming impulse in India died down, as it did in Britain itself, towards the close of the 1830s, but in the following two decades came other changes equally unsettling.

Important economic changes culminated under the governor-generalship of Dalhousie (1847–56). The most striking developments were in communications. The Grand Trunk Road from Calcutta to Delhi and Peshawar was begun in 1839. The following year other trunk roads to connect Bombay and Agra, and Calcutta and Bombay were started. The first Indian train ran over a few miles of track into Bombay in 1853. The first telegraph line, that from Calcutta to Agra, opened in 1854. The next year lines were working from Calcutta to Attock, from Agra to Bombay, and from Bombay to Madras. In 1854 too the postal system was entirely reorganised. Some of these changes had unforeseen results. The reduction in postal costs greatly facilitated the circulation of newspapers. The new railways, in India as in Europe, had profound social effects, making it possible for people to travel to new areas and form entirely new relationships. In India they had other effects too. Strict caste rules were never observed in the allocation of carriages or the serving of meals. Cracks began to appear in hitherto immutable customs.

Finally, under a succession of governor-generals, Lord Auckland (1836–42), Lord Ellenborough (1842–4), Sir Henry Hardinge (1844–8) and Lord Dalhousie (1848–56), the boundaries of British India, which had remained virtually stable since 1818, steadily expanded. It was, in effect, a new period of conquest. Britain was engaged in wars with the Afghans from 1839 to 1842 and with the Sikhs from 1845 to 1846 and from 1848 to 1849. The British were repulsed by the Afghans but the Sikhs were defeated and the Punjab annexed in March 1849. Sind had already been acquired in 1843. All three campaigns were condemned by many Englishmen at the time. Kaye considered that their ill success in Afghanistan was 'the curse of God . . . sitting heavily upon an unholy cause'.[46] Napier's famous punning telegram announcing the acquisition of Sind ('Peccavi', I have sinned) was a political comment. The British had, he admitted in his diary, no right to Sind but he thought its seizure would be 'a humane piece of rascality'.[47]

Thanks to the remarkably successful policy of the Lawrences, Henry and John, in the Punjab, the Sikhs became among Britain's most faithful allies in India. But others were not so easily conciliated. Dalhousie set out on a deliberate policy of annexation, not by the sword but by legal means, the famous 'doctrine of lapse'. It had long been customary for Indian rulers to adopt heirs, if they had no suitable sons to succeed them. Dalhousie resolved not to recognise such adoptions and to apply ruthlessly the principle that, when heirs failed, 'dependent states' reverted to the paramount power, originally the Mogul emperor, now the British. Dalhousie's actions were not entirely unprecedented but no previous governor-general had deliberately set out to annex wherever possible—especially where there were strategic advantages. Dalhousie acquired, among other states, Satara, Jaitpur, Udaipur, Nagpur and Jhansi between 1848 and 1854. The rani of Jhansi, Lakshmi Bai, strongly protested at the refusal to recognise the rights of her adopted son. Dalhousie also declined to acknowledge financial obligations to adopted heirs. The most significant example of this was his refusal to pay the pension granted to the former Peshwa, Baji Rao II, to his adopted son, Dundu Pant, better known to history as Nana Sahib. Both the rani of Jhansi and Nana Sahib were to play prominent roles in the Mutiny in 1857, although more recent Indian historians have declined to assign to them the heroic roles attributed to them by some nationalists.[48]

Dalhousie's most famous annexation was, however, that of Oudh in February 1856. Since 1801 it had been a protected state but it had retained its internal autonomy. Dalhousie's charges of misgovernment were probably well enough founded but the British self-interest in the annexation was too obvious and the ruling house of Oudh had faithfully kept their side of the bargain of 1801 to support the British. Oudh was the centre of the Mutiny of 1857.

Notes to Chapter 2 will be found on pages 238–40.

Chapter 3 THE INDIAN REACTION TO THE BRITISH CONQUEST

THE FIRST Indian reaction was one of simple military resistance to the likely conqueror and supplanter by the men in possession. In Bengal Siraj-ud-daula tried to keep the British out where his grandfather, Aliverdi Khan, had failed. He too failed and the British came to rule Bengal as agents of the Mogul empire. One of the most irreconcilable enemies of the British had been Tipu Sultan in Mysore. After his death in battle in 1799 the British found the caricatures he had ordered to be painted on the walls of the main streets of his capital of Seringapatam. One commentator wrote:

> Here were represented a row of white-faced Feringhees [Europeans], their hands tied behind them, and their faces half blackened; while others were seated on asses with their faces to the tail. Again some were being torn to pieces by tigers, while men of the true faith looked on and applauded . . . several appeared drawn up in a line, whose heads were all falling to the ground under one vigorous blow of the executioner—a man of the true faith, with a huge beard and mustachios curling up to his eyes, while streams of gore, very red and much higher and thicker than the sufferers themselves, gushed from the bodies. Here again were a group of ten or twelve seated round a table, each with a fierce regimental cocked-hat upon his head, a very red and drunken face, and his right hand upraised grasping a huge glass filled with red wine; while others, overcome by inebriation, were sprawling under the table, and wallowing among the swines and dogs . . .[1]

Clearly Tipu Sultan understood the value of psychological warfare. What is more difficult to judge is how far men like

Siraj-ud-daula and Tipu Sultan commanded the real loyalty of their own subjects. Both men were *parvenus*, the immediate heirs of adventurers who had seized their territories. They had many enemies and their own rule had been flawed by a number of cruel and arbitrary acts. In the whole of India no one man could be found strong enough, or commanding sufficiently wide support, to drive the foreigners out.

The second Indian reaction was to cling closely to old ways and old traditions. Indian society was well adapted to do this. It had survived many invasions over the centuries. The local nature of loyalties and the all-pervasive social obligations of Hinduism, which had little to do with politics—to the Indian peasant politics in any case meant little more than the unwelcome obligation to pay taxes to somebody—ensured that there need be no direct clash with the new rulers unless they were unwise enough to interfere with religious or social customs. In the early days of their rule the British understood this well enough. The ban on missionary endeavour maintained until 1813 is the best evidence of this realisation. In time they became less careful. In 1839 the British government succumbed to missionary pressure and ceased to honour the traditional obligations of Indian governments to pay for the upkeep of temples and other religious establishments. Christianity was taught in the new schools and hospitals. Evangelical army officers, like Colonel Wheler of the 34th Native Infantry, did not hesitate to say, 'As to the question whether I have endeavoured to convert Sepoys and others to Christianity, I would humbly reply that this has been my object, and I conceive is the aim and end of every Christian who speaks the word of God to another—merely that the Lord would make him the happy instrument of converting his neighbour to God, or, in other words, of rescuing him from eternal destruction.' In turn the Indians became deeply suspicious that, for example, new roads were deliberately planned along routes which would involve the destruction of temples.[2]

Battle was joined over the question of *sati*. Bentinck had forbidden it in Bengal in 1829 and in the other two Presidencies in

D

1830. He was opposed by the Dharma Sabha, a Calcutta organisation founded to defend orthodox Hinduism. Even the Dharma
Sabha, however, found it necessary to fight with western weapons,
a newspaper, and an appeal to the Privy Council claiming that
Bentinck's proclamation contravened those Acts of Parliament
which promised that there would be no interference with the
religion of the people.[3] The Privy Council turned down the appeal.
Bentinck's decrees had no force outside the Presidencies. General
Napier in Sind is said to have resorted to more direct methods.
When the orthodox urged that the burning of widows was their
custom, Napier replied, 'My nation also has a custom. When men
burn women alive, we hang them . . . Let us all act according to
national customs.'[4] *Sati* stopped.

The blind clinging to the known and traditional, however
indefensible in itself, was one understandable reaction to the
pressure of new forces and it remained one strand in Indian
reaction throughout the British raj—but it was only one. There
was substance in the belief of some European eighteenth-century
critics that India had a great civilisation which had petrified into
rigidity. The shock of the western impact compelled some Indian
thinkers to go back to examine the origins and essence of their own
philosophy. The greatest of these in the early nineteenth century
was Raja Ram Mohan Roy, who has been called the Indian Luther
since he wished to go back to the Hindu scriptures, as Luther
had gone back to the Christian ones, to strip them of the accretions
they had acquired over the centuries. Although he was not himself
a product of the new western education, his contact with western
thought was close. For much of his adult life he was an official of
the East India Company and he died in Bristol in 1833, the Mogul
emperor's ambassador to the British government. But between
1814 and the early 1830s he retired on his considerable private
fortune to study and think. Like William Jones he was a remarkable
linguist, proficient in English, Sanskrit, Arabic, Persian, Latin
and Greek. He learnt the last two in order to study the Christian
Bible more effectively. Ram Mohan Roy's aim was to combine the
best in Indian and in western philosophy. To this end he founded

a society in 1828, the Brahma Sabha, which was to be revitalised nearly twenty years later by Debendranath Tagore as the Brahmo Samaj and which, although always small in numbers and subsequently split into a number of parties, was to provide a focal point for the renaissance of Indian thought for a century. Ram Mohan Roy's view of both Christianity and Hinduism was searching and critical. In 1824 he wrote his *The Precepts of Jesus*, highly praising the ethical content of Christianity but rejecting much of its dogma, including the divinity of Christ. His attitude to traditional Hinduism was equally uncompromising. He condemned the rigidities of caste, the privileged position of the Brahmans (although he was a Brahman himself) and the depressed status of women which could lead to infanticide and child marriages, as well as to *sati*. The strength of his feeling about *sati* probably sprang from his boyhood experience when he saw his sister-in-law forced on to his brother's funeral pyre.[5]

More extreme still in their criticisms were the men associated with 'Young Bengal', mainly students at the Hindu college in Calcutta. They were as iconoclastic towards their own religion as the Utilitarians, deliberately shocking their elders by their demonstrations including, on one notable occasion, throwing beef into the house of a devout Brahman. They also condemned the British occupation of India and showed a remarkably wide knowledge of the world in so doing. One young radical wrote to a Calcutta journal, the *Reformer*, as early as 1831, pointing to the example of the United States of America as a country which had thrown off British rule and greatly profited as a result.[6]

Young Bengal was too extreme, too intent on alienating its countrymen, to have a wide influence but, as western education spread, Indian students became very aware of English political writers, of the struggles of English constitutional history and of the contemporary nationalist problems of Italy and Ireland. Burke, Macaulay and Locke were the three English writers who seem to have enjoyed the greatest vogue among the first generation of westernised Indians. The attractions of Burke and Macaulay, who had both dealt with Indian problems, are immediately

obvious but they also represented the very powerful English
Whig tradition with its strong attachment to representative government and parliamentary institutions. English history tended to be
taught in Victorian times as the story of the long battle between
Parliament and the king for control of the nation's government
with a final righteous victory going to Parliament. Later British
officials came to realise that it was unrealistic to suppose that one
could teach Indians a history in which the John Hampdens
appeared as the heroes without their applying the lesson to their
own situation. Nor indeed did those who still believed with
Macaulay that the victories of the spirit were the only ones which
had a lasting empire particularly wish to conceal such lessons.
But in time Mazzini and Daniel O'Connell, writers less congenial
to the British establishment, also came to be studied in India.

The Indians quickly learnt, too, the advantages of European-
type political organisations in pressing their views. India already
had highly developed political traditions—nothing would be more
misleading than to see them as a post-Congress development,
dating only from the 1880s[7]—but they were constantly adapted to
changing circumstances. McLane sees the 'political awakening' of
India as the transition from what he calls 'administrative politics',
small private pressure groups which antedated British rule, to
'agitational politics', involving mass communications and the
organisation of formal parties.[8] Such changes were in their infancy
before 1857 but the Indians learnt from the agitation of European
residents against the 'Black Act' as they did later from the more
important and successful opposition to the Ilbert Bill. They soon
saw the advantages of newspapers. In 1823 Ram Mohan Roy and
five other prominent Indians petitioned the Court of Directors
(unsuccessfully at that time) against a new regulation requiring
the licensing of newspapers, calling the freedom of the press a
precious right and pointing out the importance of the press both
in education and in informing the government of the true state of
public opinion. By 1839, after Metcalfe's reforms, there were nine
vernacular newspapers in Calcutta and four in Bombay. Bengal
was already beginning to take the lead in Indian politics which it

was to maintain throughout the century. But the Indians were also coming to appreciate that the place to exert effective pressure was London rather than Calcutta. They must have been well aware that dissatisfied company servants had always appealed directly to London over the heads of the authorities in India itself. They soon discovered that they had a number of sympathisers in England.[9]

Before 1857 there were developing in India radical and conservative reform movements. The latter, drawn from established society, with London links and by no means hostile to western influence was, at this time, the more important. Their allies in London were to be found on the left rather than the right of British politics but the actual links are at first sight somewhat unexpected. The Indian reformers were predominantly landowners, Cornwallis's *zemindars*. The Englishmen were interested in the economic development of India and, many of them, specifically in Indian cotton. Nowhere was this dual interest in governmental reform and economic development better exemplified than in the Quaker, John Bright.[10]

In 1837 the Bengal Landholders' Society (originally the Zemindary Association) was founded. It was pledged to work for reform and protect the rights of the *zemindars*—the two objectives were regarded as complementary, not opposed. Two years later the British India Society was formed in London. Two radicals, George Thompson and John Crawfurd, were prominent in it. Its objective was to denounce the land revenue system of British India on the grounds that it caused famine and depopulation and made cotton-growing uneconomic. Crawfurd wrote a pamphlet, interestingly entitled *An Appeal from the Inhabitants of British India to the Justice of the People of England*, in which he argued that taxation was so high in India that the accumulation of capital and consequent investment was impossible. The British India Society was not an obscure body. It held a meeting in London in July 1839 under the chairmanship of Lord Brougham (a former Whig lord chancellor) and the controversy thundered through the pages of the *Edinburgh Review*. George Thompson went out to Bengal in 1842 and the following year the Bengal British India

Society was founded. In 1851 the Bengal Landholders' Society and the Bengal British India Society joined to form the British India Association, wholly Indian in composition but essentially conservative and dominated by the *zemindars*.

Meanwhile in Britain John Bright had chaired the parliamentary select committee that met in 1848 to inquire into the obstacles to cotton-growing in India. The early 1840s had seen a number of crises with the United States, only resolved by the Ashburton-Webster treaty of 1842 and the Oregon treaty of 1846, which made Britain's dependence on American cotton seem dangerous, apart from the objections in some quarters in Britain to slave-grown cotton. Bright had become MP for Manchester in 1847 and his connections with the Manchester Chamber of Commerce were at this time close. As J. B. Sturgis says, 'an evaluation of Bright's motives in regard to India is a difficult task'. However mixed they may have been, the select committee was very critical of the East India Company and pressed for reforms, holding that good government and good commercial practice went together. Bright's views were widely known in India.[11]

The fact that the company's charter was due to come up for renewal in 1853 naturally led to a rallying of the reformers in both India and England. A remarkable meeting took place in Bombay on 26 August 1852, which crossed all the usual sectarian boundaries. It was attended by Hindus, Parsis (a very powerful community in Bombay), Moslems, Portuguese and Jews. The meeting decided to form an association which petitioned the British Parliament. One of the principal speakers was Dadabhai Naoroji who was later to sit in the British House of Commons as MP for Finsbury. Naoroji was a product of the new western-style education. He had been educated at the Elphinstone Institute in Bombay and, in 1853, had become the first Indian professor of mathematics and natural philosophy there. He had been prominent in a newly-formed Students' Literary and Scientific Society which met fortnightly to read papers on literary, scientific and social questions. Religious and overtly political topics were prudently banned. The Students' Society's predecessor, the Native Literary

Society, had however devoted a good deal of attention to classical subjects, such as Brutus's guilt in assassinating Caesar, which may well have provided opportunity for oblique political comments.

The Bombay petitions are equally remarkable for the complete understanding they show of the British political system and the forensic skill with which the Indian case is argued. They carefully avoided all extreme statements and concentrated on detailed criticisms. The dual government of the company was, they argued, inefficient, expensive and out of touch with the people. One note sounded very clearly, as it was to do later from the resolutions of the Indian National Congress—the request that a bigger share of administrative and judicial appointments should go to Indians and a reminder that the Charter Act of 1833 had laid down that no Indian should be disqualified from office 'by reason only of religion, place of birth, descent or colour'.[12]

The Bombay Association had close links with the India Reform Society which was founded in London in March 1853, to influence the terms on which the charter was renewed. Its leading spirit was once again John Bright. It included thirty-nine MPs, among them a future viceroy of India and colonial secretary (Lord Ripon), a future president of the Board of Trade (Milner Gibson) and a future home secretary (H. A. Bruce). But perhaps even more interesting are its strong links with both Ireland and India itself. It included a powerful contingent of Irish MPs. It corresponded with leading Indians and derived a substantial proportion of its finances from Indians. It also attracted a good deal more attention in the Indian than in the British press. In fact it exerted only a very limited influence on the Act of 1853 which renewed the company's charter indefinitely, but it did direct attention towards India and supplied both information and a forum for exchanging ideas. Nothing like it had existed before.[13]

Five years before the so-called 'Mutiny' of 1857 and a generation before the foundation of the Indian National Congress, leading Indians were manifesting complete comprehension of a western system of politics and the ability to play the game according to

western rules. Across these developments cut the uprising of
1857. What exactly was it? To some it was simply an army mutiny,
'the sepoys' revolt'. Others saw it as the soldiery manipulated by a
political conspiracy, directed by Nana Sahib, the rani of Jhansi
and others who had personal grievances, real or imagined, against
the British. A generation later Indian nationalists saw it in a new
light as the 'First Indian War of Independence'. Since independence a number of eminent Indian scholars such as S. N. Sen,
R. C. Majumdar and S. B. Chaudhui have re-examined it to try
to assess its full complexity.[14] It has been suggested by some that
it had within it social and agrarian elements which make it proper
to compare it with the French Revolution or the Chartist movement in England.[15]

The events of the Mutiny are easier to disentangle than the
causes. It began at Meerut on 10 May 1857. The immediate issue
was the 'greased cartridges'. The rifled barrel of the new Enfield,
just coming into use in India, required the balled cartridges to be
greased. The drill manuals instructed the soldier to bite off the
end of the cartridge to release the powder with which to prime his
rifle. It had been suggested as early as 1853 by a Colonel Tucker
that the new grease might offend the religious sentiments of the
sepoys. No one had taken much notice of him. But, in January
1857, a labourer at the Dum-Dum arsenal near Calcutta, a low
caste Hindu, taunted a high caste Brahman sepoy who had
offended him: 'You will soon lose your caste, as ere long you will
have to bite cartridges covered with the fat of pigs and cows.' The
story spread like wildfire. Nothing could have been more inflam-
matory. The touch of cow fat would be polluting to the Hindu,
that of pork fat revolting to the Moslem. It is not clear whether
either of the offending materials had in fact been used.[16] The
British authorities were willing, if a little slow, to meet what they
recognised as valid objections. Only innocuous substances, like
butter and tallow, should be used. The sepoys should grease their
own cartridges.

But it was too late. The sepoys may or may not have been reassured by British promises but what they feared was not personal

pollution but social ostracism. If it was believed that they had touched polluted substances they would be excommunicated by their own people.[17] The whole thing seemed the more sinister to the sepoys because they already suspected that the British had in mind to make them outcasts, perhaps forcibly convert them to Christianity, and so ensure their complete loyalty to their British masters. More specifically, they feared that the British wanted to make them outcasts to facilitate their employment outside India. There had been a number of army mutinies before 1857, notably those of 1806 (Vellore), 1824 (Barrackpore), 1825 (Assam), 1838 (Sholapur), several in 1839–42 (connected with the Afghan War) and 1849–50 (in the Punjab). All these had been local and easily suppressed. Most had been connected with dissatisfaction about pay and conditions—although these in turn involved questions of prestige. The Vellore mutiny of 1806 was, however, interesting because it arose from ill-judged orders to Hindus to remove their caste marks from their foreheads, to Moslems to shave their beards and to men of both religions to wear leather cockades in their headgear. The troubles of 1824 came about because of the Bengal army's reluctance to cross the sea to take part in the First Burma War which would involve a loss of caste. Dislike of crossing the Indus and fighting outside India was important in the Afghan mutinies.[18] The question of crossing the sea had come to the fore again in the 1850s with the Second Burma War.

The British had always recognised that they might lose India as the result of the disaffection of the native army. Elphinstone had written in 1819: 'I think the seed of its [our Indian empire's] ruin will be found in the native army—a delicate and dangerous machine which a little mismanagement may easily turn against us.'[19] There were in effect two armies in India, the British army which was small (rather over 45,000 in 1857) and the native army with British officers which was about four times as large (something over 233,000 in 1857). The sepoys were mercenaries with high professional traditions. They had an *esprit de corps* among themselves which the best British officers admitted they could only guess at. Woodruff recounts a story of how a regiment hid its old colours,

disgraced in battle, for thirty years and only revealed them when
the original defeat had been avenged. 'Of all this, the officers
had known nothing; the men of the regiment formed a close
hereditary corporation, knit together by blood, religion and a
deep emotional feeling for their colours.' Majumdar tells a parallel
story of how the religious relics of a Brahman, hanged for his part
in the Barrackpore mutiny in 1824, mysteriously reappeared in
1857.[20]

In the eighteenth century the sepoys had offered their services
to the highest bidder and had expected loot as a natural part of
their rewards. It was largely through them that the British had
conquered India at all. Their career prospects had worsened in
the nineteenth century. Promotion was slow. Native officers
could not rise above regimental rank and even then were subordinate to the most junior British officer and it was generally
agreed that it was the young British officers, straight out from
England, not the old Indian hands, who were the most patronising
towards and contemptuous of their Indian colleagues. It was not
beyond the bounds of possibility that the native army might look
for a new and more accommodating master. But, although a
professional force, the sepoys were recruited from the people,
often, particularly in the Bengal army, from men of high caste—
which was not necessarily synonymous with wealth—and kept
close ties with their villages. Even an army mutiny was not something that could happen in isolation.

The Meerut outbreak was preceded by two earlier incidents, at
Berhampore on the night of 26/27 February and at Barrackpore
on 29 March. At Berhampore the sepoys involved (the 19th Native
Infantry) temporarily seized an armoury of weapons. The incident
at Barrackpore was stranger. A sepoy named Mangal Pande
(corrupted to Pandy this became the popular British name for all
mutineers), who may have been drunk or drugged, challenged the
guard, calling on his comrades to join him as they had promised
to fight for their religion. His fellow soldiers neither joined him
nor obeyed an order to disarm him. After wounding two European
NCOs, Pande was eventually disarmed by the CO himself,

Major-General Hearsey. Pande was hanged. The 19th NI was disbanded and the 34th NI, which had been involved in the Barrackpore incident, was partially disbanded. The men dispersed to their homes, which were mainly in Oudh and Rohilkand (the modern Utar Pradesh), and no doubt communicated their version of events to their own people.

On 24 April Colonel Carmichael-Smyth at Meerut ordered his regiment, the 23rd Light Cavalry, to parade for firing practice. He knew that the situation was tense but he hoped that new instructions—that the cartridges were to be opened with the fingers not the teeth—might solve the problem. The men refused to take the practice cartridges, although assured that they were of an old type which had been in use for years. It seems that they feared for their reputations if they were known to have handled any cartridges.[21] They were court-martialled, disgraced on parade, and sentenced to terms of imprisonment. The punishment parade took place on Saturday 9 May. The following day, while the Europeans were preparing for church in the evening, a disturbance began in the bazaar. It spread to the infantry lines and subsequently to the native cavalry. The British officers were slow to react, at least in an organised manner, although some went immediately to the lines. By the following morning about fifty Europeans and Eurasians were dead. They included eight British officers, at least four women and four children. The murder of the pregnant young wife of Lieutenant Chambers was peculiarly revolting to European opinion. Her disembowelled body was found lying in the compound of her house. Prosperous Indian shopkeepers were also attacked and their stores looted.[22] The mutineers were on their way to Delhi to offer their services to Bahadur Shah, the pensioned Mogul emperor.

From the beginning the question was asked—was Meerut a spontaneous outbreak arising from the punishment parade of 9 May or was it part of a widespread conspiracy, possibly a premature outbreak of a movement timed to begin a few weeks later. Many British officers feared at the time that it was part of a general conspiracy. They were painfully aware that the British army in

India was in a debilitated condition in 1857. Its prestige had not
been enhanced by the comparative lack of success of British arms
in Afghanistan (1839–42) and in the Crimea (1854–6)—both of
which were perfectly well known in India. It was under strength
in 1857, with contingents serving in Persia and Burma, and its
key lines of communication from Calcutta up to Peshawar,
through Benares, Allahabad, Cawnpore and Delhi itself, were
critically undermanned. There was a widely known prophecy—
important in a country where astrology was taken very seriously—
that British rule would last only one hundred years, and the
anniversary of the battle of Plassey fell on 23 June 1857. The
British thought that they had found confirmation for the conspiracy theory in the testimony of Sitaram Baba, a Hindu holy
man, who told H. B. Devereux, the Judicial Commissioner for
Mysore, that the Mutiny was the result of a plot which had been
maturing for twenty years and had, at various times, involved
Nana Sahib, the rani of Jhansi, the Maharaja of Mysore and many
other princes who had grievances against the British.[23]

The idea of a general conspiracy became popular again many
years later with those Indian nationalists who wished to show that
1857 represented a nationwide rising against the British. But men
like Sitaram never produced any hard evidence for their views and
the weightiest modern authorities, such as Dr Sen, have rejected
the idea of an organised conspiracy, although not ruling out the
possibility of some prior consultation between sepoy regiments
who believed themselves to be confronted by a crisis of conscience.[24] Dr Palmer, in his detailed study of the Meerut outbreak, comes to the conclusion that, although it was not part of a
general conspiracy, it was not completely spontaneous and unforeseen either, and was the result of some limited conspiracy. The
telegraph line to Delhi was deliberately cut some time before the
earliest troubles in the bazaar and one British officer, Lieutenant
Gough, was warned the previous day by an Indian officer of the
likely course of events with too much precision of detail to suggest
that it was a mere guess. Again, although the decision to march to
Delhi was taken quite late in the proceedings and many sepoys

were plainly simply bewildered by the turn of events, Palmer believes that a small group among them had this in mind from the beginning.[25]

Bahadur Shah does not seem to have been in the plot, if plot there was. He was taken by surprise by the arrival of the mutineers and they terrorised his city. Casualties were high at Delhi. There were no European troups stationed there but all Christians, European or Indian, were hunted out and systematically murdered.[26] The mutineers then seem to have waited on events. There were small abortive outbreaks at Firozpur on 13 May and at Muzaffarnagar on 14 May, but it was another week before serious trouble broke out all over Oudh and the North-West Provinces, beginning with the incidents at Etawa and Mainpuri on 23 May and continuing up to that at Hathras on 1 July. The pattern generally followed that established at Meerut. Sepoys rose against their European officers. Bazaar 'mobs' joined in. Prisoners were released from jails, treasuries plundered, government offices burnt. The sepoys and their supporters set out for Delhi or roamed at large plundering rich Indians as well as Europeans. Some sepoys and others risked their own lives to protect European families. Law and order had plainly broken down over a considerable tract of northern India but the confusion and lack of any general plan of action is probably the most powerful evidence against the conspiracy theory.

Agra learnt of events in Meerut before that telegraph line too was cut at 6.30 pm on 10 May. The government in Calcutta quickly realised that it had a major emergency on its hands, although it also knew that the forces it had available to deal with it were inadequate. (It subsequently intercepted troops en route to fight in China to come to its aid.) Colonel J. G. Neill was dispatched with a force to march from Calcutta to Benares (regarded as a likely trouble spot) and Allahabad with instructions to proceed to Lucknow and Cawnpore, both important centres known to be at risk. Open mutiny broke out at Lucknow on 30 May but at Cawnpore, Nana Sahib, far from leading the movement as the conspiracy theory would suggest, resisted the pressure of the sepoys for some time and tried to negotiate with the British.[27] Serious trouble did not begin there until 4 June.

Colonel Neill has been described as a man who would have been 'in his proper environment among Cromwell's Round-heads'.[28] It may well have been his severities which caused the rising in Benares which had hitherto been avoided. On his march to Allahabad and Cawnpore he burnt villages he suspected of helping the rebels and authorised the hanging of all men he believed to be sepoys on the run. Clearly many of those summarily strung up from the nearest tree were not sepoys and may well have been innocent of any offence. Many of these actions were to draw strong condemnation from contemporary Englishmen, including *The Times*'s correspondent, W. H. Russell of Crimean War fame. He wrote: 'An officer . . . told me that the executions of Natives were indiscriminate to the last degree . . . In two days forty-two men were hanged at the roadside, and a batch of twelve men were executed because their faces were 'turned the wrong way' when they were met on the march. All the villages in his front were burnt when he halted.' He added significantly: 'These "severities" could not have been justified by the Cawnpore massacre, because they took place before that diabolical act.'[29]

Cawnpore was the best remembered atrocity of the Mutiny but it was only one link in a chain. If the murder of Europeans at Meerut and Delhi provoked Neill, Neill's actions in turn pro-voked the sepoys at Cawnpore whose home villages had been devastated. On 25 June Nana Sahib offered the small British garrison and their women and children safe conduct by river to Allahabad. On the 27th they boarded a fleet of boats. Firing then began in confused circumstances. Many died as the thatched roofs of the boats caught fire. Of those who escaped the men were shot, the women and children imprisoned in a building known as the Bibigarh. On 15 July, when it was known that British troops were approaching, sepoys were ordered to fire into the prison and kill them. The sepoys are said to have fired at the ceiling and the prisoners were hacked to pieces with knives by local roughs. Their bodies were thrown into a well. A British force, under Neill and Sir Henry Havelock, found them there when they arrived the next day. Neill ordered that those guilty should not only be executed but compelled first to help in clearing up the blood in the room where the women and children had died, so that they might die ritually polluted. This determination to make the rebels die in circumstances where they would believe themselves to be damned—by, for example, forcing Hindus to swallow beef, or Moslems, pork, or by burning Moslem bodies and burying those of Hindus—manifested itself repeatedly later when the provocation was less than at Cawnpore.[30]

It was 1859 before the last embers of the revolt were stamped out but by the summer of 1858 the main centres were back in British hands. The British were very aware that, if they had been confronted by a concerted movement, if many Indians had not been on their side and vast numbers of others had not watched the contest without committing themselves, the Europeans would have been entirely overwhelmed.[31] The ill-success of the movement provided the strongest argument for the subsequent British claim that they had not been confronted by a national war of independence at all. The rising was very limited in geographical area. It was confined for practical purposes to the Bengal Presidency. Madras, Bombay and the princely states were not involved. Even in the Bengal Presidency it was concentrated in Oudh and Rohilkhand with some overspill into Bihar, the eastern fringe of the Punjab and into the area of the Central India Agency (covering some of the territory of the old Maratha confederation), notably Jhansi. In Bengal proper only Dacca and Chittagong were seriously affected. Only a portion even of the Bengal army was involved. Dr Sen calculates that something like 70,000 sepoys joined the revolt at one time or another but they were never simultaneously involved; another 30,000 remained loyal to the British and a further 30,000 deserted or took no active part.[32]

On the other hand, the revolt was not confined to any one section of the population. Dr Sen concludes, 'No community, class or caste as such was entirely for or against the Government.'[33] Like all civil wars, it even divided families. It tapped many diverse

sources of discontent. There was the military discontent already
discussed, arising from poor career prospects and fears of attacks
upon their religion. There was the more general disquiet of the
religiously orthodox of both the main persuasions. The Moslems
had provided the ruling class before the British. The spread of
western education, to which they were unwilling to conform, had
further undermined their position and made their leaders a dis-
placed governing class with few prospects. Possibly, as A. K.
Azad suggests, this had only really been brought home to them
in the 1830s when English replaced Persian as the main language of
government and the Mogul emperor's head was removed from
the coinage.[34] The Hindus in turn had been disturbed by the Acts
of 1850 and 1856 which, respectively, safeguarded the property
rights of Hindus who became Christian converts and allowed the
remarriage of Hindu widows. They began to fear an insidious
attempt to undermine the structure of society and to convert, not
just the army, but the whole population to the alien faith.

More material grievances played a part too. The *talukdars*
(landholders) of Oudh were undoubtedly treated in a very cavalier
fashion after the annexation in 1856 when zealous revenue officers
jumped to the conclusion that the peasants were the rightful
owners of the land and the *talukdars* free-booting usurpers who
should be chased away. Even if their claims were not immediately
recognisable in western eyes, the *talukdars* were often the
acknowledged tribal or 'feudal' leaders of their districts who commanded more allegiance than the newcomers. Sir Henry Lawrence
was appointed Chief Commissioner for Oudh in March 1857
and set out to conciliate the *talukdars* and enlist their support.
Given time he might have succeeded but, within weeks, the rising
had begun.[35]

The peasantry in general felt oppressed by heavy tax demands.
The demands were not necessarily heavier than in Mogul times
but they were collected more consistently and inexorably. As in
all popular uprisings a substantial number of the participants
concentrated on rolling the financial burden off their own backs.
The scene in Saharanpur was not untypical. 'At first bankers

were robbed, or had to pay for exemption from plunder; money-lenders and traders were forced to give up their books of accounts, and vouchers for debts; old feuds were renewed; the first out-breaks were to pay off old feuds, or to clear off accounts, or for the sake of plunder . . . All the government records with the *mahajun*'s [revenue officer] accounts, bonds, etc. were torn up and scattered over neighbouring gardens . . .' These were obvious similarities with the chateau-burning of the early stages of the French Revolution.[36] Apart from the genuinely oppressed, there was inevitably a criminal element, ready to take advantage of any breakdown in law and order, who may well have been responsible for some of the worst atrocities, including possibly the original ones at Meerut.[37]

A large proportion of the population obviously waited to see which way things would go before declaring themselves. This attitude affected all classes, from men like Nana Sahib and the *talukdars* of Oudh who, despite their grievances, hesitated before committing themselves, down to the humblest peasant. Majumdar reminds us that the Mutiny was separated by barely a century from the break up of the Mogul empire. The tradition in post-Mogul India as in Tudor England was to see no disgrace in pledging one's allegiance to the *de facto* king.[38] When it seemed clear that the English were going for good, the people of a large part of northern India made what terms they could with their new rulers. When it was equally clear that the English were back, they accepted them with a good grace.

Sen sees the Mutiny as the revolt of old forces, not of new. 'The Mutiny leaders,' he says, 'would have set the clock back, they would have done away with the new reforms, with the new order, and gone back to the good old days when a commoner could not expect equal justice with the noble, when the tenants were at the mercy of the *talukdars*, and when theft was punished with mutilation. In short, they wanted a counter-revolution.' Chaud-huri, after a detailed examination of the civilian risings, agrees. It would be anachronistic to read advanced political or economic ideas into the revolt. 'Ideas of a free and independent government meant nothing further than the restoration of the power of the local chiefs.'[39] Conspicuously, the newly emergent western-educated class did not identify with the Mutiny. The British India Association in Bengal and the Bombay Association condemned it. The western-educated, the *babus*, were targets for the rebels, second only to the Europeans themselves. An English judge, Charles Raikes, recorded, 'A Bengalee Baboo at Furuckabad or Cawnpore was almost in as great peril as a Christian, so long as those cities were in the hands of the rebels . . . the students of Agra, Furuckabad, Benares, Delhi or Bareilly . . . often at the risk of their own lives openly declared their adherence to the British cause.'[40]

Was there then no 'national' element in the Mutiny at all? So far as 'nationalism' is a western concept, particularly in its assumption that loyalty to a national state should override all other loyalties, including religious and local ones, it would seem not. The men most in touch with western ideas rejected the movement. Nor is there any real evidence that there was a concept of an Indian 'nation', distinct from all other nations, to command allegiance at this time. A decade earlier the sepoys of the Bengal army had had no compunction in helping the British to subdue one of the few remaining centres of independent India, the kingdom of the Sikhs. During the Mutiny the majority of the Sikhs had equally little compunction in helping their new British allies against their old enemies the rebellious Bengal sepoys.[41] Majumdar draws attention to the fact that the real 'natural leaders' of the people, Sindhia, Holkhar, the Gaekwar of Baroda, the Nizam of Hyderabad, the ruling houses of Rajasthan, Mysore and Travancore, held aloof. The supposed leaders, Nana Sahib or the rani of Jhansi for example, were minor figures with small and doubtful followings.[42] Oudh alone formed a special case. It had only been annexed in 1856 and there the people did rally round the family of the deposed Nawab. The British recognised this at the time. The Court of Directors wrote to the Governor-General, Lord Canning, in April 1858, '. . . hostilities which have been carried on in Oudh have rather the character of legitimate war than that of rebellion'.[43] Modern historians, like Dr Sen, have agreed with this analysis. But Oudh itself was an excellent example of old-fashioned local territorial loyalty, not of new-style nationalism.

But, even if the Mutiny was a 'counter-revolution' and 'nationalism' is an anachronistic word to use, to what extent did the movement cross communal boundaries and represent an attempt to find an alternative to foreign domination? Here Indian historians differ considerably among themselves. Chaudhuri cautiously concludes 'it was not a movement of the disgruntled elements alone but a rising of the people, at any rate a considerable section of them, who felt, however dimly, the stirring of a common impulse'. As such it was the 'acorn' of the later nationalist movements. Sen is more specific. He believes 'what began as a fight for religion ended as a war of independence' and that the rebels, Hindus, Moslems, or minority groups, were prepared to sink their differences, at least in the short run 'to restore the old order of which the King of Delhi was the rightful representative'.[44] A. K. Azad, a post-independence Indian minister of education, in his introduction to Sen's work, goes a good deal further, for he says: 'The . . . important fact which attracts our attention during this uprising is the way in which Muslims and Hindus without doubt or debate looked to Delhi and Bahadur Shah.' Although most of the original rebels were Hindus, 'there was unanimous and spontaneous agreement that he alone had the right to become Emperor of India'. Azad believes that 'Indians obviously looked upon the Moguls not as foreign rulers but as their own King Emperors'. This is a point of central importance for it leads him to the conclusion, 'India faced the trial of 1857 as a united community. How is it that within a few decades communal differences became an obstacle to Indian nationhood? . . . The only explanation . . . is to be found in British policy after 1857.'[45]

Some Englishmen at the time agreed that maladroit British policy had united everyone against them. Benjamin Disraeli said in the Commons, 'For the first time in the history of your rule, you have the Hindu and Mahomedan making common cause against you.' Chaudhuri too concludes that there was, at least for a time, a coalition of usually antagonistic elements. Majumdar is less sure that even during the excitement of the Mutiny old divisions were forgotten. Although the Hindus predominated in the early stages of the revolt, the Moslems came to assume the lead in many places. Majumdar draws attention to the actual wording of the proclamations in which Moslem leaders invited Hindus to join them. They do not express great cordiality. That of Khan Bahadur Khan of Bareilly for example was full of implied threats.

> If the Hindoos shall exert themselves in the murder of these infidels and expel them from the country, they shall be rewarded for their patriotism by the extinction of the practice of the slaughter of kine. [But] the entire prohibition of this practice is made conditional upon the complete extermination of the infidels from India. If any Hindoo shall shrink from joining this cause, the evils of the revival of this practice shall recoil upon them.

Bareilly is perhaps an extreme example. It was one of the places (Bijnour and Moradabad were others) where there was actual communal fighting between Hindus and Moslems. But even in Delhi itself Bahadur Shah had to reassure leading Hindus who came to him to complain that they felt insecure: 'The Holy War is against the English; I have forbidden it against the Hindus.'[46] All in all it seems safer to conclude that the Mutiny temporarily, and not always completely, papered over the cracks of disagreement between different religious communities than that it was ever a thoroughly united movement.

What long-term effects did the Mutiny have upon Anglo-Indian relations? It has been argued that British actions during and after the Mutiny disillusioned Indian admirers. Previously they had seen British civilisation as something better than their own and their most earnest wish had been to emulate it. Now the actions of Colonel Neill and men of his stamp had shown that, under stress, the British behaved no better than anyone else. The theory seems an improbable one. Indian memories must have been very short if they had forgotten the all too 'human' actions of the company in the eighteenth century. But an even more substantial objection is that Indian interest in the West before 1858, at least as exemplified by men like Ram Moham Roy and Dadabhai Naoroji, had never been uncritical. Nor is there in fact any evidence of a turning away from westernisation on the Indian side immediately after the Mutiny. The western-educated had identified themselves with the British during the Mutiny. Their disillusionment came later.

The Mutiny certainly influenced British thinking. Stories about the Mutiny entered into English literature, including that meant for the schoolroom. Many children must have learnt poems like J. G. Whittier's[47] 'The Pipes at Lucknow', telling how the garrison was on the point of despair—

> Day by day the Indian tiger
> Louder yelled, and nearer crept;
> Round and round the jungle-serpent
> Near and nearer circles swept.
> 'Pray for rescue, wives and mothers—
> Pray to-day,' the soldier said;
> 'To-morrow, death's between us
> And the wrong and shame we dread' —

but was encouraged to hold out by a Scots girl who put her ear to the ground and heard the distant bagpipes of Havelock's relief column.

Some authorities have gone so far as to suggest that the Mutiny ruled a line across British thinking about empire and the government of alien peoples in general. The idea that one could turn Indians into English gentlemen, so popular among English liberals in the 1830s and 1840s, Professors Robinson and Gallagher suggest, 'had gone down in the Residency at Cawnpore'. Henceforth, ideally, empire meant the family of mother country and colonies of settlement. India was like 'some extra-marital responsibility incurred in youth'. It must not happen again.[48]

Did Britain, after the Mutiny, turn into a step-mother in more ways than one? It certainly opened the way for a blunter appreciation of the nature of British rule. Fewer were now inclined to say that Britain was in India with the consent and approval of the Indians. Some, like the lawyer Sir James Fitzjames Stephen, did not mince their words:

> It [the British government in India] is essentially an absolute government, founded, not on consent, but on conquest. It does not represent the native principles of life or of government, and it can never do so until it represents heathenism and barbarism . . . One great practical inference is that government in India must proceed upon principles different from and in some respects opposed to those which prevail in England, and which, since the outbreak of the French Revolution, have acquired in many parts of Europe something like the consistency and energy of a new religion.[49]

It was still a form of the doctrine of trust, because Sir James did not believe that absolute government need be bad government—indeed sometimes it was by far the best and most appropriate kind of government—but it was a harsher version of it than Edmnud Burke's. To men like Stephen it would be a long time before the Indians emerged sufficiently from tutelage to manage their own affairs.

But before attributing too much to the Mutiny, it must be remembered that views had been changing before 1857, that many earlier suggestions for improving the government of India were taken up after 1858 as if nothing untoward had happened and above all that developments in India after 1857 were part of a complex web of changing political, economic and diplomatic circumstances which affected all parts of the British empire, including the United Kingdom.

Notes to Chapter 3 will be found on pages 240-2.

Chapter 4 DID THE BRITISH CONNECTION DISTORT THE INDIAN ECONOMY?

AFTER 1858, having survived the crisis of 1857 and with the direct assumption of authority by the Crown, it seemed clear that the British were going to stay in India for the foreseeable future. Some, like John Bright, still looked to ultimate Indian independence and counselled, 'Wisdom suggests and urges a policy that will conciliate millions, and arrangements that will enable India to enter tranquilly on the path of self-government and independence.'[1] Others, like Sir James Fitzjames Stephen, saw nothing wrong with absolute government, if it was good government, and did not see why the British should 'feel ashamed' or be 'desirous to lay it down'.[2] Others again, like Charles Dilke, thought the issue simple: 'Were we to leave Australia or the Cape, we should continue to be the chief customers of those countries: were we to leave India or Ceylon, they would have no customers at all; for, falling into anarchy, they would cease at once to export their goods to us and to consume our manufactures.'[3] Even those who, like H. G. Wells, thought 'we [the British] are there like a man who has fallen off a ladder on to the neck of an elephant and doesn't know what to do or how to get down,' accepted that, as a matter of fact, the unnatural connection was there to stay for a long time.

The question obviously arises—did that unnatural connection distort the development of both countries? Did it, on the one hand, prevent India from developing from a feudal, somewhat disorganised, but comparatively advanced society in the eighteenth century, into a modern industrial state, and instead throw her back into the more primitive role of a primary producer, exaggeratedly dependent on agriculture? Did it, on the other hand, drain resources of talent and manpower from Britain which would have been better employed at home? Did it contribute to the stagnation of British industry in the late nineteenth century and so allow her to be overtaken by her rivals, the United States and Germany? Did it distort Britain's conception of her role in the world, by making her an imperial instead of a European power, and more specifically, distort her foreign policy so that, having two power bases to defend, one in Europe, one in Asia, she became obsessed with the 'route to India' and came to regard Russia as the 'national enemy', quite irrelevantly from the European point of view? It is proposed to examine the suggested distortion of Indian policy in this chapter and of British policy in subsequent ones.

It was often Englishmen (sometimes in official positions) who first drew attention to the damaging effects of the British connection on some aspects of the Indian economy. Henry Vansittart and Harry Verelst, who had both served as governors of Bengal in the 1760s, denounced, in their *Narrative of the Transactions in Bengal* (1766) and *A View of the Rise of the English Government in Bengal* (1772) respectively, the abuses to which the British trade privileges had given rise. Verelst wrote:

> It appeared that an exemption from duties had thrown the whole trade of the country into the hands of the English. This, however, was the least evil. The country government was destroyed by the violence of their agents; and individual tyranny succeeded to national arrangement. In the general confusion, all, who were disposed to plunder, assumed the authority of our name, usurped the seats of justice, carried on what they called a trade, by violence and oppression. The Nabob's officers either fled before them, or, joining the invader, divided the spoil.[4]

The merchant and one-time company servant, William Bolts, may well have been a scoundrel,[5] but his denunciation of the company's oppression of the Bengal weavers in his *Considerations on Indian Affairs* had a wide circulation; '. . . the English,' he wrote, 'with their Banyans and black Gomastahs [agents], arbitrarily decide what quantities of goods each manufacturer shall deliver, and the prices he shall receive for them.' The Gomastah compelled the weavers 'to sign a bond for the delivery of a certain quantity of goods, at a certain time and price, and pays them a certain part of the money in advance. The assent of the poor weaver is in general not deemed necessary. [If he refuses the money it is forced upon him.] The roguery practised in this department is beyond imagination . . . for the prices [fixed by the Gomastahs] are in all places at least 15 per cent., and some even 40 per cent. less than the goods so manufactured would sell in the public bazaar . . .'[6]

The decline of the Indian textile industry, although it has been questioned by some recent writers,[7] was well attested before select committees of the House of Commons and corroborated by independent writers like Bishop Heber in his *Indian Journal* and R. Montgomery Martin in his *Anglo-Eastern Empire in 1832*. James Mill had been ardent in his denunciations of many aspects of British policy in his *History of British India* and this tradition was continued by the oriental scholar Horace Hayman Wilson, who carried on the project. Wilson denounced the discriminatory tariff policy which he believed had allowed the rise of the cotton mills of Paisley and Manchester at the expense of the old Indian industry. He wrote:

They were created by the sacrifice of the Indian manufacture. Had India been independent she would have retaliated . . . This act of self-defence was not permitted her; she was at the mercy of the stranger. British goods were forced upon her without paying any duty, and the foreign manufacturer employed the arm of political injustice to keep down and ultimately strangle a competitor with whom he could not contend on equal terms.[8]

Similarly it was an Englishman, Sir George Wingate, a former revenue commissioner for Bombay, who in his *Our Financial Relations with India* (1859) first fully formulated the theory of the 'drain' of Indian wealth to Britain. The views of these men from Vansittart to Wingate were naturally taken up and elaborated by a later generation of Indian nationalists but it was important in the relations between the two peoples that it was never a question of an 'English' view and an 'Indian' view of the relationship. The English always remained self-critical—as indeed did the Indians too.

The essential moderation of the early Indian critics is well represented in Dadabhai Naoroji, who has already been mentioned in connection with the Bombay Association. Naoroji was distressed, as many of his compatriots were to be after him, by the poverty of the great majority of his countrymen. He never ceased to pay tribute to the British for bringing peace and the rule of law to India but equally he never ceased to criticise them for failing to adopt economic policies which would relieve the burden on the Indian people. He contended that the government of India was, comparatively speaking, two and a half times more expensive than the government of the United Kingdom and attributed this extravagance to the failure of the government of India to enter into proper consultations, through representative institutions, with the people of India. His books *The Poverty of India* (1878) and *Poverty and Un-British Rule in India* (1901)—unwieldy compilations though they were—inspired many later nationalists.

The most cogent detailed criticisms came from Romesh Chandar Dutt in his two-volume *Economic History of India*, covering the period 1757–1901. Like Naoroji, Dutt was very westernised. With two other young Indians he had passed the ICS examinations in London in 1869. His early career in the ICS was very successful and he became commissioner of the large province of Orissa. But he elected to retire in 1897, at the age of forty-nine. He was for a time a lecturer in the University of London and served as president of the Indian National Congress before becoming, like Naoroji before him, prime minister of the princely state of Baroda shortly before his death in 1909. Even when he was still a member of the ICS he had published a number of works in English and Bengali, translations, historical pieces and historical novels. After his resignation in 1897, he turned his considerable literary talents to publishing closely reasoned criticisms of British rule in India.

His basic position was not unlike that of Naoroji. Above all he shared his belief that essentially the British government and people had good will towards India and would try to remedy grievances if they understood them aright. Dutt freely conceded that the British had brought peace to India, a 'strong and efficacious administration' and courts of justice 'the purity of which is absolute as in any country on the face of the earth'. But against that must be set the poverty of India and the terrible toll of famine which seemed to be racing ahead uncontrolled in late nineteenth-century India. Dutt had seen disaster at first hand. As a young officer he had been sent to deal with the aftermath of the Bengal cyclone in 1876. He found the peasants of East Bengal frugal and prosperous and able to use their own savings to tide themselves over the disaster. Why, he asked, was not this more general? Why did there have to be the great famine of 1896–7 which affected, to a greater or lesser extent, 34 million people in the United Provinces, Bihar, the Central Provinces, Madras and Bombay, or the other great famine, beginning in 1899 and continuing for several years in Bombay, the Central Provinces, the Punjab, Rajputana, Baroda and the Central India Principalities?

To Dutt the answer seemed clear. It was because 'the sources of national wealth in India have been narrowed under British rule'.[9] He identified four main ways in which this had come about. There was the rapacious conduct of the company in the late eighteenth century, exemplified by its seizure of the internal trade of Bengal and the so-called 'Investment' by which it had paid for its goods for export from funds virtually stolen from the revenues of India, which had stunted Indian development. Secondly, there was the tariff policy of the British government which had favoured British industrialists, particularly the Lancashire cotton-manu-facturers, at India's expense. Thirdly, there was the burdensome land tax, which kept the peasant at subsistence level and made it impossible for him in most parts of India to build up any reserves to meet famine situations. Dutt believed that the situation in Bengal was better because of the 'Permanent Settlement' and recommended that it be extended to other areas. Fourthly, there was the continual 'drain' of Indian capital to England through the 'home charges', that is, salaries, pensions, interest on loans, etc. It will be seen that Dutt had welded together, with an impressive array of facts and statistics, the main charges which had already, but more tentatively, been brought against British rule.

R. C. Dutt's analysis was closely followed by many other Indian writers in the twentieth century. Among the most important was a namesake (but no relation) Rajani Palme Dutt, who used R. C. Dutt's facts but fitted them into a strictly Marxist framework. Palme Dutt identified company rule in the eighteenth century with the stage of 'merchant capital', in which the sole object, efficaciously achieved, was plunder. The industrial revolution in Britain, however, ushered in the second phase, that of 'industrial capital', when the manufacturers dominated the British government and India was valued as a producer of raw materials and a market for finished products. This was followed by the third stage, that of 'finance capital', which began to assume importance in the closing years of the nineteenth century. This, he regarded as the most gigantic fraud of all for, in his view, the British did not even 'export' capital to India as they did to other underdeveloped areas but by clever manipulation (since they were the government) assigned Indian capital to themselves. He concluded: 'Thus the British capital invested in India was in reality first raised in India from the plunder of the India people, and then written down as debt owed to India by Britain, on which she had henceforward to pay interest and dividends.'[10]

Pandit Nehru also used Romesh Dutt's ammunition in his attacks on British rule before independence in 1947, notably in works like *The Discovery of India* (1946). But the change in attitude is demonstrated by the much more marked bitterness in Nehru's work compared with that of Naoroji or R. C. Dutt. He too attributed Indian poverty to British rule and, indeed, believed that those areas of India which had been longest under British rule were the most impoverished. But, unlike the two earlier writers, he no longer believed in British good will. (The book was, of course, written while he was imprisoned by the British and is not completely representative of his views.) Instead he accused the British of deliberately holding back Indian development. 'Change,' he wrote, 'came to India because of the impact of the West, but it came almost in spite of the British in India. They succeeded in slowing down the pace of that change to such an extent that even today the transition is far from complete.' He would not agree that even in the educational field Britain had wished to advance India. He believed, 'That government feared the effects of the spread of modern education and put many obstacles in its way [but it] was compelled by circumstances to arrange for the training of clerks for its growing establishment. . . . So education grew slowly, and though it was a limited and perverted education, it opened the doors and windows of the mind to new ideas and dynamic thoughts.'[11]

These attacks naturally led in time to British replies. Some were uncritical panegyrics of the benefits British rule had conferred, but others were serious attempts to draw up 'balance sheets' to try to determine whether the period of alien government had done more good or harm to the Indian economy. Among the most important of these were Dr Vera Anstey's chapter on 'Economic Development' in O'Malley's *Modern India and the West* (1941), Sir Reginald Coupland's *India: A Re-statement* (1945) and Sir Percival Griffiths's *The British Impact on India* (1952). They were all well aware, as in a different way Nehru had been too, that they were examining a double problem. Griffiths put it very succinctly when he wrote:

> . . . in considering the economic impact on India of the British connection we are in reality studying a dual process. The first element in that process was the assumption of political authority in India by a Western power; the second element was the impact on the primarily agricultural economy of India, of the industrial revolution in Europe.[12]

This is a fundamental point which should never be forgotten.

In examining modern opinion on the effect of British rule on the Indian economy it will be convenient to consider each of

R. C. Dutt's charges in turn. The first charge concerned the late
eighteenth century. No weighty English writer has been found, at
least in the modern period, to defend the company's monopoly of
the Bengal inland trade or of their use of what was euphemistically
called the 'Investment' drawn from the revenues of Bengal to
finance their commercial operations. These charges of plunder
have generally been admitted and deplored by English writers
as belonging to the period of 'power without responsibility'. But
behind them there lies an even more serious and fundamental
charge, namely, that foreign intervention stunted the natural
industrial and commercial development of India. R. C. Dutt reminded his readers that 'India in the eighteenth century was a
great manufacturing as well as a great agricultural country, and
the products of the Indian loom supplied the markets of Asia and
Europe'. Dr Anstey in her *The Economic Development of India*
agreed that, in the eighteenth century 'Indian methods of production and of industrial and commercial organization could stand
comparison with those in vogue in any part of the world'.[13] Palme
Dutt did not doubt that India was ready for the take-off into industrial society in the eighteenth century. He wrote:

> The internal wars which racked India in the eighteenth century
> after the decline of the Moghul Empire represented a period of
> inner confusion (comparable in some respects to the Wars of the
> Roses or the Thirty Years War in Germany) necessary for the
> break-up of an old order and preparing the way, in the normal
> course of evolution, for the rise of bourgeois power on the basis
> of the advancing merchant, shipping and manufacturing interests
> in Indian society.

This normal course of evolution was interrupted by the invasion of
'the more highly developed European bourgeoisie'. They not only
forcibly superimposed themselves on the old society, they also
'smashed the germs of the rising Indian bourgeois class'.[14]
Nehru, although attracted by the idea, was less confident. He
thought that by the eighteenth century:

The economy of India . . . had advanced to as high a stage as it could reach prior to the Industrial Revolution. Whether it had the seeds of further progress in it or was too much bound up with the rigid social structure, it is difficult to say . . . Though the Indian merchant and manufacturing classes were rich and spread out all over the country, and even controlled the economic structure, they had no political power. Government was despotic and still largely feudal . . . Hence there was no middle class strong enough to seize power, or even consciously of thinking of doing so, as in some Western countries.[15]

Dr Misra, in his analysis of the growth of the Indian middle classes, essentially agreed with Nehru's reservations. India, he believed, had institutions conducive to capitalist growth before the period of British rule. Artisan industry and occupational specialisation was highly developed. She had long enjoyed a money economy. But against that must be set the political and social systems of the country, the rigidity of the caste system and the conviction of the priestly and warrior classes that trade and industry were inferior callings, and the bureaucratic despotism imposed by the Moguls. The radical changes that allowed the development of a western-type middle class in India came only with British rule.[16]

This, of course, raises the question whether the Indians had any desire for a capitalist revolution in the eighteenth century. Until late in the nineteenth century when, at least in Bombay, the situation was changed by the lead given by Parsi families like the Tatas, wealthy Indians were reluctant to offer capital to develop industries, preferring the traditional securities of gold and jewels or, a little later, the profits of land speculation. At an even deeper level, motivation may have been lacking. 'In the West,' Dr Anstey once remarked, ' "material progress" is almost a spiritual thing to the philosophical mind. It entails the possibility of a higher level of life for the mass of the population . . . But in India earthly exis-tence is still [1929] looked upon but as a passing phase, preparatory to the life or lives to come. Hence the ideal of the religious leaders is to subdue the appetites rather than to satisfy them.'[17] This in itself made it exceptionally difficult to stimulate economic effort. Karl Marx, indeed, held that the destructive British intervention was necessary to break the rigid shell of Hindu society. He lamented the passing of the Indian village community and thought it 'sickening... to witness those myriads of industrious, patriarchal and inoffensive social organisations disorganised and dissolved into their units, thrown into a sea of woes'. But he thought it inevitable: 'The question is: can mankind fulfil its destiny without a fundamental revolution in the social state of Asia? If not, whatever may have been the crimes of England, she was the unconscious tool of history in bringing about that revolution.'[18]

Some modern commentators have challenged even the proposition that the economic conditions generally considered necessary for an industrial take-off existed in eighteenth-century India. Professor Morris, for example, has held that it would be more realistic to compare Indian development to that of late medieval Europe.[19] But even if economic factors would have allowed a 'take-off', the co-existence of the social, political and ideological factors—noted by both Nehru and Marx—which were likely to hold back developments, must leave the proposition that, without British intervention, India would have progressed to the status of an industrial nation much more quickly, at least unproven.

There was a corollary to the charge that British intervention stunted Indian development. An American, Brooks Adams, developed a thesis in 1895 that it was the influx of 'treasure' from Bengal after Plassey that provided the capital necessary for the British industrial revolution.[20] The theory caught the eye of Nehru. Palme Dutt arrived at similar conclusions. 'The spoliation of India was the hidden source of accumulation [of capital] which played an all-important role in making possible the Industrial Revolution in England.'[21] The meticulous investigations of another American, Holden Furber, have however demonstrated that the actual 'drain' from India to England in the late eighteenth century was not huge, perhaps £1,800,000 per annum. Even if there was further 'spin-off' in profits from re-export to Europe and in stimulation of industry, it is hardly sufficient to account for such a massive change.[22] Eric Williams, the former prime minister of Trinidad, developed a similar thesis in his *Capitalism and Slavery* —the only difference being that he attributed the source of the capital to the 'triangular trade' in slaves and other commodities between Britain, West Africa and the West Indies.[23] The reader begins to feel a little like a mathematician confronted by too many 'proofs' of a theorem, in this case the proposition that western industrialism was entirely based on the exploitation of the third world. Plainly there were adequate capital resources for the industrial revolution in Britain. Plainly, too, overseas trade played a part. But it is impossible to identify any one trigger factor such as the wealth of Bengal.

There would seem to be a good deal more substance in the contention of Indian nationalist writers that the British connection helped to ruin the existing industries of India, especially the textile industry. Indian textile exports fell sharply in the early nineteenth century and the decline of the textile trade undoubtedly brought unemployment and suffering to many. R. Montgomery Martin recorded, '. . . many millions of Indo-British subjects have been totally ruined in their trade . . . while thousands of men and women have perished of want'. The Governor-General, Bentinck, spoke dramatically of 'the bones of the cotton-weavers bleaching the plains of India'. The very fine Dacca muslins were particular casualties. Sir Charles Trevelyan, who had served under Bentinck in India, told a Commons select committee in 1840: 'Dacca, which was the Manchester of India, has fallen off from a very flourishing town to a very poor and small one; the distress there has been very great indeed.' The population had declined from 150,000 to between 30,000 and 40,000 and 'the jungle and malaria are fast encroaching upon the town'. He also told the committee, 'The only cotton manufacturers which stand their ground in India are of the very coarse kind and English cotton manufactures are generally consumed by all above the very poorest throughout India.' Such a fundamental change affected men from the highest to the lowest. It disrupted the village community where the weaver, like the potter and other craftsmen, traditionally received a set

E

share of the village crops every year. At the other end of the social scale Bishop Heber told of a Moslem family 'formerly of great wealth and magnificence' who had to sell off their very fine library in order to live.[24]

Indian handicrafts did not, however, decline to vanishing point. Even in 1950–1, over 4 million people in the sub-continent were still engaged in the handloom industry.[25] India imported large quantities of yarn in the nineteenth century and, in some areas, the handloom industry declined only when it came into direct competition with the Indian factory industry in the late nineteenth century. The question whether the British connection 'de-industrialised' India is a difficult one. It has been widely accepted that in the nineteenth century the proportion of the Indian population engaged in agriculture rose and that engaged in industry and commerce fell. This has been questioned by Professor and Mrs Thorner, who have demonstrated that the figures available up to 1881 are difficult to interpret and that those after 1881 reveal stagnation rather than 'de-industrialisation'.[26] Stagnation is perhaps a serious enough charge in itself but it leads to a further question. How far was this the inevitable result of the European industrial take-off which wrested markets, even Indian ones, from the more backward Indian craft industry? How far was it due to the deliberate policy of the British government? More specifically, did the British government manipulate Indian tariff policy in such a way as to give an overwhelming advantage to British manufacturers?

It had originally been English workers who feared Indian competition and who demanded, and got, high duties (in some cases as high as 70 per cent) to try to keep Indian goods out. These tariffs had in fact failed to exclude Indian goods and it may be that no Indian tariffs would have been effective in keeping out English textiles, once factory methods had produced good quality goods very cheaply. Indian consumers took to them with enthusiasm—in some areas, for example, cheap Lancashire cottons replaced the coarse jute cloth previously in use—and it has been fairly pointed out by English apologists that, however disastrous this turn of events may have been for the Indian manufacturer, the Indian consumer benefitted.

If Indian interests were not always uniform, equally there was nothing monolithic about the British manufacturing and commercial interests confronting India. On the contrary the manufacturers and the company were often at odds. The company was for a long time compelled to transport a proportion of unwanted woollen exports to India to its own embarrassment. In the late eighteenth century the company began to build up both the cotton and the silk industry of Bengal so successfully that it caused alarm at home. The adoption of the Italian method of silk-winding led to a short-lived boom in the 1770s. The investment in the Bengal cotton piece-goods industry was sometimes marred by the kind of oppression noted by William Bolts but it also led to the establishment of flourishing commercial centres like that at Beerbhoom in which W. W. Hunter calculated, in his *Annals of Rural Bengal*, that £45,000 to £65,000 was invested every year. At one time about one-sixth of the textile workers of the whole of Bengal were given employment by the company. It is not surprising that in 1783 the directors of the company were as dismayed as the Bengal weavers would have been if they too had known the facts at the rise of a hitherto unknown place called Manchester, and wrote to their agent in Bengal directing him to 'exert yourself to the utmost in causing the manufacturers of Bengal to pay every attention not only to an improvement in the fabric of the muslins but also to a reduction of the prices, as on both the one and the other will depend very much our future success in this article'.[27]

The British duties on muslins (as distinct from calicoes which were higher) had never been prohibitive. In 1812 they were only 27 per cent and in 1832 British duties on both calicoes and muslins were only 10 per cent. Indian goods were driven out of the British market because they had ceased to be competitive with Lancashire. Lancashire goods, however, now began to drive Indian goods out of their home market. The British-controlled government of India did nothing to check this. The older generation of English apologists generally took the view that there was no deliberate intention on the British part of ruining Indian industry or even of keeping India as a captive market for British goods. Their action was dictated by the fact that they were completely committed to free trade policies, often in a doctrinaire way, believing that markets would find their own levels and that artificial attempts to interfere with economic processes were usually disastrous. This was sometimes linked with the view that the 'Victorian gentlemen' who generally held the political power had little instinctive sympathy with the business classes.[28] It was accepted by this school of thought that the British government of India did not act as an Indian government probably would have done or indeed as the Canadian government did in a famous case in 1859. In that year the Canadians put on a tariff, partly for revenue purposes, partly to protect infant industries, which was regarded as seriously damaging by the Sheffield hardwear manufacturers. The Sheffield men protested to the British colonial secretary. He passed on their complaints to the Canadian government but it rejected them sharply, maintaining that it was the best judge of its own needs. The British government acquiesced in the Canadian claim and henceforward did not try to interfere in the tariff policy of the British colonies of settlement.[29] The difference was noted in India but it was not until after World War I that India gained a comparable control of her fiscal policy.

In the last twenty years, however, there has been growing scepticism among scholars as to whether the British policy in India was really one of *laissez-faire*. Doubts were expressed by Professor Habakkuk in his contribution to the second volume of the *Cambridge History of the British Empire* and, in a famous article in the *Economic History Review* in 1953, Professors Robinson and Gallagher suggested that, on the contrary, India 'was subjected to intensive development as an economic colony along the best mercantilist lines'. The whole question has become part of the wider controversy of the 'imperialism of free trade' of the mid-nineteenth century. Peter Harnetty has recently undertaken a detailed investigation of one aspect of this in his *Imperialism and Free Trade: Lancashire and India in the mid-nineteenth century*.[30]

Harnetty studied the period from the assumption of Crown responsibility in 1858 to 1882. He found very steady pressure from the Manchester manufacturers on the British government to support their interests, which was often successful—but not always. Manchester influence always had to compete with other influences, including that of the British government of India—which by no means identified its interests with those of Manchester.

In 1859 the government of India decided to raise the import duties on cotton goods which had previously stood at 5 per cent to 10 per cent to help to pay the huge extra costs of the Mutiny. Manchester protested strenuously but it did not get its way. Manchester kept up the pressure during the early 1860s which were the abnormal years of the American Civil War and the cotton famine, but only in 1862 was the duty restored to 5 per cent.[31]

The next critical period was during the Tory administration, 1874–80. From 1873 onwards Manchester began to be affected by that mysterious phenomenon, the 'Great Depression'. In January 1874 the Manchester Chamber of Commerce petitioned the government, protesting that the prevailing duties of $3\frac{1}{2}$ per cent on yarns and 5 per cent on British cotton manufactures imported into India were based on out-of-date valuations and were consequently more burdensome than in the past. They were further alarmed by rumours that long-stapled Egyptian and American cotton was to be imported into India free of duty and that what they termed 'a protected trade in cotton manufacture' would spring up in India, eventually to compete with the British industry. They asked that, in order to prevent this, the existing duties on cotton yarn and cotton manufactures should be abolished.[32]

The Secretary of State for India, Lord Salisbury, felt compelled to take notice of the Lancashire argument, although the explanation he gave privately to the Viceroy, Lord Northbrook, is interesting. He told him on 27 January 1875 that he thought the 'Manchester people' were mistaken about the probable results of abolition, but if this request was granted it would 'take the steam out' of other 'more unreasonable' demands. Much later in the

year, on 29 September, he wrote again advising Northbrook not
to take too much notice of the Anglo-Indians, that is Britons
resident in India, who were opposing the Manchester pressure.
Salisbury considered them 'more noisy than important' but he
added: 'The feelings of the Native community, if really excited,
would be more important, and it may be that a few years hence it
will be sufficiently awakened to be open to the irritants applied
by the Anglo-Indians. Therefore I am anxious to remove this bone
of contention out of the way while there is yet time.' He expounded
further on this on 5 November:

> The problem to be solved requires a knowledge both of English
> and Indian opinion . . . I am . . . strongly moved by the feeling
> that the one great danger for an Indian Empire of the future will
> be the jealousy of the two populations. If some time hence the
> natives should think they are being 'exploités' for English interests,
> and should be led in that discontent by Anglo-Indians, the
> collision will be serious. But the danger is some way ahead, for
> the Native consciousness is only half awakened.

He repeated that the cotton duties could not be maintained and had
better be abolished before the opposition was still better organised.
'Their abolition now will create much outcry, and I shall no doubt
be sufficiently abused. But later it will create something worse
than outcry; whereas, if they are now abolished, it will soon be
seen that they were in no way necessary for the prosperity of the
Indian manufacture, and the conflict will be speedily forgotten.'[33]
    In the course of 1875, however, Salisbury and Northbrook had
got completely at cross-purposes on the tariff. Northbrook was a
Whig, appointed by the previous Gladstone administration, and,
as a member of the great banking family of Baring, something of a
financial expert in his own right. He had embarked on a major
review of Indian finances and tariff policy. Salisbury's dispatch
of 26 March only generally commended the Manchester views to
Northbrook and a more specific dispatch drawn up in May was
for some reason not sent off until July. It arrived too late to affect
the tariff measure introduced by Northbrook on 5 August. This

reduced many import duties but kept those on cotton manufactures at 5 per cent. It did meet Manchester wishes by imposing a duty of 5 per cent on raw cotton imports. Salisbury 'disallowed', as he was entitled to do, the clauses relating to the import duties. Northbrook resigned as viceroy at the end of 1875. It is quite true that he did not resign specifically on the cotton duties, as Indian opinion was inclined to suppose at the time.[34] He had quite genuine family reasons for wishing to return to Britain and he had first suggested resignation on 12 September before the quarrel became acute (although he had known since 30 August that the British government was going to object to his tariff measure). Nevertheless, as the Northbrook papers in the India Office Library and the Salisbury papers in Oxford demonstrate, there had been a long build-up of strain and misunderstanding between the two men on both economic and military questions.[35]

The incident of the cotton duties in 1875 has been dealt with at some length both because it became central to the Indian nationalist case that Indian interests were always sacrificed for those of Lancashire and also because, investigated in depth, it seems to show not a single-minded machiavellian policy on the part of the British government so much as a remarkable tangle of conflicting interests and human fallibility. Even when Northbrook had been replaced by the Conservative nominee, Lord Lytton, and even though the government was frightened by the bogey of the loss of fourteen seats in Lancashire in the 1880 election if the cotton interest was not satisfied,[36] the India Office was still unable to force through the abolition of the 5 per cent duty and it was not in fact removed until another Liberal viceroy, Lord Ripon, abolished all general import duties in 1882.

The case of the excise duty in 1894 does seem to be a clearer example of a Manchester success. In 1894 the state of the Indian finances compelled the reimposition of import duties including, eventually, a 5 per cent duty on cotton goods. The government of India was persuaded to impose a 5 per cent excise duty on those Indian cottons which competed with Lancashire goods. In 1896 the excise duty was reduced to 3½ per cent but extended to all cotton goods. Some Indian authorities regarded this as more oppressive than the 1894 arrangement because it included even the coarsest cottons bought by the poorest which were not in competition with Manchester.[37] The import duty was later raised to 11 per cent but the excise duty remained at $3\frac{1}{2}$ per cent until it was finally abolished in 1925. Even this then was, in the long run, a qualified success for Manchester.

The British government undoubtedly left Indian industry exposed to outside competition in a way in which an Indian government probably would not have done. That this was, in part at least, a genuine attachment to free trade doctrines and not simply a camouflage for Manchester interests is perhaps demonstrated by the fact that they felt that it would have been improper and 'weakening' to try to protect India from foreign competition either. This is illustrated by correspondence between another secretary of state for India, John Morley, and another viceroy, Lord Minto, in 1908. Morley wrote on 3 September, 'Then the Japanese have their eyes on it [India]. They are meanwhile flooding the Indian Banyans [merchants] with their wares and beating the English traders.' Minto wrote back on 23 September agreeing that India was full of Japanese 'on the look out for something' and 'Japan is to a certain extent getting hold of the Indian market [because they had modern machinery and could make goods cheaply] but this is fair competition'.[38]

The suggestion that Britain governed India as a colony in the mercantilist tradition, however, relates not only to tariff policy but to her management of the internal economy of India. In some ways plainly Britain did not pursue a classical mercantilist policy. There was no attempt in nineteenth-century India, as there had been in eighteenth-century America, to prevent the development of industries by prohibitions and directives. There was, however, investment, with government blessing, and this investment was guided into the channels regarded as necessary or desirable from the government point of view.

This was the period when the 'infrastructure' of roads, railways, posts and telegraphs was laid down. Indian critics protested that these roads and railways ran, not where India wanted them, but where British military and commercial needs dictated. There is no question but that many roads and railways built by the British in India were strategic ones. This was particularly true on the north-west frontier where the possibility of one day having to counter a Russian attack was never far from the military mind. Some roads in Bombay and the Central Provinces were certainly 'cotton roads', designed to facilitate the transport of raw cotton to the ports.[39] Some roads and railways fulfilled the function of transporting British manufactured goods to the interior—although it is more difficult to establish particular instances of this being done with specific goods in mind. Nevertheless, looking at a railway map of India in the early twentieth century (such as that in Anstey's *Economic Development of India*) when 25,000 miles of track were open, it is difficult to see where else an independent government would have placed them since most of the major lines followed ancient and obvious lines of communication. Even John Strachey in his highly critical *End of Empire* found this argument hard to accept. But all the critics, including Karl Marx himself, were agreed that whatever the British motives for putting the railways in, once they were there they would cause a revolution. Marx wrote, 'I know that the English millocracy intend to endow India with railways with the exclusive view of extracting at diminished expenses the cotton and other raw materials for their manufactures . . . [But] the railway system will . . . become in India truly the forerunner of modern industry . . . Modern industry, resulting from the railway system, will dissolve the hereditary divisions of labour, upon which rest the Indian castes, those decisive impediments to Indian progress and Indian power.'[40]

Many British officials would have given a very different account of the justification of the road, rail and canal system. They saw them, *inter alia*, as important weapons in the battle against famine. There had always been famines in India. Particularly bad ones were recorded in 1345, 1474, and 1630-2 before British rule. Famines have occurred since independence. But there was a general feeling in the late nineteenth century that famines were becoming more frequent. This may have been due in part to better information and more public sensitivity, but from the Orissa famine of 1866 onwards there was a succession of serious crises in different areas. It has been calculated that as many as 28 million people died as the direct result of famine between 1854 and 1901. The British despairingly attributed much of the trouble to the rising population. Indian critics replied that the rise was no steeper than in Europe and that, except in a few areas, India was not so densely populated as Britain.[41] No one doubted that the basic cause of famines was the violence and unpredictability of the Indian climate. The monsoon failed partially one year in five, totally one year in ten. Great rivers changed their course without warning. Cyclones and tidal waves created disaster areas. It was realised, however, that the famine was always limited in area. India was so vast that disaster never struck everywhere at once. The problem was to get food from 'normal' areas to regions of acute shortage.

A famine policy was hammered out between the Orissa famine of 1866 and the promulgation of the famous Famine Code in 1883. There was a small famine in Bengal in 1874 and an extremely serious one in 1877-8 which affected Madras, Bombay, Mysore, Hyderabad and the United Provinces. The 1877 famine took the British government in London by surprise. Lord Salisbury, the Secretary of State for India, had gone to the Constantinople Conference and left Lord Carnarvon, the Colonial Secretary, in charge of Indian affairs. Carnarvon was angry that he had received no warning of the impending crisis and canvassed opinion widely for emergency measures to deal with the situation. British opinion had vacillated a good deal. In 1866 Britain had observed a strictly *laissez-faire* attitude. Grain exports from Orissa had not been checked even when the shortage of supplies was becoming apparent. Relief had at first been left to private charity. But as the death toll mounted, British opinion became angry. It was still sensitive in 1874 and 1877. In 1874 the London press called for the impeachment of Northbrook, the Viceroy, and of the Duke of

Argyll and Lord Salisbury, successively secretaries of state, if a 'single life' were lost. The result was a certain amount of extravagant and misdirected public charity. In 1877 the India Office was rather grimly resolved that things should be managed better this time. Sir Louis Mallet, the Permanent Under Secretary, was irritated by what he regarded as the hypocrisy of public opinion in Britain. He accused the public of 'hugging itself, at Indian expense in a cheap and selfish philanthropy' while being unwilling to 'sacrifice a single shilling' to help. Carnarvon, however, stated:

> I am clearly of opinion that neither the local nor the Imperial Government of India can acquiesce in the death by starvation of a single individual so long as they have the power to prevent it. And though I admit with you that this country expects that India shall bear the burden of whatever measures may be necessary, yet in so deciding she is bound, and I believe would be prepared on the failure of India—to accept the share of the cost.[42]

The tension always remained in British policy between the genuine shock and horror they felt at Indian famines and the difficulty of persuading the British tax-payer that it was unrealistic to simply tell the Indian peasant that he must 'stand on his own feet'.

The solution of the dilemma was obviously to increase Indian prosperity and, more specifically, improve Indian communications, so that these embarrassing famines did not happen. In January 1877 a very experienced Indian official, Sir Bartle Frere, had put a comprehensive plan for such public works, including railways, canals and roads, before Carnarvon. He had insisted that the money for them would have to be raised on the London money market.[43] The Famine Commission of 1880, presided over by Richard Strachey, reported in much the same sense. As a result the government encouraged private companies to construct new lines, with varying degrees of government backing. The British government did not entirely solve the great technological problems connected with famine control in the nineteenth century but, thanks in large part to the improved communications, the first half of the twentieth century was very much better than the previous half-century. According to British statistics no life was lost from starvation between 1901 and 1943,[44] although some deaths did occur from diseases such as cholera which are frequently associated with famines.

R. C. Dutt, however, writing under the shadow of the last great famine of the nineteenth century, bitterly accused the British government of having pursued policies which had aggravated the situation. He charged them with neglecting irrigation in favour of railways. This particular accusation does not seem to be well founded. The British found the irrigation system of northern India in considerable decay at the end of the Mogul period. Even in the period of company rule, although there was much foot-dragging and objection to expense, the East and West Jumna Canals and the Ganges Canals and the dams on the Coleroon and Krishna rivers—all important for irrigation purposes—were completed. The famines of the latter half of the century did direct British attention to the irrigation problem. After the Orissa famine of 1866 it was agreed that irrigation works should be financed by public loans and by the 1890s sufficient expertise had been gained to bring under cultivation large tracts of the Punjab which had previously been barren. By World War II over 32 million acres, or one-eighth of the cultivated land in India, was irrigated from state irrigation schemes, the largest area in any country of the world.[45]

Dutt also accused the British of taxing the peasant so heavily that he had no reserves with which to buy food in times of scarcity and suggested that the Bengal Permanent Settlement should be extended to other areas. Dutt's criticisms attracted a reply from the Viceroy, Lord Curzon, in a famous memorandum. Woodruff fairly points out that Curzon had the advantage of a team of expert advisers, which Dutt did not have, and that on many questions of fact he demolished Dutt—in particular demonstrating that extending the Bengal Permanent Settlement to other areas would actually have increased taxation in many places—but that the warm humanity of Dutt's indignation won more sympathy than the statistical logic of Curzon's reply.[46]

There were undoubtedly flaws in Dutt's argument. Famines were caused more by bad transport than by lack of savings with which to buy alternative foods. But the traditional system had been disrupted in many ways. The realisation that there was now a market for cash crops may in itself have encouraged the peasant to sell reserves of cereals which he would otherwise have kept for his own use and this may have had at least a marginal effect on the famine situation. But there is no doubt that the British did not solve and in some ways aggravated the enormous problem of rural poverty in India. They were confronted at the outset with the great complexities of Mogul and Hindu systems of land tenure which they spent a century trying, not always successfully, to understand. Land taxes had been high in Mogul times. The state's share of the gross produce of cultivated land was theoretically assessed at one-third. In each village other specific shares went to village craftsmen, who were not themselves cultivators, and the rest remained with the individual cultivator and his family. The Moguls had rarely succeeded in exacting their full one-third. Under British rule the screw certainly tightened. Bishop Heber wrote in 1826, 'No Native Prince demands the rent which we do.' (In nineteenth-century India the land revenue was frequently described as 'rent' on the assumption that the Mogul empire had been a feudal state in which the emperor was the ultimate owner of the land.) At their worst taxation demands were allowed to rise to 55 per cent of the gross produce. But, particularly after 1858, the British knew that they were a long-term government. They had no interest in ruining agriculture for the sake of a temporary quick money return. Land taxes at the end of the nineteenth century were not excessive, probably, allowing for the changing value of money, not more than 10 per cent of the produce.[47]

But the British had dislocated the system in other, more subtle ways. In order to collect taxes conveniently they wanted an 'owner' of every piece of land on their books. They found him in the *zemindar* or 'landlord' in Bengal, in the *ryot* or peasant in most other areas. They also wanted the taxes paid in money. These two factors together led to the sale of land, an idea essentially foreign to the Hindu system, and provided a field day for land speculators and for the money-lenders, who gave the peasant a low price for his standing or just-harvested crops and then sold them at a profit. It did much to destroy the autonomy and practical democracy of the village community—over which even Marx shed a tear, although believing it inevitable.[48] By the end of the century it had created a class, scarcely known before, of landless agricultural labourers.

The British also introduced the idea of large-scale cash crops, particularly cotton, indigo, jute and tea. In the eyes of Indian nationalists this was part of the British plan to keep India as an area of primary production to supply British needs. British manufacturers, especially cotton manufacturers, did see India as a source of raw materials; but to be a primary producer, in itself, need not have held back Indian development, any more than being a primary producer of raw cotton held back the development of the United States. British interest in the growing of cotton in India was intermittent, only rising when troubles threatened with the United States as in the 1840s and 1860s. Lancashire machines were adapted for the long-stapled American cotton. New varieties were introduced into India but often they were not suitable for the climate.[49] Real progress was not made until after 1895 when, during the viceroyalty of Lord Curzon, a much more scientific approach was adopted to Indian agriculture. Between 1895 and World War I the area under cotton in India increased by nearly 70 per cent.

Indigo had always been grown in India but it had not been important for export purposes until the West Indian supplies were drastically reduced as the result of the slave rising in Santo Domingo in the 1790s. European private enterprise then moved into indigo-growing in Bengal. Commercially the industry was a success but it gave rise to serious scandal. The planters rented land to the *ryots* on condition that they would grow indigo on one quarter of it. On the face of it this was not unfair, but the planters also put the *ryots* heavily in their debt by advancing money for the start of the enterprise and the resulting relationship became a disguised form of slavery. The case of indigo was particularly interesting because it gave rise to a play in Bengali—*Nil Durpan*, the Mirror of Indigo—exposing the evils of the system. The play was translated into English by a missionary named Long. The Planters' Association brought a legal action against Long for defamation and he was fined and imprisoned. The indigo plantations finally declined at the end of the century under the competition of German synthetic dyes.

Jute was first exported on a regular basis to the mills of Dundee in 1838 but it was the Crimean War, during which Russian flax and hemp became temporarily unobtainable, which really stimulated the Indian production. Tea too became a prosperous industry in the late nineteenth century. Tea plants grew wild in Assam and other varieties were introduced from China. The opening of the Suez Canal in 1869 brought India into easy touch with world markets. On the face of it the Indian economy was steadily expanding and she should have had an excellent balance of payments situation. Between 1834 and 1910 Indian exports increased from less than £8 million per annum to £137 million, and imports from £4½ million to £86 million. There were, however, two drawbacks from the Indian point of view. First, the planter element was not a happy one in Indian society. It was they, for example, who led the outcry against the Ilbert Bill in 1883. Sir George Trevelyan considered that there was not 'a single non-official person in India . . . who would not consider the sentiment that we hold India for the benefit of the inhabitants of India a loathsome un-English piece of cant'.[50]

The second reason why the Indians felt that they were deprived of the benefits of their own productivity was the famous 'drain'. One aspect of this has already been dealt with in considering whether it was Indian wealth which triggered off the British industrial revolution. But, although the high priest of nineteenth-century free traders, Adam Smith, had roundly condemned the drawing of 'tribute' from colonies as bad economics as well as bad morality, it was contended that this process went on so long as the British raj lasted. The tribute or 'home charges' rose from

five main categories—the dividends to the proprietors of East
India Company stock, interest on loans raised in England, the
administration in London of Indian affairs, the salaries and pensions of British officials in India which were transmitted home
and payment on account of British troops serving in India. In
addition there were occasional overseas campaigns, such as that
in Abyssinia in 1868 and in Egypt in 1882, which were partially
charged to the Indian account because they were viewed in London
as being undertaken partly for Indian interests.

It was admitted that some of these charges would have had to
be met in one form or another even if India had been independent.
British politiciams argued that it was entirely reasonable that
Indians should pay for the administration of India. Why should
the British tax-payer foot the bill? Indian critics (and their British
sympathisers like Sir George Wingate in 1859)[51] pointed out that
if the administration had been an Indian one the money would
at least have stayed in the country. Dutt wrote, 'Taxation raised
by a king, says the Indian poet, is like the moisture of the earth
sucked up by the sun, to be returned to the earth as fertilising
rain; but the moisture raised from the Indian soil now descends
as fertilising rain largely on other lands not on India.'[52] A certain
proportion of goods and services were, of course, bought by
serving officers and officials in India. But the upkeep of the India
Office in London was a considerable item and it was perhaps the
harshness of the bargain that the British treasury drove—the
government of India had to pay for everything down to the
wages of the charwomen—which, although entirely typical of
the nineteenth-century treasury's attitude to all 'spending' departments, served to emphasise the British determination that
every penny of the burden was to be on the Indian not the
British tax-payer.

Dividends on the East India Company stock were a major item.
In 1834, when the company ceased to trade, stockholders were
guaranteed a yearly dividend of 10½ per cent out of the revenues
of India. India frequently found it impossible to meet this new
charge on her revenues and when the Indian revenues could not

be sufficiently stretched, the difference had to be made up with loans raised in London, on which interest subsequently had to be paid. In 1858 the company surrendered its rights to the Crown but Section 42 of the Government of India Act of that year provided that the dividend on the capital stock of the company and its debts in England should be 'chargeable upon the revenues of India alone'. R. C. Dutt subsequently commented bitterly, 'The Crown took over the magnificent empire of India from the Company without paying a shilling; the people of India paid and are still [1903] paying, the purchase money.'[53]

The total Indian debt rose much more rapidly after the assumption of full government responsibility than before. Between 1792 and 1857 it rose from £7 million to just under £70 million, that is an average rise of less than £1 million *per annum*. The rise had not in fact been a steady one but had rapidly increased in time of war, for example during Wellesley's wars at the turn of the century or during the Afghan War of 1839–42. Bentinck's careful administration in the early 1830s actually decreased the debt. But the considerable cost of suppressing the Mutiny, over £40 million, was, despite the protests of men like John Bright, all charged to the Indian account. By 1860 the public debt was over £100 million. By 1877 it was in the region of £139 million and by 1902 over £226 million. The connection between the total debt and the 'tribute' was that whenever the Indian revenue was insufficient to meet the charges on the debt new loans had to be raised in London. The total Indian debt in London rose from £3½ million at the time of Victoria's accession in 1837 to over £133 million at the time of her death in 1901.

Indian responsibility for the upkeep of the British army in India was resented, more particularly because, as a result of historical accidents, neighbouring Ceylon did not have to carry a comparable burden. Britain was in fact able to maintain a considerable army overseas in the nineteenth century at someone else's expense. Apart from day to day expenses, there were the costs of campaigns, sometimes internal campaigns like the Sikh Wars of the 1840s, at other times campaigns on the borders of

India like those in Burma or Afghanistan, or overseas campaigns like that in Egypt in 1882. The last was regarded as questionable even in British circles and the India Office fought a hard battle to have its share of the expenses reduced. Indian nationalists came to regard all military expenditure as an unnecessary expense which took away money from the real needs of the country, such as combating poverty. This was not altogether realistic. All countries, even professional neutrals like Switzerland and Sweden, have found it necessary in the modern world to expend a substantial proportion of their budget on defence. Independent India and Pakistan have certainly found it necessary to do so. India spends 30 per cent and Pakistan 45 per cent of her national budget on defence.[54] If Britain did exploit India militarily she did in return keep other powers out during the competitive days of the nineteenth century and provide naval cover.

Some of the sterling debt was for the establishment of public works, especially the railways. Indeed R. C. Dutt complained that the British public naïvely supposed that it was all for productive works of this kind.[55] In 1911 Sir Theodore Martin wrote a powerful reply to the Indian exponents of the 'drain' theory in his *The Economic Transition of India*, in which he argued that the British connection had enabled the Indians to borrow capital for public works at substantially below the figure exacted from the Japanese for similar enterprises—he put it at $2\frac{1}{2}$ per cent less—and argued that this in itself was enough to wipe out the so-called 'tribute'. He did not convince his critics, who maintained that the guarantee of a 5 per cent minimum return, secured on Indian revenues, which the British government promised to railway investors, only served to encourage wasteful speculation. With the dividend guaranteed it did not matter if the money was 'thrown into the Hughly or converted into bricks and mortar'. The parliamentary inquiries of 1872 and 1873 certainly revealed a degree of extravagance and carelessness in drawing up contracts but witnesses doubted whether, without the guarantees, Indian railways would have attracted much capital. As it was, British capital did build the railways and by the end of the century both canals and railways were making a profit and beginning to contribute to the Indian revenues.[56]

Finally, it must be said that Indian industries had begun to develop before World War I whether because of, or in spite of, the British presence. Some, although not all of the capital came from Britain. Bengal became an area of jute manufacture as well as producing raw jute. The first Indian jute-spinning mill was established near Serampore in 1855 by two Scots and an Indian. The first power loom began to operate in 1859. Dundee protested but to no avail and by 1908 the Indian production surpassed that of Dundee. The Indian group most active in establishing new industries were the Parsis of Bombay. One such man, Cawasji Daver, established a cotton-spinning factory at Bombay in 1854. Indian cotton manufacture boomed during the American Civil War. By 1914 India was the fourth greatest cotton-manufacturing nation in the world and Sir Percival Griffiths draws attention to the fact that Lancashire provided the machinery and a great part of the technical know-how.[57] If Lancashire wished to repress the Indian industry it spoke with a divided voice. In 1907 another Parsi family, the Tatas, founded the great Tata iron and steel works and insisted that the capital should come from Indian sources.[58] It developed into the largest such works in the British empire and India became sixth among the steel-producing nations of the world. Other industries too were developing, paper, brick, hardware, soap and cement among them. Hydro-electric works were established in the Mysore gold fields in 1903 and just before World War I the Tata family were completing a project to supply hydro-electric power to Bombay.[59] In 1914 India was certainly not an industrial desert, kept as an area of primary production for the British manufacturer.

When, about the time of Indian independence, a number of men tried to draw up 'balance sheets' of the advantages and disadvantages to India of the British connection, most of them safeguarded themselves by the remark that it was too early to try to strike a balance. A quarter of a century later the task seems no easier and is indeed probably a permanently impossible one because two imponderables must always remain. The first is that one cannot establish what would have happened in India but for the British conquest. Secondly, even if it could be demonstrated beyond reasonable doubt that the pace of Indian economic development would have been very different without British intervention, it would still involve a subjective judgement to determine whether that would have been a good or a bad thing. As Griffiths put it, one would be called upon to 'arbitrate between Mr. Gandhi with his spinning wheel and Tatas with their great steel factory at Jamshapur'.[60] The only thing that can be said with any confidence is that Indians' own diagnosis of what had gone wrong with their country's development during the British period was very influential in formulating their own policy both during the closing years of British rule and after independence.

Notes to Chapter 4 will be found on pages 242–4.

Chapter 5 DID INDIA DISTORT BRITISH FOREIGN POLICY?

BRITAIN IS a European power. Few statements are less accurate than the headline with which some newspapers greeted Britain's entry into the Common Market in 1973—'We have become Europeans'. Britain has always been a European power, culturally, geographically, and in her primary political interests. She has also, for several centuries, been a world trading power. In the latter role she would necessarily have been interested in developments in the Indian Ocean and, after 1869, in the Suez Canal, whether or not she had had any special territorial interest in India. Nevertheless it can hardly be denied that her possession of an Asian as well as a European power base fundamentally affected her role in Europe and in the world. Other nations' assessments of British policy—whether accurate or not—in turn influenced their actions. Some saw India as a British hostage to fortune, as Bonaparte did in 1798. Others attributed British industrial prosperity in the nineteenth century at least in part to her possession of an empire and believed that if they too acquired an empire similar prosperity would follow—hence those French and German colonialists who never tired of advocating 'an India in Africa'.

As the century progressed it became increasingly apparent that Britain could not afford to lose her Indian empire to another European power. As long ago as 1819 Elphinstone had written to a friend, Sir James Mackintosh, speculating that the British empire in India would not be long-lived and suggesting that it might fall to 'Russian and other foreign attacks'.[1] Elphinstone regarded the possibility, if not with equanimity, at least as something for which Britain should be prepared. By the late nineteenth

century such a thing was regarded as intolerable in Britain. It
was not only that many Englishmen now regarded England's
prosperity as being bound up with that of India; England's
prestige too was now heavily committed and, however contemptuous the Manchester school might profess to be of that kind of
prestige, it was almost a tangible weapon in a world of power
politics created by men like Otto von Bismarck. India affected
British policy in a number of areas, the Ottoman empire, Persia,
Afghanistan, Tibet, South-East Asia, South Africa and, possibly,
other parts of Africa. In many of these areas Britain was brought
into direct conflict with Russia. By the 1870s many were saying
that a war between Britain and Russia, those two peripheral
powers in Europe who might seem to have no clash of interests
in Europe, who even operated in different military spheres, the
'Bear and the Whale', lay 'in the logic of history'—and that the
explanation was India.

The decline of the Ottoman empire began in the late sixteenth
century but it did not become manifest until the Russian War of
1768–74 as a result of which Turkey lost control of the Crimea
and ceded Azov to Russia by the treaty of Kuchuk Kainardji.
The fate of the Ottoman empire remained a major question in
European diplomacy until the treaty of Lausanne in 1923. The
European powers most immediately concerned were Turkey's
neighbours, Russia and the Austrian empire. Russia was anxious
about free access to the Mediterranean through the narrow straits
of the Bosphorus and the Dardenelles, although scholarly opinion
differs as to whether she was more concerned with an offensive
pushing out into the Mediterranean or with a defensive desire to
prevent any other powers gaining access to the Black Sea.[2] In
the latter half of the century Russian policy was also intermittently
influenced by Pan-Slav sentiments on behalf of the Slav subjects
of the Ottoman empire. Austrian interests until 1866 were generally
directed westwards towards Italy and Germany but after the
defeats of 1859 and 1866 Austrian policy became more orientated
towards the Balkans and more concerned about Russian expansion
and the possible influence of Pan-Slav ideas on her own Slav

subjects. France with a long Mediterranean coast had many commercial interests in the Near East. Germany took little interest in the fate of the Ottoman empire until late in the century when considerations of European politics made her anxious to avert a clash between Russia and Austria and when German commercial interests in the Ottoman empire itself began to expand.

How did British concern for the fate of the Ottoman empire fit into this pattern? Was Britain primarily concerned to protect her routes to India or was her policy determined by more general considerations of European politics and would it have been much the same without the Indian dimension? Writers in the late nineteenth and early twentieth centuries tended to assume that British policy had always been dominated by her anxiety about her routes to India. Lady Gwendoline Cecil wrote of her father's policy in 1876, 'England was concerned in these continental rivalries only so far as they might react upon the independence of Constantinople. Her road to India—not yet safeguarded by her occupation of Egypt—lay through regions subject to the Sultan's suzerainty.'[3] Lord Salisbury himself wrote in 1892, 'The protection of Constantinople from Russian conquest has been the turning point of the policy of this country for at least forty years, and to a certain extent for forty years before that.'[4]

Some twentieth-century writers have developed this theme. The Zinkins, in their book *Britain and India: Requiem for Empire*, suggest in the chapter entitled 'The Lake and the Route':

> The centre of British strategic concern was the Route, the Mediterranean way to India; Disraeli's 'lifeline of empire'. This concentration ... is one of the odder oddities of the British connection with India.

They date it from as early as 1800 and quote Horace Walpole's comment: 'This little Britain is to cover Constantinople ... I am right sorry for it.' The *Cambridge History of the British Empire* lends some support to this theory when it says of the battle of Trafalgar, 'Nelson's last and greatest triumph safeguarded the overland route to India.'[5]

Historians who have concerned themselves primarily with Europe have, however, come to some very different conclusions. A. J. P. Taylor, in characteristically trenchant fashion, states the opposite case in his suggested interpretation of the Crimean War.

> The Crimean war was fought for the sake of Europe rather than for the Eastern question; it was fought against Russia, not in favour of Turkey . . . The real stake in the Crimean war was not Turkey. It was central Europe, that is to say, Germany and Italy.[6]

In other words the Crimean War was about general balance of power considerations in Europe.

Professor Anderson in his study of the eastern question comes to the conclusion that British 'fears of Russia in the Near East were always exaggerated, even unreal' and that their antagonism at least from the 1830s to the 1880s was 'greater than the facts really warranted'. He doubts whether Russian expansion posed any really serious threat to Britain so long as she retained command of the seas and points out that Britain gave her blessing to the Russo-Turkish alliances of 1799 and 1805 when Britain still regarded France as the main enemy in the Mediterranean. Russia only begins to emerge as the villain of the piece in the 1830s and Anderson agrees with Taylor that 'until the 1850s anti-Russian feeling in Britain was based on resentment of the oppression of Poland and fear of Russian influence in Europe generally rather than on Near Eastern considerations'.[7]

It is by no means easy to disentangle the different threads in this complicated story. It is not made easier by the usual reluctance of nineteenth-century British ministers to enunciate general principles or explain their motives. On the comparatively rare occasions when they did appear to be expounding principles, it is necessary to bear in mind that this was almost always in relation to a particular issue, usually in reply to a challenge in Parliament or the press. What may at first sight appear to be a general statement may in fact only be an explanation of a particular decision. No doubt most of his predecessors felt like Sir Edward Grey that the grand schemes and strategies attributed to them by scholars were the inventions of the study and that the minister actually in office was compelled to deal piecemeal with events as they arose.[8] This very absence of overall plans makes it necessary to take very seriously Professors Robinson and Gallagher's suggestions concerning the 'official mind' of the Victorian Foreign Office,[9] the possibility that some reactions became so traditional, so built in to the system, that they were no long examined rationally on each occasion. It is possible that this was operating as late as 1956 when, a decade after Indian independence, Sir Anthony Eden could still regard the Suez Canal as the 'jugular vein of the empire'.

British power first became established in India at about the same time as the decay of the Ottoman empire first became apparent. This was a coincidence but it meant that British policy towards the Ottoman empire developed parallel with the increase of British obligations in India. The main British route to India at this time was, as it remained for several generations, by sea round the Cape of Good Hope. But there were other ways to India from Europe, the old land routes by which the spices had come in pre-Ottoman days. There was the route through Persia and down the Persian Gulf. There was the route across Asia Minor and down the Euphrates river. Finally there was the 'overland route' through Egypt.[10]

Attempts were made at various times in the nineteenth century to develop all these routes. A Royal Artillery officer, Captain F. R. Chesney, surveyed the Euphrates route in the 1830s. In 1836 two steamers, the *Tigris* and *Euphrates*, were launched on the Euphrates with the eventual intention of opening up a regular service; but the *Tigris* was wrecked in a sudden storm, with heavy loss of life, and the project was abandoned. The Euphrates route came to the fore again after the Crimean War with the proposals for the Euphrates Valley Railway. This commanded quite wide business support in England where it was seen as an alternative to the French-sponsored scheme of a canal through Suez. It was also, by the 1870s, seen by some as the only possible quick counter to a sudden Russian advance from Kars and the general area of northern Persia. But once the Suez Canal was in operation, it was not an economically viable project and it was allowed to languish.

The overland route through Egypt was opened up in the 1830s. Passengers sailed to Alexandria, went overland to Suez and took another ship for Bombay. A railway was built from Alexandria to Cairo in 1855 and from Cairo to Suez in 1858. From the beginning the overland route was useful for the transport of non-bulky goods of high value. More particularly, it was very valuable for the quick transmission of news and dispatches and it was much used for this purpose during the Mutiny.

Even before the building of the Suez Canal Britain had interests in the Near East connected with her Indian possessions, but British policy seems to have evolved quite slowly. The first real challenge to the security of India, after the Seven Years' War, came at the time of the Napoleonic Wars. Bonaparte's Egyptian campaign of 1798 certainly had an Indian dimension. One of the three alternatives allowed him by the Directory's instructions of 14 November 1798 was 'to pass into India, where he will find men ready to unite with him'.[11] It would have been incredibly short-sighted of any British government to have forgotten this challenge and indeed the first British pronouncements on the desirability of keeping the Ottoman empire intact do date from the period of the French wars.

The next threat to the integrity of the Ottoman empire came from a more purely European question, the Greek War of Independence in the 1820s. The issue was complicated for the British government by the strong philhellenic feelings of men educated in the classics, including the archaeologist Foreign Secretary, Lord Aberdeen. Fear of the extension of Russian influence westward into Europe was present too—men had not forgotten the 'Mongolian' troops who helped to pursue Napoleon to Paris in 1814. One unexpected upshot was the battle of Navarino when the western powers helped to expose the Ottomans to the Russians by destroying the Turkish and Egyptian fleets. The treaty of Adrianople of 1829 by which Russia made significant gains in Asia and the Balkans alarmed Britain, although, if she had but known it, it was shortly after this that the Tsar's committee on Turkish affairs reported in favour of upholding the integrity of the Ottoman empire.

It was during the next decade, the 1830s, that British opinion began to harden. The treaty of Unkiar Skelessi of 1833 by which the Turks agreed to close the Straits to warships in time of war in return for Russian assistance against the rebellious Pasha of Egypt, Mehemet Ali, caused undue alarm in Britain. The British Foreign Secretary, Lord Palmerston, however held no brief for Mehemet Ali. He was now clearly concerned with Egypt's role on the route to India and told his brother in March 1833 that the Turks were safer 'occupiers of the route to India' than an independent Mehemet Ali would be.[12] The same motives were behind Palmerston's actions in the eastern crisis in 1839–40 although his tactics were different. This time he allied with Russia to keep some control over her policy, while putting pressure on Mehemet Ali to check his dangerous challenge to the Sultan.

It is interesting, though, that Palmerston himself did not think that the Crimean War was fought about the route to India. He told the Commons, 'We fear nothing for our Indian possessions.' The war was a 'battle of civilisation against barbarism' and fought to maintain the independence of Europe—in other words it was about the balance of power against tyrannical Russia.[13] The Russian role in suppressing the revolutions of 1848 was a recent memory.

When did British priorities change? When did preserving the integrity of the Ottoman empire become, not an integral part of maintaining the balance of power of Europe, but strictly directed towards defending the route to India, so that eventually Britain was prepared to consider bargaining about Constantinople and control of the Dardanelles (unthinkable earlier in the century) so long as she was sure of her base in Cairo and her control of Egypt? The change seems to have begun in the 1870s and to have been connected with developments in the 1860s. In the 1860s Russia embarked on an unprecedentedly rapid advance in Central Asia and in 1869 the Suez Canal was opened.

The canal was built by French enterprise, French capital and French technology. Britain had always opposed it. Palmerston had commented on the impossibility of controlling a 'two hundred foot ditch' through someone else's territory. Even while the canal was being built British naval officers were still writing memoranda hopefully concluding that the project was an impossible one. But on 17 November 1869 it was officially opened in the presence of half the crowned heads of Europe. Britain was now faced with a dilemma. Because of British opposition to the scheme Britain had no stake in the canal. Opinions differed as to the importance of the canal in time of war. Some held with Randolph Churchill that, though it was an important highway in time of peace, it would be closed in war and the old route round the cape would still be the vital strategic one. Others held that, so long as Britain kept command of the high seas, she had nothing to fear from the canal. But this only led to the conundrum—would Britain's chances of keeping command of the seas be materially less if the canal were in enemy hands?

British opinion had toyed with the idea of taking Egypt for a generation. A writer in the *Oriental Herald* in the 1830s had written: 'It will be well, if Egypt really is to be possessed by any European power, that England shall be the first to plant her standard on the banks of the Nile.'[14] When Disraeli bought the bankrupt Khedive Ismail's canal shares in 1875 there were journalistic suspicions (or hopes) that this was the preliminary to a 'protectorate'. If such a thought was in Disraeli's mind he shrank from the probable international complications. The Khedive held only 45 per cent of the total shares and, because they had been mortgaged, they had temporarily lost their voting rights. Nothing was more inaccurate than Disraeli's boast to the Queen, 'You have it [the canal], Madam.' Nevertheless, the purchase made a profound impression on contemporary English opinion. Henceforth, the British public did believe that in some way the Suez Canal was their property.

The British occupation of Egypt in 1882 came at the end of long but ultimately unsuccessful attempts to keep in step with France in an Egyptian policy. It was totally at variance with the declared policy of the Gladstonian government. Nevertheless it had been the logical step since the 1830s. There were undoubtedly other factors besides the route to India involved, among them the British capital invested in Egypt and the destructive effect this had had on Egyptian government. However much Gladstone might deny that he was fighting a 'bondholders' war', the activities of the bondholders had helped to create the situation in which intervention seemed necessary. But the reason why intervention was deemed essential, why Egypt could not be allowed to collapse into anarchy and misgovernment, was undoubtedly the strategic importance of the Suez Canal. This was the decisive factor in the minds of Gladstone's ministers in the critical months of June–July 1882. It also explained why withdrawal, the avowed policy of the Gladstone government, was so difficult to accomplish. If a power vacuum were left in Egypt, who would fill it? Another power hostile to British interests?

Some historians have seen in the British occupation of Egypt the trigger which set in motion the whole spectacular 'scramble for Africa' which led to the partition of all tropical Africa between the European powers in considerably less than a decade.[15] The present author would not go so far as that, believing that there were many other factors in the economic condition of Europe at the time which influenced the movement. Nevertheless in certain areas and at certain times the British need to protect their position in Egypt was of critical importance. Once it had become apparent that Britain was not going to be able to extricate herself from her Egyptian entanglement, there seemed no alternative to Salisbury's carefully planned campaign for Kitchener to conquer the Sudan in 1896–8. It would have been far too dangerous to allow the area to fall into French hands.

Earlier generations had believed that Constantinople was the key to all, that 'Constantinople was the first strategic position in the world, and no Great Power could allow another to possess it'.[16] By the 1890s the British were compelled to modify their attitude. In 1891 the directors of naval and military intelligence reported that it was no longer practical in the event of a general war to concentrate a sufficient proportion of the British fleet in the eastern Mediterranean to ensure that Russia could not seize Constantinople. The politicians were reluctant to accept this but eventually Salisbury was convinced.[17]

The final change of policy was not accomplished, however, until the great upheaval of World War I. The Turks had joined the Germans and by the secret agreement of March–April 1915 Britain and France agreed that, after the war, the Ottoman empire should be dismembered and Russia come into possession of Constantinople. The agreement was only cancelled by the Russian revolution and the Russo-German treaty of Brest-Litovsk. The British were prepared to surrender Constantinople because they felt secure in Egypt. They had stumbled into Egypt as they had stumbled into India but they had begun to take an immense pride in their efficient government in Egypt—modelled very much on the lines of Indian administration, sometimes with personnel from India, drawing ICS salary rates. They were no longer thinking of leaving hurriedly and in 1915 they regularised their position in international law by proclaiming a protectorate.

British interest in the fate of the eastern Mediterranean from the time of Catherine the Great onwards was not entirely governed by concern for the safety of the routes to India but they were always a factor and her final willingness to concede Constantinople so long as she felt secure at Cairo suggests that by the end of the century concern for the route to India was the dominant consideration in British thinking.

The original route to India round the Cape of Good Hope also involved Britain in African affairs. The Dutch had established a base at Table Bay in 1652 for the convenience of their ships sailing to the East Indies. The British captured the base at the Cape during the Napoleonic Wars. It was one of the comparatively few areas they chose to retain at the peace. Generations of English statesmen had no doubt that their only interest in Cape Colony was its importance as a naval base. As late as the 1850s a governor of Cape Colony, Sir George Grey, could say, 'Beyond the very

limited extent of territory required for the security of the Cape of
Good Hope as a naval station, the British Crown and nation have
no interest whatever in maintaining any territorial dominion in
South Africa.'

Unfortunately for British plans, even in the days of Dutch
control, settlement had begun to spread out along the coast and
into the interior. Endless 'Kaffir' wars followed. When disgruntled
Boers trekked out of the British colony into what became Natal
the British felt compelled to forestall them because they dared not
risk a Boer colony with diplomatic links with a rival European
power on the coast of South Africa. The British involvement in
southern Africa was even more closely linked, at least in its origins,
with the British position in India than was British concern with
the Ottoman empire.

The Zinkins, however, develop their theory beyond the hypo-
thesis that British anxiety about her routes to India fundamentally
influenced her foreign policy. They quote Lord Rosebery's
remark of 1892, 'Our great Empire has pulled us out of the European system—our foreign policy has become a colonial policy'
and suggest:

> The vacuum which was created in British nineteenth-century
> foreign policy by Britain's safety in Europe was filled by the British
> Government's adopting an Indian foreign policy. This policy was
> not always made in Calcutta, but it was always, at least until the
> early 1900s, a policy of which India was the centre.[18]

Britain's 'safety in Europe' in this period may be the matter of
some dispute but it is true that she reacted with great vigour to
any movement that seemed directly to threaten her Indian
possessions.

Such a threat was most likely to emanate from Russian activities
in Central Asia. As early as 1838 Britain went to war with Afghanistan to prevent the Amir, Dost Mohammed, from cementing a
friendship with Russia. British policy was politically inept—
Dost Mohammed had tried to secure British friendship before
turning to Russia as second-best—and militarily disastrous. A

British army fought its way to Kabul in 1839 only to be overwhelmed in 1841. Of the 16,000 British troops who left Kabul on
6 January 1842 only one man, the famous Dr Bryden, rode into
Jalalabad wounded and exhausted a week later. It is hardly surprising that, despite Palmerston's conviction that 'sooner or later
the man from Calcutta and the man from the Caucasus must meet
in Central Asia' and that Britain should ensure that it would be as
far from her Indian possessions as possible, Britain lost her taste
for Central Asian adventures. But in the 1860s Russia began to
advance with unprecedented rapidity in Central Asia. In 1863 the
Russians completed their conquest of the Kirgniz Steppes. In
1865 they captured Tashkent and began to set up the province of
Turkestan. In 1866 they broke the power of the Khanate of
Khoquand and the following year they invaded the Khanate of
Bokhara. By 1868 they had conquered Samarkand and Bokhara.
Bokhara bordered Afghanistan, although no one had as yet clearly
defined the frontier.

There was a formidable natural barrier between the Russian
sphere and Afghanistan and British India, the Hindu Kush. Some
men believed at the time, and some historians have agreed with
them, that it was in the late nineteenth century a sufficient barrier
in itself. Earlier armies of lightly equipped marauders had been
able to pass it; a twentieth-century army with mechanised transport and air support could overcome it; but a nineteenth-century
army which needed heavy guns but had only horse-drawn transport to move them would have been completely halted by it. On
each side all the advantages would have lain with the defenders.
So runs the argument—but not everyone believed it.[19] In any
case there was a possible danger point at the western end commanded by Herat. Herat itself lay in an area which had long been
in dispute between Persia and Afghanistan. Britain also became
anxious about places in the vicinity of Herat like Merv which,
although of little strategic significance in themselves, seemed to
provide a test of the advance of the Russian threat.

Opinion was sharply divided on the best way to counter the
threat. Two schools of thought emerged, dubbed by their enemies

the 'mischievous activity' and the 'masterly inactivity' schools.[20] The latter held that the best security for British India would be a broad band of no-man's land in Central Asia with a comparatively short and easily defensible frontier served by strategic railways to bring up supplies. The former held that it would be madness to let the Russians come down to the frontiers of British India and that it would be better to go out and meet them in the wilds of Central Asia as Palmerston had said, as far from British India as possible—even though this meant longer lines of communication. The question was complicated by the fact that British prestige in the eyes of the Indian masses was believed to be heavily involved. By the 1870s the British were seriously concerned about the possibilities of Russian-inspired subversion in India. Salisbury wrote to Northbrook on 19 November 1875 spelling out the three different dangers he foresaw if the Russians became masters of Afghanistan: first, actual invasion of India; second, subversion; and third, the permanent tying up of a large British army to watch them.[21]

Salisbury, however, was not the first to have to formulate a policy to counter the new Russian threat; that fell to the Gladstone administration of 1868–74. They were inclined to try negotiation and the British Foreign Secretary, Lord Clarendon, and his Russian opposite number, Gortchakoff, began to negotiate in 1869 to define the frontiers of Afghanistan and so lessen the dangers of an accidental clash. In January 1873 Gortchakoff seemed to have met British wishes by assenting to a 'hands off' policy as far as Afghanistan was concerned. Unfortunately from the British point of view, he seems to have believed that this included a British acquiescence in Russian advance elsewhere and, in the spring of 1873, the Russians took Khiva. This was almost as unacceptable from the British point of view as intervention in Afghanistan.[22]

In the previous Conservative administration the then Secretary of State for India, Sir Stafford Northcote, had agreed with the policy of negotiation later pursued by Clarendon[23] but when the Conservatives came back to office in 1874 they were in a different frame of mind. Serious differences of opinion built up between

F

Lord Salisbury as Secretary of State for India and the Viceroy, Lord Northbrook, as to increased expenditure for intelligence work both on the frontier and to counteract subversion. Northbrook's successor, Lord Lytton, was a very different man. He was a strange choice for viceroy, a diplomat and poet with no previous Indian experience. The job had first been offered to two more suitable candidates, Lord Carnarvon who became Colonial Secretary, and Lord Dufferin, who became viceroy in 1884. Both declined in 1876 for family reasons.

Lytton's plans were from the first expansive. Even on the way out he bombarded both Disraeli and Salisbury with lengthy letters explaining his intentions. Salisbury may have been cautious in his reception but Disraeli was in an expansive mood himself. He was currently toying with ideas of acquiring a port on the Black Sea and a 'commanding position' on the Persian Gulf.[24] Lytton wrote that since Russia had now an easily defensible mountain frontier from Bokhara eastwards, Britain was entitled to a similar 'material guarantee'. 'And from Herat to the North Eastern extremity of Cashmire, one great continuous watershed [presumably that of the Hari Rud river] seems to indicate the natural defensive bulwark of British India.' Lytton considered that India would be safe if they took this with some 'margin to the north' to give them command of all the passes. The Oxus river should be recognised as the northern boundary of Afghanistan, and Britain might establish a station in the Kurram valley to command Kabul and Jalalabad. Salisbury might ruefully tell Disraeli a little later that he was 'telegraphing hastily back to prevent the immediate annexation of Central Asia',[25] but Salisbury too held 'My feeling as to Afghanistan is that the idea of neutral territory is fundamentally impossible. The country must either be within our attraction or that of Russia' and, since he believed Persia would pass to Russia, Afghanistan must not go too.[26]

In 1877 the British occupied Quetta by arrangement with the Khan of Kalat. A British agent was stationed at Herat. But matters reached a crisis when, in July 1878, a Russian mission, backed up by a military force, reached Kabul and negotiated a treaty of friendship with the Amir. A British mission was stopped at the Afghan frontier in September. Lytton dispatched an ultimatum to the Amir and, when it was ignored, invaded Afghanistan on 20 November. The Afghans agreed to a treaty with Britain too but on 3 September 1879 the British envoy, Cavagnari, was murdered. Hostilities were renewed. Afghan affairs were, however, influenced by events in Europe. The original Russian mission had been dispatched during the period of tension resulting from the Russo-Turkish War of 1877–8. After the Near Eastern disputes had been settled peacefully at the Congress of Berlin in June 1878, Russia became much less interested in an immediate challenge to Britain in Central Asia.

In April 1880 Disraeli's government was defeated in a general election. Gladstone and the Liberals had always condemned the Conservative policy in Afghanistan and vowed they would withdraw. When it came to the point they were reluctant to do so, particularly to cede the key point of Kandahar. They did in fact retain control of the Khyber Pass, the Kurram Valley and Quetta. But, beyond that, they took the considerable risk of trying to make Afghanistan a genuine buffer state under a new Amir, Abdur Rhaman, who had spent the previous twelve years in Russia. The gamble paid off. So long as he was left a free hand in domestic matters Abdur Rhaman was quite prepared to keep out Russian or other foreign influence.

This, however, did not entirely settle the matter. Boundaries were still in dispute. This led to the famous Penjdeh incident of 1885. A Russian force defeated a small Afghan force at the Penjdeh oasis, a fertile area south of Merv. The object of the attack was apparently to establish a Russian claim before the boundary commission delimiting the Afghan-Turcoman frontier reached that district. Public excitement in Britain was considerable. The pacific Gladstone asked the House of Commons for a vote of credit of £11 million and the crisis led to the coining of the word 'Jingoism' from the briefly popular music hall song: 'We don't want to fight but, by Jingo, if we do/We've got the ships, we've got the men, we've got the money too.' The problem was eventually

solved peacefully by the mediation of the king of Denmark.
Penjdeh usually appears as a curiously incongruous incident in
Gladstone's second administration, yet another distraction from
his attempts to 'pacify Ireland', but the British public showed good
judgement in according it considerable importance. Men had
long prophesied that when the Russian and the British spheres
finally met in Central Asia there would be a thunderous crash.
This was the moment at which Anglo-Russian war was supposed
to lie in 'the logic of history'. In fact that matter was peacefully
resolved. In the very last resort the European powers never
wanted colonial disputes, whether in Africa or Asia, to lead to
European war.

Central Asia continued to give rise to British anxiety after 1885.
As late as 1899 the Tsar thoughtfully remarked that he could alter
the course of the war in South Africa by mobilising in Turkestan.
In that sense Central Asia, like Egypt, continued to be a British
hostage to fortune but there seemed now to be no problems that
could not be negotiated. Tentative negotiations with Russia
began in 1901. They were delayed by the Anglo-Japanese alliance
of 1902 and the Russo-Japanese War of 1904-5 but they finally
came to fruition in 1907. The Russians, with certain minor
reservations, renounced any interest in Afghanistan. Both powers
agreed not to deal with Tibet, into which a British mission had
penetrated in 1903-4, except through her suzerain power, China.
The third part of the bargain concerned Persia.[27]

Britain could not afford to ignore Persia[28] which, even more than
Afghanistan, commanded the traditional invasion routes into
India from the north-west. With the development of steam naviga-
tion and talk of a Berlin-Baghdad railway, there seemed a new
threat of the development of rival steamship lines on the Persian
Gulf. Although the challenge might in the first instance be commercial, it also had strategic implications. As early as 1808 the
then Governor-General, Lord Minto, had sent Charles Metcalfe
to negotiate with Ranjit Singh to secure a Sikh alliance against a
possible French invasion through Persia. In 1814 the British
concluded the treaty of Teheran with the Persians by which the

latter promised not to admit armies hostile to Britain. But, by the 1830s, this agreement had worn thin and the British helped the Afghans to defend the region of Herat which was in dispute between the Afghans and the Persians. Britain again fought with the Afghans against Persia in 1856-7. The Russian advances in Central Asia put Persia under continually increased pressure. The Anglo-Russian agreement of 1907, so far as it concerned Persia, seemed at first sight to favour Russia—and was vigorously condemned by some English statesmen including Lord Curzon in consequence. It divided Persia into three zones, a Russian sphere of influence in the north, a large neutral zone in the centre and a small British sphere of influence in the south. The Russian sphere included most of the main towns and trade routes of Persia, among them the capital Teheran. But the British and neutral zones included the whole of Persia's coast on the Gulf and by this time Britain was more concerned to prevent a Russian base on the Gulf than to combat her influence on land.

Most of the international complications in which the possession of India involved Britain related to the Near and Middle East and brought her into conflict with Russia. But Britain also became involved in the affairs of South-East Asia and here her rival was France. Britain's first two Burmese Wars, those of 1824-6 and 1852, the second of which led to the annexation of Lower Burma, were brought about by purely local disputes. But the third, that of 1885-6, was triggered by Anglo-French rivalry. The French had acquired Saigon in 1859. By 1885 they were in control of Cochin China, Cambodia, Annam and Tonkin. In 1885 they signed a trade treaty with the king of Burma and, even more disturbing from the British point of view, agreed to allow the importation of arms into Burma through Tonkin. The British took advantage of an ill-advised Burmese molestation of a British firm to intervene. The war ended in the annexation of Upper Burma.

Between Burma and French Indo-China lay the independent state of Siam. British commercial interests began to penetrate from the west, French from the east. In 1893 Siam caused a serious incident between Britain and France when a French ship blockading the Menam river in the course of a dispute with the Siamese threatened a British ship. The Anglo-French agreements of April 1904 recognised a British sphere of influence in the west, a French one in the east and a neutral zone in the middle, rather like the subsequent Anglo-Russian arrangements concerning Persia.[29]

Britain's Indian possessions thus caused some degree of estrangement from both France and Russia. She had long drawn out quarrels with Russia over the eastern Mediterranean and Central Asia. She had minor quarrels with France over South-East Asia. More important, there was French irritation at Britain's unilateral policy in Egypt after 1882. The old liberal Anglo-French *entente* which flourished intermittently in the nineteenth century could not be resumed until, in 1904, the French recognised the British position in Egypt in return for British acquiescence in French plans for Morocco. 'Splendid isolation'—so-called—was never a preferred British policy.[30] It was never practical in the late nineteenth century to turn one's back on the power politics of Europe and concentrate on an overseas empire—too many imperial problems were linked with the policy of a European rival. But since she was at odds with both France and Russia Britain was driven to the policy of 'leaning on' the Triple Alliance of Germany, Austria and Italy. Sir Edward Grey has recorded that, when he became Under Secretary at the Foreign Office in 1892, 'The traditional policy which the new Government took up was that of distinct friendship with the Triple Alliance.'[31] Despite the personal preference of some ministers for French rather than German culture, this was not politically uncongenial to Salisbury and the Conservatives or to his Liberal successors. France and Russia were traditionally the 'restless' and ambitious powers and the policy of co-operating with Austria in particular to check Russian ambitions was an old one. But an Anglo-German understanding at any time after 1871 meant the abandonment of another traditional policy—that of maintaining the 'balance' in Europe by throwing Britain's weight against the strongest continental *bloc*. In that sense Britain's imperial interests, a high proportion of which were directly connected with her possession of India, fundamentally affected European alignments in a critical period between 1882 and 1904–7. In 1904 and 1907 respectively, however, Britain came to general arrangements with her two main imperial rivals, France and Russia. A position of stability, or at least stalemate, had been reached in many of the sensitive areas. The alignments of World War I, with Britain fighting beside Russia and France against the central powers, were not those which might have been expected if Asian considerations had dominated British foreign policy. In the last resort Britain was a European power and responded as balance of power considerations on that continent demanded.

EPILOGUE TO CHAPTER 5

It was during the British period that considerable communities of Indians moved into Africa. With de-colonisation some African states have come to bitterly resent the presence of these enterprising and prosperous Asian communities in their midst and to feel that Britain must directly bear the burden of them. How far was Britain in fact responsible for these emigrants?

It used to be held that, prior to the British period, Hindu India was a very insular society—if such an adjective can reasonably be applied to a sub-continent. Modern opinion doubts that. Indian traders had actively penetrated into South-East Asia, and even into Indonesia, before the British appeared on the scene. Indian traders had to some extent replaced Arab ones on the sea routes of the Indian Ocean when the Portuguese arrived at the end of the fifteenth century.[32] Indian firms had certainly assumed importance in Zanzibar before the British acquired any kind of political control there—indeed the need to protect these British Indian subjects was one argument in favour of British intervention in that region.[33]

It is not uncommonly suggested that the Asian communities in Uganda and Kenya owed their origin to the indentured Indian labour brought in to build the railway line from Mombasa to Lake

Victoria. The British government had initially been reluctant to give permission for the use of indentured labour, which had a bad reputation for degenerating into a disguised form of slavery. But in 1896 the Indian Emigration Act was amended to permit such recruitment. Between 1896 and 1901, 32,000 were recruited and crossed to Africa, at first usually from Bombay, later from Karachi. These, however, were not the main originators of the East African Asian communities. The vast majority returned to India on the expiry of their three-year contracts and only just under 7,000 stayed on.[34]

But from 1898 there was a steady stream of independent emigrants, Goans, Punjabis, Parsis and Gujeratis. Many were traders and spear-headed a revival of East African commerce. They were not always popular, partly because they also added money-lending to their activities. Richard Burton called them 'the Jews of East Africa'. They were pioneers in the Uganda cotton industry, their products going to supply the mills of Bombay. A large number, however, also came to take clerical posts in local administration or clerical and supervisory jobs on the new railways. A committee reported in 1909, for example, that almost all the station masters on the Uganda railway were Indians. Harry Johnston called East Africa the 'America of the Hindus' but schemes for officially sponsoring large-scale emigration in the early twentieth century came to nothing. The British in fact cooled towards the idea of encouraging the build-up of Asian communities in East Africa, partly because they were so successful commercially and so advanced in their political demands.

Modern British responsibility for some East African Asians seems to derive from a quite different root from any encouragement of their settlement. It springs from the concept, dearly cherished for several generations, of the common citizenship of the empire. Just as the Government of India Act of 1858 followed the Charter Act of 1833 in forbidding any distinction between the Queen's subjects, as they now were, on grounds of race or religion, so it was held as axiomatic that the Queen's subjects must be free to move anywhere in her empire. As a result the

Australians were compelled in the beginning to disguise their 'White Australia' policy under educational and similar qualifications. The initiative in defining a narrower citizenship than that of a subject of the British Crown was taken by the self-governing dominions like Canada.[35] The United Kingdom clung longest to the concept of a common citizenship, only eroded under the pressure of immigration in the 1960s. It is from that idea of a common citizenship, unless superseded by the adoption of a local citizenship, that there has arisen the strange anomaly of Indians with no citizenship except that of the United Kingdom which must by all the normal tests of birth and kinship be a totally foreign country to them.

Notes to Chapter 5 will be found on pages 244–5.

Chapter 6 THE IMPERIAL PERIOD

THE MOST obvious political result of the Mutiny was that the East India Company finally surrendered its rights to the Crown by the Government of India Act of August 1858. But the company did not lose all its stake in Indian affairs. Apart from the fact that the revenues of India continued to provide a guaranteed return to the old stockholders, the new secretary of state for India was to be assisted in his duties by a council of fifteen. Seven of the fifteen were to be appointed by the Court of Directors of the company. The majority of the council were always to be men who had served in India for at least ten years and had left India not more than ten years before. This provided the secretary of state for India with a reservoir of expert knowledge that his colleague at the Colonial Office might have envied but it meant that the influence of the company lingered on; and as late as 1885 the Indian National Congress resolved that 'the abolition of the Council of the Secretary of State for India, as at present constituted [is] the necessary preliminary to all other reforms'.[1]

The British Parliament had had some say in Indian affairs since North's Regulating Act of 1773 but British parliamentary interest increased in the late nineteenth century. Macaulay had lamented in the 1830s that India was a 'dinner bell' that emptied the House and his biographer, G. M. Trevelyan, commented 'with an Indian question on the paper, Cicero replying to Hortensius would hardly draw a quorum'.[2] John Bright found the situation little better in 1860. He wrote, 'Parliament cares about India little more than the Cabinet. The English people, too, are very slow and careless about everything that does not immediately affect them.'[3] But by the 1870s Lord Salisbury was complaining that the House of Commons was beginning to take a very active,

although very ignorant, interest in India.[4] Sir Charles Wood
(Lord Halifax) had written to Sir Bartle Frere a decade earlier,
'The worst of all governments is a popular government of one
race over another.'[5] Wood had then been cautioning against the
bestowal of political power on the small group of British settlers in
India but his apprehensions might also be applied to some aspects
of British parliamentary involvement.

There were both advantages and disadvantages for India in
being brought more directly into the arena of British party politics.
The most obvious disadvantage was that it made her more vulner-
able to the pressures of sectional interests like the Lancashire
manufacturers. On the other hand it made it more possible for
Indian reformers to look for allies among British parliamentarians.
Indian issues became one dimension in the rapidly changing
views of British politicians in the late nineteenth and early
twentieth centuries. This, of course, had been true to some extent
since the fortunes of Britain and India first became intermeshed
in the eighteenth century. British fears about the potential dangers
to the delicate balance of the British constitution had led to
disapproval of corruption in India and the evolution of the whole
doctrine of trusteeship. Ideas about 'natural laws' which should
govern society, deriving in many cases from French philosophers
of the eighteenth century, came to fruition in the Utilitarians and
were transplanted to Indian soil. In the late nineteenth century
many different and often contradictory currents were flowing in
British political thinking.

There were the flamboyant views of Benjamin Disraeli who
chanced to be particularly interested in India and the East. Disraeli
represented a new, more articulate, more extravagant Toryism,
far removed from the sober, business-like conservatism of a Robert
Peel or even the cautious traditionalism of a Lord Liverpool.
Disraeli himself was, it is true, a unique phenomenon, a 'sport'
in British politics, but the fact that he rose to lead one of the two
great historic parties in the 1860s and '70s seems to show that,
briefly, he reflected some important element in English life.
To Disraeli India was indeed the 'brightest jewel' in the British

crown, proof that Britain was a great power. His official biographer, G. E. Buckle, wrote, 'It was the fortune of Great Britain at a time when the British Empire in Asia and the highway to the East were threatened, to have a Prime Minister of Oriental extraction and imagination, whose whole outlook had been coloured at the most impressionable period of his life by his travels in the Levant....'[6] Disraeli's personal influence aside, the shift in British thinking towards 'imperialism' in the late nineteenth century was bound to have profound effects on Britain's attitude to India. In the mid-nineteenth century at least lip service had been paid by almost all politicians and public men to the idea that colonies were a burden but would soon become independent. Now colonies were regarded as important economic assets, major status symbols without which no European power could attain the first rank. When other powers talked enviously of building 'Indias in Africa', Britain could hardly think of voluntarily relinquishing India herself.

Race consciousness, too, had become very much more marked. Competent critics who discussed the question at the time were agreed that colour-consciousness was a very recent growth in European thinking.[7] Possibly they were to some extent mistaken and elements of racial prejudice had a long history but the unanimity of contemporary opinion shows that they themselves were conscious of a striking change. Lord Salisbury, himself a severe critic of many Indian developments, deplored the growth of what he termed the 'damned nigger' school, who had no good word to say for Indians or Indian opinions. The Queen was highly indignant at this new contempt for her Indian subjects. She was angry at disparaging remarks alleged to have been made to and about the Indian princes by British officials at the time of the Prince of Wales's visit to India in 1875.

Disraeli agreed with her. He wrote to Salisbury, 'Nothing is more disgusting, than the habit of our officers speaking always of the inhabitants of India—many of them descended from the great races—as "niggers". It is ignorant and brutal—and surely most mischievous.'[8] But Lord Mayo, a reforming if conservative vice-

roy, could write to Sir Henry Durand, the Lieutenant-Governor
of the Punjab, 'Teach your subordinates that we are all British
gentlemen engaged in the magnificent work of governing an
inferior race.'[9] The very term 'inferior race' was a comparative
novelty, a reflection of a new mode of thinking that owed its
origins to popular (and inaccurate) understanding of Darwinian
theories of evolution and the survival of the fittest. Races could
be classified into superior and inferior according to how far they
had progressed in the evolutionary scheme. Europeans were
naturally at the top; other races still struggling along the way. It
implied a relationship between the 'advanced' and the 'backward'
very different even from that implicit in Charles Grant's compas-
sion for the benighted heathen.

India posed a great dilemma for English liberals in the late
nineteenth century. R. J. Moore sums up the problem acutely:

> Well into the nineteenth century the ideal of all liberals was even-
> tual self-government, and the interim objective was good govern-
> ment. The achievement of the former implied the progressive
> loosening of the imperial connection, whereas that of the latter,
> by the lights of the West, implied the commitment to India of
> British expertise, administrators and capital. In the last quarter
> of the century, the doctrine of the trust and the ideal of political
> liberty were seen to be ultimately incompatible.[10]

This liberal dilemma was to be inherited by the Fabians and other
progressive groups. 'Progress' in India might mean a paternalistic
approach, a continuation of the inconoclasm of the Utilitarians.
Even Karl Marx had seen the need to break the old mould. On
the other hand as equality came more and more to rank with liberty
as the progressive goal, the subordinate position of India came to
be more and more of an embarrassment.

Immediately after the Mutiny, however, the problems facing
the British government turned on the best way of restoring the
Indian situation to 'normal' and ensuring tranquillity. The
Governor-General, Lord Canning, earned the nickname 'Clemency Canning' by his policy of offering amnesty to all Indians who

had not actually been concerned in the death of Europeans.[11] The British took rather literally some of the warnings of the Mutiny. The annexation of Oudh had been a major factor. There should be no more annexations of princely states. Even when the Gaekwar of Baroda got rid of a British 'Resident' whom he disliked by what Salisbury termed the 'simple expedient' of poisoning him, the British deposed the Gaekwar but stopped short of annexing his state. Henceforth the boundaries between British India and the princely states were fixed and did not change again.

The British also pursued for a time a cautious policy of eschewing innovation and relying on the established governing classes. Even the *talukdars* of Oudh were restored to their former position.[12] This policy was congenial to both Lord Derby's Conservative government of 1858-9 and the Whig government of Lord Palmerston which succeeded it. It was in some ways a reversion to Cornwallis's policy. But it made the position of the newly westernised classes, who had generally supported the British during the Mutiny, increasingly difficult. Where were they to find a role in their own society? Salisbury saw the dangers clearly when he referred to them as 'a deadly legacy from Metcalf [*sic*] and Macaulay'.[13]

On the other hand British policy towards India immediately after 1858 was by no means rigidly conservative or negative. The British had been appalled by the suddenness of the Mutiny and their own lack of foreknowledge. They recognised that their communications with the Indian population had broken down. New bridges must be built. The reforms of 1853, the work of Dalhousie and the president of the Board of Control, Charles Wood, had brought the governor-general's legislative council into existence.[14] This was a conservative enough body, entirely official in composition, indeed simply an extension of the governor-general's executive council, summoned from time to time to help in formulating laws and regulations. But throughout the British empire legislative councils, however modest in origins, had provided the germ from which parliaments grew. Dalhousie himself had attracted criticism in the 1850s by treating the council from the beginning as a quasi-parliamentary body with parliamentary-type standing orders, public debates and its own 'Hansard'. No one had been very pleased with how this first legislative council worked but after 1858 men like Sir Bartle Frere saw it playing a new role as a sounding-board for the newly awakened Indian public opinion. The Indian Councils Act of 1861 empowered the governor-general to summon between six and twelve additional members, at least half of them 'non-officials', to join his legislative council. It was intended, although not specifically laid down, that some of the 'non-officials' were to be Indians. Sir Charles Wood, now Secretary of State for India, wrote to Canning, 'the introduction of intelligent Native gentlemen into the Council will bring to its deliberations a knowledge of the wishes and feelings of the Native population, which cannot fail to improve the laws passed by the Council by adapting them to the wants of the great mass of the population of India'.[15] The governor-general retained his executive council of five officials, who increasingly came to assume departmental responsibilities for law, finance, military matters, education and public works and so to fulfil something like the role of ministers in a western-style government —but there the resemblance ended. They were all Europeans and did not depend for their position in any way on the legislative council. On the other hand, legislative councils similar to the governor-general's were to be set up in Madras and Bombay and subsequently in other provinces. The 1861 Act did therefore represent a real, if very modest, step on the way to representative government in India.

Another pressing problem after 1858 was the army.[16] The Bengal army had to be completely rebuilt. Here again there was emphasis both on precaution and on closer association. The anomaly of company troops disappeared. Henceforth all British troops in India belonged to the regular army. European troops in Bengal were to be more nearly equal in numbers to Indian troops and British and Indian battalions were to be mixed together in the same regiment. Only European officers could hold the

Queen's commission. Indian officers held their commissions from the viceroy. This later caused some dissatisfaction among well-born Indians and Lord Salisbury sided, unsuccessfully, with those who believed that any subject of the Queen should be entitled to hold her commission. For a time Moslems and Hindus and men of different castes were purposely mixed in each battalion so that no unit could assume a sectarian character. When the British government wanted Moslem troops for the Egyptian intervention in 1882 they were told that they could not be made available because the Indian army was deliberately not organised on that principle.[17] This policy was, however, reversed in the late 1880s and from 1892 recruitment was again on a religious and caste basis.

The post-Mutiny period also saw the emergence of the idea that there were 'martial' and 'non-martial' races in India. Gurkhas, Sikhs and Punjabis were regarded as 'martial races' *par excellence*. It was naturally suspected that this supposed distinction between good and bad soldiers was merely a convenient device for distinguishing between those who were loyal to the British connection and those who, like the men of Oudh, were no longer trusted. No doubt this entered into it. But the post-Mutiny reforms—some of which were also applied to the still separate Madras and Bombay armies—rebuilt an efficient professional army with a strong *esprit de corps*, which did not again concern itself with politics.

The main pressure against the British establishment came from a quite different source, the new westernised classes. For them the great objective was entry into the ICS. The Queen's Proclamation of November 1858 had reiterated the promises of the Charter Act of 1833, disclaiming discrimination on grounds of race. 'And it is our further will that, so far as may be, our subjects, of whatever race or creed, be freely and impartially admitted to offices in our service, the duties of which they may be qualified, by their education, ability, and integrity, duly to discharge.' They were ringing words but the odds were heavily stacked against the Indian candidate. Since entry became competitive in 1853 the examination had been held in London. The upper age limit was twenty-one and most marks were awarded for classics and mathematics, the subjects in which English public school boys might be expected to acquit themselves best. A few Indians did enter the service, one in 1864, three in 1869. The 1869 entry included both Romesh Chandra Dutt and Surendranath Banerjea. Merely taking the examination involved serious conflict with their own community, not because it seemed to be 'selling out' to the enemy but because it involved the ritual pollution of crossing the sea. Banerjea later wrote that although his own family supported him in what he was doing, 'the whole attitude of Hindu society, of the rank and file, was one of unqualified disapproval. My family was practically outcasted . . . those who used to eat and drink with us on ceremonial occasions stopped all intercourse and refused to invite us.'[18]

Banerjea's experience of the ICS was almost uniformly unhappy. After he had passed the examination it was discovered that the age he had given did not tally with the age he had given earlier for a school examination. He was disqualified as over-age. Banerjea appealed to the High Court on the grounds that the discrepancy was due to a misunderstanding of the Indian method of calculating age. He won and was reinstated. But a few months after taking up his first appointment in India he was accused of submitting a deliberately false report concerning a difficult case. The circumstances were obscure. Banerjea was probably guilty of no more than an error of judgement of the kind which many young Englishmen must have fallen into in the early days of their service. But the suspicion which immediately rose to the minds of his superiors was that, being an Indian, he had been subjected to personal and communal pressures which he could not resist. This was already becoming an important argument against the further employment of Indians—they could not be expected to attain the degree of impartiality an Englishman could. Banerjea was dismissed from the service. He subsequently became active in Congress politics. It is interesting, however, that he always remained a member of the moderate party, eventually becoming very much the elder statesman of the party and accepting a knighthood in 1921. However unfortunate their own experiences, men of Banerjea's generation saw the future progress of their country as being closely linked with Britain.

The late 1870s saw some worsening in the position of the westernised classes. Of the post-Mutiny viceroys, Lord Lawrence (1864–9) and Lord Northbrook (1872–6) deliberately pursued quiet, unspectacular policies. Lawrence showed little of the flair he had been famous for earlier in the Punjab. Northbrook quarrelled with London. But both Lawrence and Northbrook succeeded in their aim of keeping the political temperature down in India. Lord Mayo (1869–72) might, in the eyes of some critics,[19] have developed into a great reforming viceroy but he was struck down by an assassin in the Andaman Islands in February 1872. His assassination came only a few months after that of the chief justice of the Calcutta High Court and at first it was suspected that it was the work of an extreme Moslem organisation, the Wahabis. Further investigation, however, seemed to show that it was non-political.

Lord Lytton, who arrived in India in April 1876, was an altogether more flamboyant character than his predecessors. Much of his energy was, of course, directed towards his frontier policy in Afghanistan, but he also held strong and sometimes idiosyncratic views on domestic questions. He was a complex man, capable of generous enthusiasms. He maintained a warm friendship with his fellow-poet, Wilfrid Scawen Blunt, who stayed with him in 1878 and became one of the most vocal critics of British rule in India—without apparently damaging his friendship with the viceroy.[20] It was typical of Lytton that he intervened personally in the notorious Fuller case to reprimand the judicial authorities who had let an English barrister named Fuller off with a modest fine for the manslaughter of an Indian.[21]

But another side of Lytton's character was revealed in his enthusiasm for the proclamation of the Queen as Empress of India. The origins of this decision are obscure. It had been talked of since the 1850s. The Queen herself was enthusiastic for it but its timing in 1877 was probably a deliberate political reply to Russian challenges. It was extremely unpopular in England where

'Emperor' was regarded as an adventurer's title associated with the Bonapartes. The debate in the Commons, which provided a rallying point for radical protest, disgusted Lytton. He wrote to Salisbury, 'Parliamentary Govt. is becoming annually more and more incompatible with the elementary conditions of Imperial Govt.'[22] But the new title gave Lytton an excuse to call a great durbar and emphasise the honoured position of the Indian princes in the British empire.

Lytton's flair for the dramatic may have had some success with the aristocracy but it did not extend to a similar astuteness in dealing with the westernised professional classes. In this Lytton shared Salisbury's views. Salisbury was disturbed by the growing intransigence of the Anglo-Indian community in India who, he complained, thought that they could, like the West Indian planters, defy both the home government and the 'native millions'. 'In the distant future, the Empire if it is to endure must stand not on one leg but on two . . . If England is to remain supreme she must be able to appeal to the coloured against the white as well as the white against the coloured. It is therefore politic as well as humane to conciliate the natives.' The 'literary classes,' he admitted, were 'politically alive' but Britain could look for no support there. The masses were still inert so they must bid for aristocratic support.[23]

In 1878 Lytton introduced the Vernacular Press Act, which he himself did not hesitate to call a 'gagging Bill', which allowed in some instances for the confiscation of the plant of vernacular newspapers if they offended against the new regulations. Although the government had been irritated for some years by what it regarded as exaggerated and irresponsible criticism in some newspapers, there seemed no immediate crisis to justify such draconian legislation. The educated classes were particularly offended.

They were also angered by a measure in 1877 which lowered the maximum age for taking the ICS examination to nineteen. This was a particularly sensitive point with Indian opinion which was always pressing for the raising of the age to allow their candidates to compete on more equal terms. It was in fact part of Lytton's, and Salisbury's, plan to revert in India to the system, comparatively recently abandoned in England, of recruitment by nomination from the traditional governing classes. 'I can imagine no more terrible picture for India than that of being governed by competition-baboos,' Salisbury wrote in April 1877.[24] There was already an Act of 1870 on the statute book which allowed for the appointment of Indians recruited in India. In 1879 it was laid down that a proportion, not exceeding one-sixth, of the covenanted service, was to be recruited from 'natives selected in India', to be drawn from 'young men of good family and social position possessed of fair abilities and education'. In fact the Statutory Service, as it came to be called, was always regarded as an inferior one by the Indians and failed to attract good men.

Lytton's appointment was so obviously a political one that he resigned immediately on the Conservative defeat in 1880. His successor was Lord Ripon. Ripon was the son of Frederick Robinson, Viscount Goderich, who had been prime minister in 1827. Indeed Ripon was actually born in No 10 Downing Street. Despite this Conservative background Ripon had been much interested in the Christian Socialist movement as a young man. He had also risked his career by becoming a convert to Roman Catholicism. Despite these rather unorthodox antecedents his biographer, Leonard Wolf, is probably right in seeing a strong streak of Whiggism in Ripon's views throughout his life.[25] Ripon had been associated with John Bright, a much-respected personal friend, in the India Reform Society, and he maintained a close friendship with the former viceroy, Lord Northbrook. The 1880 election had been preceded by Gladstone's Midlothian campaign in which he had flayed British policy in India and Afghanistan. Gladstone was now Prime Minister.

It seemed likely that Ripon's viceroyalty would be the antithesis of Lytton's. Ripon did in fact become the hero of westernised Indians. It was said that if a speaker lost the thread of his argument at a meeting he had only to mention Lord Ripon's name and the prolonged applause would give him ample time to recover himself.[26] Ripon repealed Lytton's hated Vernacular Press Act and in 1882, with the help of Evelyn Baring, the future British agent-general in Egypt, he introduced the famous Local Boards Resolution. It was envisaged that these local boards would supplement the municipal and local governments which already existed and that they would have a majority of elected non-official members. Ripon thought that such bodies would be administratively helpful and take some of the burden from overworked district officers but his main object was rather different. 'It is chiefly desirable,' he said, 'as an instrument of political and popular education.'[27] In the face of misgivings in both India and London he was, however, unable to carry out his scheme in its entirety. Indian hopes were raised, only to be dashed again, and the full implementation of the Resolution remained an Indian demand for many years.

In the long run, however, the most controversial and, probably, the most influential measure of Ripon's viceroyalty was what came to be known as the Ilbert Bill. Ilbert was the legal member of Ripon's council. In 1883 he introduced what he envisaged as a 'tidying up' measure, which would give Indian magistrates jurisdiction over Europeans in criminal cases outside the Presidency towns. They already had jurisdiction in criminal cases in the Presidency towns and in civil cases everywhere. Despite some misgivings,[28] Ripon's government hoped that the measure would be uncontroversial. The number of Indians eligible for such jurisdiction was as yet very small but it was anticipated that it would grow, especially if Lytton's Statutory Civil Service worked as it was originally intended. The absurd situation might soon arise when an Indian magistrate would lose some of his powers if he were promoted from a Presidency town to a post in the country and might have to hand over certain cases to a European subordinate.[29] Ripon reckoned without the reactions of the non-official Europeans, mainly planters, who lived in the *mofussil* (country districts), and their alliance with the Calcutta bar.

There was a tremendous explosion of feeling. The Calcutta bar had its own grievances in what Ripon himself called the 'ill-judged' reduction of their salaries to the levels obtaining in Bombay and

Madras, and the appointment of an Indian, Romesh Chandra
Mitta, to act as Chief Justice of Bengal.[30] But the protest was
widespread and well organised. It began with a great meeting of
over 3,000 people in Calcutta Town Hall. Ripon told Northbrook
privately that the organisers had sent an 'expurgated' version to the
press at home because they were afraid of the effect which would
be produced in England by the 'violent contempt & hatred which
the speeches expressed for the natives'. He added, 'It fills me with
shame for my fellow-countrymen, of whom I had expected better
things, and it makes me almost despair of the future of India.'
He suspected that what was really at the bottom of it was 'not an
opposition to this particular measure but to the admission of
Natives to the Covenanted Civil Service at all'.[31] Ripon's suspicions
on this seem confirmed by a number of letters which flooded in
to the government, such as that from John Beames, the Commissioner of the Burdwan Division of Bengal, warning that the
outcry was 'the explosion at last of long pent-up discontents' and
expressing his own view that the employment of Indians in high
positions was premature. He had never met a native fit to be more
than a deputy collector. 'As second in command, a native is
admirable, but as first he is utterly deficient.'[32]

The more extreme speakers at the Calcutta meeting played on
the fact that the European alone in the *mofussil* would be at the
mercy of false charges, supported by bribery and corruption.
'What the stiletto is to the Italian, a false charge is to the Bengali.'
English women could be dragged before a native magistrate.
Even in Turkey and China Europeans had the right to be tried
by European courts.[33] Even sober-minded British officials
expressed doubts whether a European in the country would get
justice from a judge who might be 'only too glad to pay out the
grudges which his class bear against the English'. Others in-
stanced cases where an Indian judge had found it difficult to
execute justice against his co-religionists.[34] Planters and railway
employees were foremost in signing petitions. Some dropped
dark hints that capital would no longer be forthcoming if this
condition of insecurity was created.[35] In the end Ripon, who still

professed to consider the whole matter one of secondary importance on which it was not worth risking other achievements,
compromised. Europeans in country districts should be tried
by juries, at least half of whom should be Europeans. Since he
hoped to see the jury system brought into more general use in
India in any case, he contended that this was entirely acceptable.

Educated Indian opinion had watched the contest with the
closest interest. Petitions indeed had come in from some Indian
sources which compared very favourably both in common sense
and knowledge of the law with those emanating from Anglo-
Indian interests. One from the Howrah Peoples' Association
made the practical point that in many districts there was no
European magistrate, and Indians had therefore put up with
offences from Europeans rather than expend the time and money
necessary to reach the nearest European judge. It made short
work of the argument that capital would be withdrawn. It was
contrary to human nature to withdraw capital when profits
could be made. Similar threats had been made in 1836 (at the
time of Macaulay's Black Act) and in 1858 (in protest against
Canning's leniency) and not carried out. But more fundamentally
the petition asked 'in whom the government of 200 millions of
Indian subjects is really vested? Is it vested . . . in the Crown and
its responsible servants, or in the handful of Europeans making
India their temporary home and who quit the country as soon
as they have secured a competence . . . ?' The Queen's Proclamation of 1858 had promised legal and political equality to British
subjects. All states tend to 'the gradual political equalisation of
the different orders of people comprising them . . . At first there is
inequality, then comes the period of aspiration and transition,
then equalisation . . . one can no more prevent such final equalisation than stop the waters of the mighty river swollen with tropical
rains from finding their way to the ocean.'[36] Indians had heard
the expression of overtly racialist views of an intensity never
experienced before. They had seen the fear of the European
planters and their frank admission that the Indians disliked them
and wished to be rid of them. They had also had a chance to study

some very effective methods of political agitation. They knew
that Ripon's government in India and Gladstone's government
in London had wanted the Bill but had been unable to maintain
their position in the face of determined and, at times, unscrupulous agitation. The lesson was not lost.

Less than two years after the Ilbert Bill failed the Indian
National Congress met for the first time. The Congress as it
assembled in Bombay in December 1885 was the work of Alan
Octavian Hume, a retired official and the son of the British radical
Joseph Hume, and it had the blessing of Lord Dufferin who had
succeeded Ripon as viceroy in 1884. Dufferin had previously
been British ambassador in Turkey and had just been engaged in
trying to secure a constitutional settlement in Egypt. His views,
like those of Ripon, could reasonably be described as those of an
enlightened Whig but, unlike Ripon, he did not much care for
the 'Bengalee baboo' whom he compared to the unpredictable
Celt.[37] According to W. C. Bonnerjee, the Congress's first
president, it was Dufferin who persuaded Hume to amend his
original plan for a society which should only discuss social
questions to an annual meeting of an assembly which should
consciously represent Indian opinion to the government, which
might otherwise be unaware of it.[38] Membership of the Congress
was self-elective by the simple payment of a subscription and the
original members were recruited by a canvas of the graduates of
Calcutta university.

But although Hume certainly sponsored the assembly that met
in Bombay in 1885, the Congress did evolve from a long line of
Indian developments as later Indian nationalists contended. In
1876 Surendranath Banerjea who, after his dismissal from the
ICS, had become a lecturer at the University of Calcutta, founded
the Indian Association of Calcutta which was to be 'the centre of
an All-India movement', based on 'the conception of a united
India, derived from the inspiration of Mazzini'. The association
began to find its strength in the agitation against the lowering
of the age for the ICS examination in 1877 and in its support of
the Ilbert Bill. In connection with the first, Banerjea himself

undertook a remarkably successful tour of Upper India, speaking at Agra, Delhi, Lahore, Allahabad and Benares and many other places in the Punjab and the United Provinces. A shrewd official, Sir Henry Cotton, saw the significance of this when he wrote, 'the tour of a Bengalee lecturer lecturing in English in Upper India, assumed the character of a triumphal progress' and remarked that Lord Lawrence would have found the idea of Bengali influence in the Punjab incredible.[39] The national dimension, missing in 1857, was beginning to emerge. An Indian National Conference, attended by delegates from all over India, met for the first time in Calcutta in 1883. Its second session, also in Calcutta, coincided with the meeting of the first session of the Congress in Bombay in 1885. Banerjea and the other leaders of the Conference appreciated the greater political possibilities of the Congress and the following year the Conference was allowed to lapse and its members attended the Congress.

The first meeting of the Congress consisted of seventy highly respectable men, mostly lawyers, teachers and journalists. It was drawn therefore from a very narrow class basis and, potentially disturbing, only two delegates were Moslems. Nevertheless, the early omens seemed good. The debates and the resulting resolutions were well informed and moderate, and for several years, the British authorities continued to look very benignly on the Congress. The Congress expressed strong, sometimes effusive, loyalty to the Crown but a clear pattern began to emerge from its annual resolutions. First, Congressmen wanted more say in their own government, both through the further development of representative institutions and by the greater employment of Indians in the administration. The very first Congress resolved, 'That this Congress considers the reform and expansion of the Supreme and existing Local Legislative Councils, by the admission of a considerable proportion of elected members . . . essential.' They wanted these councils to be allowed to consider the budget, and to be allowed to question the executive on all administrative matters—they were plainly familiar with both the history and the procedures of Parliament in formulating these demands. Further they asked that a standing committee of the House of Commons should be constituted to receive complaints from majorities on the legislative councils if they were overruled by the executive. The first Congress also resolved that competitive examinations for the ICS ought to be held simultaneously in Britain and in India and that the maximum age should be raised to at least twenty-three. Two years later they added the plea that the highest military appointments should be open to Indians.[40]

The second theme that ran through Congress resolutions was the poverty of India. This was coupled with complaints about excessive military expenditure and extravagant civil administration. As the Indian nationalist case began to develop this was bolstered by charges of inequitable taxation, ruined industries and the 'drain' of national wealth.

Throughout this period the Indians never lost sight of the fact that the most direct way to influence British government opinion was by political action in London. Dadabhai Naoroji had pioneered this, as so much else. He came to Britain in 1855 as the representative of the Bombay firm of Camas. He lived for a time in Lancashire and formed connections with Liverpool and Manchester business interests. But he also, with W. C. Bonnerjee, formed the London Indian Society with the object of bringing Indians and Englishmen together at social gatherings. They were to exchange views on Indian subjects, but religion was not to be discussed and the society was not to pledge its support to any political party. Naoroji campaigned on a number of matters including the recruitment of Indians to the ICS, but he was moved to take his next step to 'educate' the British public by the increasing prevalence of racialist views, exemplified by John Crawfurd's presidential address to the Ethnological Society of London in February 1866, in which he set out to prove scientifically the inherent inferiority of Asiatics to Europeans. Later that year Naoroji helped to found the East India Association with the object of informing the British public about India. It had a highly distinguished membership and by the 1870s was able to exercise some parliamentary influence, mainly through Henry Fawcett, who earned the nickname of the 'member for India', and John Bright, who had begun to resume his earlier interest in Indian topics.[41]

In the 1870s too India found entirely new champions in the Irish nationalists and especially in F. H. O'Donnell, the member for Dungarvan. To some extent the Irish were simply interested in any cause which might obstruct and embarass the British government, but there was an ideological element too. O'Donnell himself told the House in March 1884, 'Parliamentary agitation would not be very effective until the Irish people, crushed down under their present tyranny, effected a coalition with the oppressed natives of India and other British dependencies, and all regarded England as the common enemy.'[42] Irish allies might in some ways be a liability to Indian reformers, anxious to impress moderate opinion in the House, but they pointed the way to useful lessons in political organisation and agitation. Banerjea said in 1876, 'Let us have political associations on the model of the Catholic Association of Daniel O'Connell.' By 1886 Dufferin was complaining to Lord Kimberley, the Secretary of State for India, that all the arts of Irish agitation had come to India.[43]

With the surge of political activity in India in the mid-1880s, provoked partly by the hopes roused by Ripon's liberalism but more by the controversy over the Ilbert Bill, Indians began to take a more direct interest in British elections. The Ilbert Bill itself divided British opinion. Ripon was irritated to find that *The Times* came out against the Bill. Northbrook promised to 'scold' Chenery, the editor, for him and to get the Liberal, Hobhouse, to write something on the other side. But Northbrook's considered view was that the articles in *The Times* 'represent only the superficial view of London Society'. If the question were well argued 'the mass of the people of England will side with you against the clamour of Calcutta Anglo-Indian society backed by London society'. He was 'surprised at the sympathy there is for them [Anglo-Indian society] among the upper ten here'. He contrasted this sharply with what he regarded

as working-class opinion on the subject. 'The feelings of the mass
of the working classes in this country are very generous and
disposed to be a little romantic.' He expected them to support
the Ilbert Bill in India just as they had supported the abolition
of slavery in America.[44] As a rare piece of contemporary evidence
about working-class opinion Northbrook's views are interesting.
Indians too must have seen some chance of directly influencing
the British electorate. The Bombay Presidency Association
(which had replaced the older Bombay Association) sent a
delegation to Britain to take a hand in the 1885 election. They
drew up a list of candidates to support (which naturally included
John Bright) and to oppose. They were not particularly successful
in helping their candidates to secure election but for the first time
Indian affairs were put before well-attended election meetings.[45]

A year or two after its foundation the Indian National Congress
began to maintain an informal organisation in London in which
Naoroji, W. C. Bonnerjee and Sir William Wedderburn, another
retired Indian civil servant associated with the early days of the
Congress, were prominent. They gained a doughty if unorthodox
ally in the radical member for Northampton, Charles Bradlaugh.
Charles Dilke, still in the political wilderness after the divorce
case, also lent them some support. Banerjea came to England to
help lobby MPs in 1890. Naoroji, however, had come to the
logical step of standing for Parliament himself. An Indian in
England automatically had all the civil rights of franchise he did
not possess in his own country. After an unsuccessful contest in
Holborn in 1887, he stood for Central Finsbury in 1892. Lord
Salisbury in an extraordinary political *gaffe*—which was not even
altogether fairly representative of his own views—helped Naoroji
to victory by his speech at Edinburgh in November 1887 when
he laughed to scorn the idea of a British constituency electing
a 'black man'. Naoroji was a fair-skinned Parsi and Salisbury's
opponents did not lose the opportunity to retort that Salisbury
was probably the 'blacker' of the two. More seriously, leading
English politicians headed by Gladstone himself demanded an
apology for such a remark, not from a political nonentity, but

from the Prime Minister of England. Even the Queen was reported to have expressed displeasure. The outcry against Salisbury's ill-considered remark should perhaps be weighed against the view of men like Crawfurd in considering how colour-prejudiced England was in the late nineteenth century.[46]

The moderate position represented in England by Naoroji was represented in India by men like Gopal Krishna Gokhale, who earned the nickname of the Indian Gladstone. Gokhale was a Brahman from Bombay, a teacher by profession. He was prepared to work for liberal reforms by gradual methods. A further instalment of reform had come with the Indian Councils Act of 1892 which slightly enlarged the membership and powers of the governor-general's and provincial councils. Gokhale became a member of the Bombay council and subsequently of the governor-general's. Gokhale did not pull his punches. He gave evidence before Lord Welby's Royal Commission on Indian expenditure in 1897, severely critical of the 'drain' on Indian revenues caused by British military policy. But his argument was couched in strictly liberal terms. In 1905 he founded the Servants of India Society to train what he termed 'national missionaries'. But his ultimate objective was Indian self-government within the British empire. He won the respect of many British politicians and officials and was particularly important in the influence he exerted on the veteran radical, John Morley, who was to be secretary of state for India, 1905–10.

The contrast to Gokhale was provided by Bal Gangadhar Tilak.[47] Like Gokhale, Tilak was a Maratha and a Brahman. Both indeed were born in the Ratnagiri district of the Konkan south of Bombay, members of the Chitpavan community which had once directed the destinies of the Maratha confederation from Poona until its final defeat in 1818. But they chose to fight the British with very different weapons. Tilak had trained as a lawyer but he saw his life's work as leading a great Hindu revival. He was a Sanskrit scholar who looked back to a golden age, not only before the British raj but even before the Moslem invasions. He rejected western education and western political concepts and saw social reform and the battle against poverty, which was so important to the moderate party in Congress, as secondary to the purification of India and freeing her from the taint of foreign rule.[48]

Tilak was not a voice crying in the wilderness. From the beginning there had been two Indian responses to the intellectual assault of the West. First there had been those who, like Ram Mohan Roy, tried to synthesise the best in both traditions. Secondly, there had been those who, like the adherents of the Dharma Sabha, were mainly concerned to reassert their own traditions. A number of organisations were founded in the latter half of the nineteenth century to carry on the traditions of the Dharma Sabha—although some were also pledged to extirpate abuses from Hinduism. Among the most important was the Arya Samaj, founded by Dayanand Saraswati in 1875. 1882 saw the establishment of the Cow Protection Society which also became a focus of Hindu feeling. The Ramakrishna Mission, founded by the disciples of Ramakrishna Paramahansa, a mystic priest who had lived in a temple near Calcutta, was rather different. It did not altogether reject the West and laid stress on social reform and pacificism. Nevertheless it too became a recruiting ground for Hindu nationalists.

The Hindu revival attracted some western sympathisers, of whom the most important was Annie Besant. She settled in India in 1893 and became the mainstay of the Theosophical Society which had been founded in the United States in 1875 by Madame H. P. Blavatsky and Colonel H. S. Olcott. The mystical and rather confused doctrines of the Theosophical Society did not win too much respect from either eastern or western philosophers but Annie Besant's understanding of what was going forward in India was not without importance. She wrote, as early as 1893:

> The Indian work is, first of all, the revival, strengthening, and uplifting of the ancient religions. This has brought with it a new self-respect, a pride in the past, a belief in the future, and, as an inevitable result, a great new wave of patriotic life, the beginning of the rebuilding of a nation.[49]

Despite his emotional attachment to the old, Tilak was forced, like the Dharma Sabha before him, to work through the new. He founded two newspapers, the *Mahratta* in English and the *Kesari* (Lion) in Marathi. He was an active member of the National Congress and of the Bombay legislative council. His approach was, however, the opposite of that of Gokhale. He opposed female education and vaccination as both being entirely contrary to Hindu custom. He fought with passionate intensity against the Age of Consent Bill of 1891 designed to stop child marriages. He wrote justifying political assassination in certain circumstances. In 1896 he mounted a campaign to prevent the enforcement of sanitary measures designed to stop the spread of plague in Bombay because they violated caste traditions. Two British officers were murdered. Tilak was tried for incitement to violence and suffered his first spell of imprisonment.

The test for both moderate and extremist protest came with the viceroyalty of Lord Curzon, 1899–1905. Curzon's viceroyalty had a quality almost of Greek tragedy about it.[50] He was a man of exceptional intellectual brilliance. His interest in India had been roused as a boy at Eton when Sir James Stephen had said in the course of a lecture, 'There is in the Asian Continent an empire more populous, more amazing, and more beneficent than that of Rome. The rulers of that great dominion are drawn from the men of our people.' Curzon said nearly twenty years later in 1896, 'Ever since that day the fascination and *sacredness* of India have grown upon me.' In the last year of his viceroyalty he asserted, 'If I felt that we were not working here for the good of India in obedience to a higher law and nobler aim, then I would see the link that holds England and India together severed without a sigh.'[51] Not only were Curzon's ideals exceptionally lofty, his practical knowledge of India was outstandingly good. He had travelled widely in India and Central Asia in 1887 and 1892— financing his expeditions by journalism, for he was not a wealthy man—observing everything of strategic, commercial, archaeological and human interest. As viceroy he saw very clearly many of the real problems. Like the Indian nationalists, he was distressed by Indian poverty. He was very active in furthering irrigation schemes and railways. He set up an Agricultural Department with research facilities to try to put Indian agriculture on a scientific basis. Furthermore, he was interested in India's cultural past and set up the Archaeological Department to record and preserve antiquities.

But for all its promise, Curzon's viceroyalty was a disaster. He had no belief in the Indian's capacity to govern themselves. He wrote to Balfour in 1901, 'It is often said why not make some prominent Native a member of the Executive Council? The answer is that in the whole continent there is not one Indian fit for the post.'[52] His very desire to do good to India made him impatient of any criticism or interference from what he never ceased to regard as a small self-seeking group of westernised Indians who were only interested in jobs for themselves. He began as a popular viceroy but by 1903 he was complaining, 'No angel from Heaven could satisfy the Native party or escape being the victim of their incessant abuse.' One Indian criticism is extremely revealing. Dinshaw Wacha, who had been president of the Congress in 1902, wrote to Gokhale in 1904, 'The person who said that Lord Curzon was an *Asiatic* viceroy will prove true. He has forgotten English methods of governing India and is daily growing in love with *Asiatic* ways of ruling. What a fall is here.'[53] Gokhale himself compared Curzon with Aurungzabe.[54]

Authoritarianism was no longer popular in India. The two measures by which Curzon particularly offended educated Indian opinion were the Universities Act of 1904 and the partition of Bengal. Neither was meant illiberally. Curzon thought that the proliferation of colleges, aided by loosely controlled government grants, was no real asset to Indian education. He intended to rationalise the system and concentrate more resources on the University of Calcutta which he thought the only Indian institution likely to develop into a world-class university. Educated India, however, was deeply involved emotionally with the schools and colleges which it saw as its own special creation. It was generally suspected that Curzon's motive was to bring education more directly under government control.

The partition of Bengal was equally well meant. Over the years Bengal had grown into an enormous, untidy, straggling province. A rationalisation had been suggested several times before. Curzon cut the province into two parts, East and West Bengal. Again it was immediately suspected that Curzon's motives were entirely political and sinister—he wanted to divide the politically active Bengalis, to set the predominantly Hindu west against the predominantly Moslem east.

Curzon resigned the viceroyalty in 1905 as a result of his quarrels with his commander-in-chief, Lord Kitchener. He subsequently regretted the resignation, feeling that it could too easily look like a surrender of his principles on matters more far-reaching than his disagreements with Kitchener. But attitudes were changing by 1906. In that year the Liberals won a landslide victory in a British general election. John Morley, a radical of almost impeccable credentials, became Secretary of State for India. Lord Minto succeeded Curzon as Viceroy. Minto had been appointed by the out-going Conservative government and his own background was Whig, but he represented a return to more conventional traditions. He had no intention of governing India on 'Asiatic' principles.[55]

Morley and Minto were, however, agreed that the first priority must be to put down the disorders which had assumed serious proportions in Bengal. Isolated acts of terrorism had already occurred in the Maratha districts of Bombay in recent years but the movement in Bengal was much more widespread. Political meetings were held. Demonstrating processions came into the streets. Black armbands were worn as a sign of mourning. But politically the most significant development was the *swadeshi* movement. Indians pledged themselves to 'boycott' British goods. The original resolution passed at Calcutta Town Hall on 7 August 1905 spoke of protesting at the indifference of British opinion to Indian affairs. The idea of a boycott demonstrated familiarity with Irish and American precedents. The growing

G

conviction of Indian nationalists that their industry had been ruined for the sake of British manufacturers added to the attractiveness of the boycott plan. But it reflected something even more fundamental. *Swadeshi* literally meant 'of one's own country'. It was meant as a re-affirmation of their loyalty to their own traditions. Gokhale, who disapproved of the boycott as only likely to aggravate ill-feeling, tried to draw a distinction between the two. A boycott, he said, was negative and, if meant literally, impossible, but *swadeshi* in the sense of a positive preference for things Indian could be strengthening.[56]

Gokhale and Tilak parted company entirely on the tactics to be adopted after the partition of Bengal. Tilak wholeheartedly approved of the boycott. It was at this time that the words 'Moderate' and 'Extremist' came into general use to describe the two rival parties in the Congress. The Moderates still hoped for a great deal from the new Liberal government in England and, moreover, they still attached importance to the attitude of the British electorate. Tilak poured scorn on this. 'It is said,' he commented in 1907, 'there is a revival of Liberalism, but how long will it last?' Everyone was agreed that nothing could be expected from the Anglo-Indians and the 'bureaucracy', that is the government of India as well as the ICS.

> So then it comes to this that the whole British electorate must be converted . . . The whole electorate of Great Britain must be converted by lectures. You cannot touch their pocket or their interest, and that man must be a fool indeed who would sacrifice his own interest on hearing a philosophical lecture . . . To convert the whole electorate of England to your opinion and then to get indirect pressure to bear upon the Members of Parliament, they in their turn to return a Cabinet favourable to India and the whole Parliament, the Liberal party and the Cabinet to bring pressure on the bureaucracy to yield—we say that is hopeless.[57]

Tilak, however, was far from commanding a majority. He stood as a candidate for the presidency of the Congress at the 22nd session at Calcutta in 1906 but was defeated by Dadabhai. The 1907 Congress which met at Surat was excited and irritable.

The first disorders occurred when the veteran Moderate, Dr Rash
Behari Ghose, was proposed for president. On 27 December Tilak
and his Maratha supporters deliberately resorted to violence to
close the session which was now unlikely to pass their resolutions.
The *Manchester Guardian* correspondent later recorded:

> . . . as at a given signal, white waves of turbaned men surged up
> the escarpment of the platform. Leaping, climbing, hissing the
> breath of fury, brandishing long sticks, they came, striking at
> any head that looked to them Moderate, and in another moment,
> between brown legs standing upon the green-baize table, I
> caught glimpses of the Indian National Congress dissolving in
> chaos.[58]

Many Conservatives on the British side did indeed rejoice in
1907 at what they saw as the final dissolution of the Congress as a
serious political force.

Apart from the split between the Moderates and the Extremists,
the alienation between Hindus and Moslems had become much
more marked. The Congress had always wished to represent all
India; that, indeed, was the chief claim of a body which was
essentially self-elected to speak for its countrymen. But the
Moslems had always been a minority within the Congress and
over the years their numbers had dwindled. As early as 1887 one
of their most respected leaders, Syed Ahmad Khan, had anticipated all the main Moslem fears if the aspirations of the majority
of Congress were ever fulfilled. Congress was asking for elected
representatives on the viceroy's council. But, if universal suffrage
was achieved, what would happen to the Moslems? They would
be a permanent minority, outnumbered four to one. 'It would,'
he said, 'be like a game of dice, in which one man had four dice
and the other only one.' Who would safeguard the Moslem
interest then? He was equally disturbed by Congress demands
that Indians should have a much greater share in the administration, with recruitment by competitive examination. Because the
Moslems had been reluctant to take up western education, the
Hindus would have a great advantage. 'There would remain no

part of the country in which we should sit at the tables of justice and authority except those of Bengalis.'[59] Moslem anxieties were naturally increased by the emergence of the aggressive Hinduism of Tilak and his school. In December 1906 they set up the all-India Moslem League as a direct reply to the Indian National Congress.

In subsequent years the British were strenuously attacked by Indian nationalists for deliberately driving wedges between the Hindu and Moslem communities in an attempt to delay the ultimate inevitability of Indian independence. The British would have been either extraordinarily stupid or extraordinarily altruistic if they had not seen the advantages of not having all their potential critics and opponents united against them. It was also natural that, as the Moslems began to regard the British as their protectors against an unpredictable Hindu majority, the British began to warm towards them. But it does not seem to be in accordance with the facts to suggest that it was a British policy of 'divide and rule' which created all the problems between the two communities which would otherwise have reached a *modus vivendi* without difficulty. Hindu-Moslem tensions reached far back into history. They represented the whole complicated relationship of conquerors who were no longer dominant to their once-subject but now resurgent neighbours. The problem was not readily solvable along geographical lines since the Moslems were now spread all over India, many being the descendants of converts rather than of the original conquerors.

At the grass-roots level generations of local officials had dealt with manifestations of communal rivalry. They had little material force at their back, at least readily available force. The nearest troops, in any case few in relation to the size of the population, might be 300 miles away. In these circumstances a man had to rely on his wits. Woodruff tells the anecdote of how annually, on the tenth day of the month of Moharran, the images of the tombs of Hasan and Husain, the grandsons of the prophet, had to be carried along the processional route at, say, Pitampura. Unfortunately, they had to pass under a pipal tree sacred to the

Hindus. The Hindus, armed with staves, would not let the tree be cut back. The Moslems would not lower the ceremonial 'tombs'. One year an Indian inspector of police solved the problem by persuading the local unemployed to dig the road lower. Another year a British district officer let two elephants, semi-sacred to the Hindus, graze in the neighbourhood and remove the offending branches.[60] Crises of this sort were not provoked by the authorities. They were woven deep in the fabric of Indian society.

At the centre too there is at least equal evidence that the British thought that stable government demanded a *modus vivendi* between the major communities as that they wished to emphasise communal differences. It is true that Minto once told Morley that the Mohammedan population 'ought to be of real assistance to us in dealing with much of the one-sided agitation we have to face'.[61] But of course the British did not accept the Congress claims to speak for everyone. They still regarded it as one party among others. The test came over the question of communal electorates. In bringing the 1892 Indian Councils Act into operation Lansdowne had wished to leave the way open for some measure of at least indirect election. A system had evolved by which the elected district boards and municipal authorities helped to choose the non-official members of the provincial legislative councils. These in turn had a voice in the selection of four of the non-official members of the viceroy's council and the Calcutta Chamber of Commerce suggested one other. It was clear that in the next instalment of reform the elective element was likely to be greater. The next reform measure was, in fact, the Indian Councils Act of 1909, which became popularly known as the Morley-Minto reforms. The Act took a very long time to finalise.

In October 1906 Minto received a Moslem deputation, led by Mohsin-ul-Mulk, at Simla. They asked for separate Moslem electorates and 'weightage' of Moslem representation beyond what a crude count of heads would allow them. Minto agreed in principle. The latest Indian historian of Minto's viceroyalty has come to the conclusion, 'It is not correct to suggest that the Muslim deputation and their demands were inspired or engineered by the Government.' He acquits Minto of proceeding on a 'divide and rule' principle and thinks, 'He [Minto] sincerely thought that separate representation would eliminate the causes of irritation between various classes and that the Government would benefit by the presence of all important interests on her Councils.'[62]

At one time Morley considered the possibility of electoral colleges in which Hindu and Moslem voters would be mixed but he was compelled to acknowledge the validity of the Moslem objection that Moslems, elected in part by a Hindu vote, might not be representative of their community. It would, he admitted, be like Roman Catholics voting for a Protestant—they would probably choose a 'Romanising Protestant'.[63] The idea of electorates based on religious allegiance was uncongenial to British liberals but there was already a precedent in Cyprus where separate representation was provided for the Greek and Turkish communities. In the end the regulations made under the 1909 Act provided for the election of the non-official members of both the viceroy's and the provincial legislative councils by municipalities, district boards, chambers of commerce and special groups. In practice the 'special groups' were landlords and Moslems. Much though this last point was criticised by Congress, it was to be enshrined in the Lucknow Pact of 1916 which temporarily brought Hindus and Moslems into alliance. However much the British may have thought of the Moslems as a 'counterpoise' to Congress, Moslem fears were genuine and had to be respected.

The 1909 Act provided for non-official majorities on the provincial councils but retained an official majority on the viceroy's own council. Morley and Minto had also been earnestly discussing for some years whether an Indian could be admitted to the holy of holies, the viceroy's executive council. Neither man saw any insuperable objection in principle but both were extremely nervous of Anglo-Indian reaction. In 1909 they overcame their fears sufficiently to appoint Sir Satyendra Sinha as the first Indian on the executive council.

The Morley-Minto reforms had only a limited time to take effect before the outbreak of World War I. They were too cautious to satisfy Indian opinion for long. Some historians have seen them as essentially a holding operation—an attempt to quieten Indian demands without conceding anything of substance.[64] Morley and Minto were emphatic that they were not trying to establish a parliamentary system in India—although their public utterances were themselves distorted by the need to conciliate Conservative opinion in Britain and 'Anglo-India'. But the Indian leaders saw them as an advance to parliamentary government and their interpretation was of lasting importance.[65]

In 1906 Congress had adopted dominion status as its goal. Since the establishment of the series of colonial and imperial conferences which began in 1887, the concept of dominion status had become gradually clearer. By this time it meant virtually complete internal autonomy and some right to be consulted about foreign affairs where the dominion's own interests were involved. Canada, Australia, New Zealand and South Africa had attained this state. But the British empire was still a unitary state in international law. The king was the king of all. The Westminster Parliament alone could speak for the empire as a whole. More specifically, when London declared war the whole empire was at war. To most Indian nationalists in 1906, a status similar to that of Canada, still within the empire, was the maximum that seemed attainable. A few, however, were irreconcilable.

In 1905 the Japanese defeated the Russians. It was the first victory in modern times of an Asian over a European power. It was greeted with excitement in some sections of the nationalist press. One paper went so far as to say, 'We [the people of the East] who are hated as cowards and imbeciles, are proud of this triumph of the East in its terrible struggle with the West.' Another journal asked its readers directly, 'If the rice-eating Jap is capable of throwing into utter rout and disorder the Russian soldier, cannot the rice-eating Indians also if properly trained,

do the same?' It is difficult to assess how widespread such
sentiments were, but leading Indians certainly took note. Nehru
promptly bought a large number of books on Japan. Gokhale urged
the Congress to follow the Japanese example in patriotism and
discipline. Japanese business interests had already begun to
penetrate India and some fraternal solidarity was expressed. In
1906, for example, some Japanese took part in the Shivaji festival,
which had been founded by Tilak in 1896 to commemorate the
birth of the Maratha hero Shivaji. Prominent Indians, including
Rabindranath Tagore, visited Japan.[66] The spectacle of another
Asian power making rapid political and material progress, free
from the tutelage of a European power, inevitably increased
Indian impatience.

In the short run, however, the moderates were willing to co-
operate with the Morley-Minto reforms, hoping for further
instalments. Some terrorism continued in Bengal but it was
fanatical and backward-looking. 'The mother is thirsting after
the blood of the Feringhees who have bled her profusely,'
screamed one pamphlet. 'Satisfy her. Killing the Feringhees we
say is no murder . . . With the close of a long era the Feringhee
empire draws to an end, for behold Kali [the goddess who had
been the patron of Thuggee] rises in the east.'[67] The prolongation
of this terrorism led to some repressive measures. A new Press
Act was passed in 1910. In 1908, following the murder of two
Englishmen, Tilak had been arrested again for incitement and
sentenced to six years' imprisonment.

The general emphasis, however, was on conciliation and
emphasising that India had an honoured place within the empire.
A great durbar was held in 1911 to mark the coronation of George
V. George V and Queen Mary attended in person, the first time
a reigning British monarch had visited India. Indian leaders,
especially the princes, were feted and honoured. The durbar
was held at Delhi and marked the removal of the British seat of
government in India from Calcutta to the ancient capital. The
opportunity was quietly taken to undo Curzon's work and re-
unite most of Bengal in one province. This policy paid dividends.

When war broke out in 1914 India responded with a loyalty to the British Crown that took many British commentators by surprise. Indian forces played an important part in the allied struggle.

Notes to Chapter 6 will be found on pages 246–8.

Chapter 7 THE TWENTIETH CENTURY

THE MAGNITUDE of her effort in World War I brought India on to the international stage in an entirely new way. Her contribution to the allied cause had been much larger than that of many small independent powers. She, like Britain's older colonies of settlement such as Canada, had played the part of a nation state; and yet neither was a nation state. India's problem was, of course, more acute than that of Canada because Canada, as a dominion, had a defined place in the hierarchy of the British empire. India as yet had not. In the series of colonial and imperial conferences before the war India had been represented, admittedly by British officials, at those of 1902 and 1907 but not at that of 1911. Ironically, this was because of the enhanced status of the 1911 conference. Henceforth conferences were to consist of the prime ministers of the self-governing dominions, presided over by the British prime minister.

The war brought entirely new developments. The imperial conference which should have met in 1915 was postponed until 1917 but, in 1917, it was envisaged that the first conference that met after the war would be a great constitutional conference which would re-define the relationships of different parts of the empire one to another. India was invited to the 1917 conference and represented not only by the secretary of state for India and an official, Sir James Merton, but also by the Maharaja of Bikaner, on behalf of the Indian princes, and by Sir Satyendra Sinha on behalf of British India. Henceforth India was represented at all imperial conferences. The year 1917 saw other important developments such as the establishment of the imperial war cabinet. Lloyd George, on forming his coalition government in December 1916, had decided that the ordinary cabinet was far too

large for the transaction of war business and had set up a small
inner cabinet of five as his 'war cabinet'. At the time of the 1917
conference the dominion prime ministers were invited to attend
this to discuss matters of common interest. The Canadian Prime
Minister, Robert Borden, remarked with satisfaction, 'We meet
there on terms of perfect equality' and called it a 'Cabinet of
Governments'.[1] India was represented at the imperial war cabinet
by the secretary of state for India, assisted by three assessors
who again included two Indians, Sir Satyendra Sinha and the
Maharaja of Bikaner. It was one sign among others that India's
status in international affairs was running ahead of her constitutional development at home. The anomaly became even more
marked after the war with the setting up of the League of Nations.
India was an original member of the League and the only one
which was not self-governing. India also played an active role in
other international organisations, notably the influential International Labour Organisation. Indeed she gained a seat on the
Council of the ILO as one of the eight leading industrial nations
of the world.

On 20 August 1917 Edwin Montagu, as Secretary of State for
India, made his famous declaration that dominion status was the
British goal in India. It was an essentially cautious statement.
Montagu said:

> The policy of His Majesty's Government, with which the
> Government of India are in complete accord, is that of the in-
> creasing association of Indians in every branch of the administra-
> tion and the gradual development of self-governing institutions
> with a view to the progressive realisation of responsible govern-
> ment in India as an integral part of the British empire.

'Responsible government' within the British empire was not, of
course, a generalisation, but bore the technical meaning it had
acquired in Canada in the 1840s of a ministry 'responsible' to the
majority in the (elected) legislature. Montagu promised that he
would himself proceed to India to consult a wide body of opinion
about the methods to be adopted but he added this sombre
warning:

The British Government and the Government of India, on whom the responsibility lies for the welfare and advancement of the Indian peoples, must be judges of the time and measure of each advance, and they must be guided by the co-operation received from those upon whom new opportunities of service will thus be conferred and by the extent to which it is found that confidence can be reposed in their sense of responsibility.[2]

This caution was repeated in the report issued in the name of the secretary of state and the viceroy—the Montagu-Chelmsford Report—the following year. The report distinguished three levels of administration, the local, the provincial and the centre (the Government of India). Its authors believed, 'As we go upwards, the importance of the retarding factors increases; and it follows that popular growth must be more rapid and extensive in the lower levels than in the higher.' At the local level matters might safely be left to those most concerned. 'There should be, as far as possible, complete popular control in local bodies and the largest possible independence for them from outside control.'[3] At the provincial level, governments should be given some measure of responsible government immediately and completely responsible government as soon as possible, provided only that they did not encroach on the proper sphere of the central government. The Government of India, on the other hand, must remain responsible to the British Parliament, although the report recommended that the viceroy's legislative council might be enlarged and made both more representative and more powerful.

These principles were carried into general effect in the Government of India Act of 1919. The viceroy was to be assisted by a two-chamber legislature, the Council of State and the Legislative Assembly. The Council of State was to consist of 60 members, not more than 20 of whom were to be official members. The Legislative Assembly should have 140 members, made up of 26 officials, 14 otherwise nominated and 100 elected. The most interesting experiment was, however, at the provincial level. At least 70 per cent of the members of the provincial governors'

councils were to be elected and not more than 20 per cent were
to be official members. Their functions were to be determined
under the system which became popularly known as 'Dyarchy'.
Some subjects, mainly police, justice, famine relief, irrigation
and land-revenue administration, were 'reserved' for the consideration of the provincial governor, responsible to the
Government of India and, ultimately, to London. Other subjects,
notably education, public health, public works, agriculture and
some aspects of industrial development, were 'transferred' to
the governor, acting with ministers appointed from the provincial
legislatures. This attempt to distinguish between 'imperial'
subjects and 'local' subjects had a long history in the British
empire, going back at least to the Durham Report on Canada of
1839. Such distinctions always proved to be artificial and un-
workable in the long run but it was a useful interim device which
featured in many British colonial constitutions in the twentieth
century.

Although to the British the 1919 Act seemed a considerable
step along the road towards creating real parliamentary government in India, to some Indians it appeared derisory. World War I
had drawn a line across history in a way which few other historical
events have done. European supremacy over the rest of the globe
which had lasted for, perhaps, two centuries had ended—although
this was not to be fully apparent for another generation. Indeed
the British empire actually expanded again after World War I
with the acquisition of some of the former German colonies as
mandated territories. But the old confidence was not there.
Much had perished in the mud of Flanders. It was difficult to
resume the old certainty in the superiority of European civilisation
after such a holocaust. In some ways, of course, the war only
intensified and accelerated feelings and tendencies which were
already there, but it did so in an unusually brutal fashion. For
the first time the Indian Civil Service, which had always been
the prestige service with keen competition for places, began to
experience difficulty in attracting a sufficient flow of first-class
recruits.

If belief in the 'civilising mission' was faltering, great problems were becoming apparent at home. The war, and new factors like conscription, had shaken society from top to bottom. However much some people might talk of the return to 'normality' by which they meant pre-war conditions and the pre-war balance of society, it was not a practical possibility. The war was followed in the 1920s and '30s by inflation, unemployment, the slump and the great depression. Previously inarticulate classes in British society were finding leaders to demand a share in the government and entirely new social demands were being formulated.

The new British empire of the late nineteenth century had been forged in a time of economic crisis and social unrest in the 1880s. Vast new possessions had been acquired, mainly in Africa, the bonds with India had been drawn tighter and attempts had been made to draw closer the bonds even with the self-governing colonies of settlement. Then it had seemed that imperial possessions might be the answer to domestic problems. This belief had swept right across the political spectrum. There had been Liberal imperialists and Fabian imperialists, as well as Conservative imperialists. So long as belief in the superiority of western forms of government remained intact and popular belief in progress and the 'backwardness' of non-European peoples was pervasive, even good liberals and socialists could—and did—persuade themselves that, although the acquisition of empire was usually a reprehensible business, the good government of an empire was a noble duty.

The challenge to those beliefs had begun before the war, notably in J. A. Hobson's famous and widely read book *Imperialism: A Study*, published in 1902 under the immediate impact of the Boer War. Hobson contended that imperialism was not a remedy for, but a distraction from, the solution of the real problems at home, which he believed sprang ultimately from the maldistribution of wealth. He also questioned whether the spread of British rule had in fact led to the dissemination of 'the arts of free self-government which we enjoy at home', as its apologists claimed. Hobson's economic arguments were taken up by both

Marxist and non-Marxist critics of imperialism. His political arguments also reached a wide audience on the British left. Hobson had raised the question incidentally whether democracy at home could co-exist with the quasi-despotic rule of an overseas empire. (The same question had occurred in a different form to Salisbury and Lytton in the 1870s.)[4] Was authoritarian rule infectious? For the growing labour movement the subjugation of India was associated with those very classes whom they had most reason to distrust in British society. A number of radical critics began to identify the struggle for equality in Britain with the struggle for self-government in India, although many of them were still conservative enough to hope that the ultimate outcome would be a self-governing India within a British commonwealth of nations—a newly fashionable idea.

Annie Besant played a unique role, identifying herself totally with the Indian nationalist movement. She was imprisoned in Madras in 1917 and became president of the Indian National Congress in 1918. She also played a crucial part in rousing the women of India to assume a political role. Women's Indian Associations were established in Madras and Bombay and an All-India Muslim Ladies' Conference was founded in 1914. In 1925 Sarojini Naidu became the first Indian woman president of the National Congress. From 1926 onwards an All-India Women's Conference met annually to press for those social and educational reforms which particularly affected women. Only a small minority of Indian women became politically conscious— the same, of course, was true of Indian men—but the women's movement was of special importance because a particular stumbling block for English liberals who wished to press for more self-government in India was the depressed status of women in Indian society. Conservatives who resisted change could plausibly argue that, without the restraining hand of British rule, the lot of the weakest members of Indian society, the women[5] and the Untouchables, would perceptibly worsen. In some ways, however, Indian women had an easier task than their sisters in England. Their husbands and brothers did not already have an entrenched political position. The movement for women's suffrage marched side by side with a general demand for the franchise.

Annie Besant was unique but she found supporters among other British socialists. Keir Hardie visited India in 1907 and was appalled by the poverty of the Indian peasants. He found it hard to believe that their condition had ever been worse than it was then. He wrote in the *Labour Leader*:

> The Government of India is a huge bureaucracy in which every form of popular rights is supposed to be a menace to the stability of the Empire. The men in charge of affairs are broad-minded, enlightened, competent, and capable in most of the affairs of life, but concerning India and its Government they have but one idea —to maintain things as they are.

Hardie's visit caused considerable excitement in England. A *Times* leader on 2 October thundered that Hardie was 'Fostering Indian Sedition'. A cartoon in *Punch* showed Britannia expelling Hardie, who was depicted holding a burning torch labelled 'Sedition', from the sub-continent and advising him to come home where they knew better than to take him seriously. Hardie's recommendations were in fact moderate. He wrote, also in the *Labour Leader*:

> It may be that the people of India are not yet fit for the Colonial form of self-government, but between that and the present soul-less bureaucracy there are many degrees of expansion in the direction of modifying bureaucratic power and enlarging the rights and liberties of the people.[6]

In the book he wrote on his return, *India, Impressions and Suggestions*, he put the case for Indian advancement in terms which, to a later generation, look almost racialist. He urged his fellow countrymen:

> Let it not be forgotten that the India people are of the same Aryan stock as ourselves. Take a gathering of Indians. Remove their graceful, picturesque costumes, and clothe them in coats and trousers, wash the sun out of their skins, and then a stranger suddenly set down into the midst of them would have difficulty in saying whether he was in Manchester or Madras.[7]

Ramsay Macdonald was just as cautious as Keir Hardie in his original approach to the Indian problem. He visited India in 1909 and was actually offered the presidency of the Indian National Congress in 1911. In the interval he too had published a book, *The Awakening of India*, in which, although he had avowed that he saw 'the future as belonging to Nationalism', he had also said:

> Britain is the nurse of India. Deserted by her guardian, India would be the prey of disruptive elements within herself as well as the victim of her own too enthusiastic worshippers, to say nothing of what would happen to her from incursions from the outside.

Perhaps, however, the most interesting passage in *The Awakening of India* is that in which he anticipated, in 1910, the form which Indian government was to take by the Act of 1935, prepared while Macdonald himself was Prime Minister. He wrote, 'Responsible government in the Provinces, a federation of the Provinces in an Indian Government—that seems to me to be the way India is to realize herself.'[8]

The sympathy of the British Labour movement was valuable to the Indian nationalists but it was only one symptom of a new world in which many of the old political landmarks had disappeared and had been replaced by new forces and new goals. World War I had become an ideological war. It had not started as one. In 1914 it had been a simple old-fashioned European war for national interests and national survival. But as it had become a 'total' war, involving civilian populations to a much greater extent than the wars of the previous century, it had become necessary to establish the righteousness of one's own cause and the wickedness of the enemy. The propaganda war was in full swing. It was a war for 'freedom', for 'democracy', for 'national self-determination'. Moreover, the allied powers bid for American support by emphasising the purity of their own war aims. The culmination of this process was President Wilson's Fourteen Points. Different men took these declarations with varying degrees of literalness. Some believed in them passionately. To others they were never more than the small change of politics. Few European statesmen thought of them as applying seriously to areas outside Europe, or at most beyond the Ottoman empire. But, like Burke's earlier exposition of the doctrine of 'trusteeship', they were now on public record. Educated Indians could, and did, read them. They saw no reason why they should only apply to Europe. If self-determination was appropriate for the states of the Austrian empire, why not for those of the British empire?

World War I had caused one great revolution, that in Russia in 1917. It attracted interest in India as the Russo-Japanese War had done. Both the February and the October revolutions were greeted with approval in most Indian nationalist circles. Another pattern for overthrowing a despotic government and overcoming poverty had been provided. The Russian example had some influence on the nascent Indian labour movement, particularly perhaps in the great strike in the Bombay cotton mills in 1918–19 and the British were undoubtedly nervous about the infiltration of Russian-inspired communists into India. For a brief time after the revolution Russian leaders were still under the influence of Lenin's arguments that world revolution would be achieved by a combination of proletarian civil war against the bourgeoisie in advanced countries and 'a whole series of democratic and revolutionary movements, including movements for national liberation in the undeveloped backward and oppressed nations', even where they were too undeveloped to have an urban working class to spearhead a true proletarian movement. The Russians countenanced the activities of M. N. Roy, an Indian expatriate who had participated in the revolution, in setting up a training school in Tashkent for an Indian revolutionary army.[9]

British alarm and suspicion was understandable but was to prove exaggerated. The Indian communist movement never commanded mass support. Educated Indians, although interested in the Russian experiment, were by no means uncritical of it. Many were distressed by the bloodshed of the civil war and wished to avoid anything comparable in their own country. Even Roy's own recruits, who were mostly Moslems, were alienated by the antireligious nature of Russian communism. On their side the Russians, especially after Stalin came to power in 1926, abandoned any attempt to actively foster revolution in the colonial territories of other European powers, even when they still paid lip service to the idea. The Indian communist movement had little Russian backing. Even as late as the Yalta Conference of February 1945 to decide the pattern of the post-war world, it was the American President, Roosevelt, not the Russian Prime Minister, Stalin, who espoused the cause of Indian independence.[10]

The most fundamental reason for the failure of Russian communism to take root in the apparently promising soil of India was that the Indians had a powerful indigenous alternative to it in the Congress movement, and the remarkable new generation of leaders who came to the fore after World War I. The old generation was passing away. Gokhale died in 1915, Tilak in 1920. But Mohendas Karamchand Gandhi returned to India in 1915 and Jawaharlal Nehru became converted to the radical cause in 1919.

Gandhi was born in Porbandar on the north-west coast of India in October 1869. His family belonged to the merchant caste but his father and his grandfather had both been prime ministers of the tiny princely state of Porbandar. Porbandar was remote, an ancient Jain stronghold, although the Gandhis, like most of their neighbours, were devout Hindus of the Vaishnava tradition. Gandhi's mother, Putlinai, was a woman of exceptional piety. Her son in his fragmentary autobiography (which he characteristically sub-titled 'My experiments with Truth') told of the severity of her religious observances and how once, when observing the long Chaturmas fast during the rainy season, she vowed that she would not eat except when she saw the sun. Her children would wait and call her if the sun appeared but, if it had disappeared before she came out, she would say cheerfully, 'God did not want me to eat today'.[11] A child of such a home was likely to grow into an unusual man.

All his life Gandhi was troubled by conflicting duties and the reconciliation of the highest claims of the spiritual life with the resolution of practical problems. This was brought home to him as a boy by the question of meat-eating. His religion forbade meat but he had been persuaded by a school fellow that only meat-eating made a man grow big and strong and fit to govern, a sentiment expressed in the jingle:

> Behold the mighty Englishman,
> He rules the Indian small,
> Because being a meat-eater
> He is five cubits tall.

He joined in secret feasts of goat's meat until he had a nightmare of a live goat bleating inside him. Later in life he was equally troubled by the conflict between his duties as an orthodox Hindu husband—he had been married to a wife of his parents' choice at the age of thirteen—and his conviction that celibacy was his highest duty.[12] There was much in Gandhi's background which was totally alien to western ways of thought and consequently much in his character which it was very difficult for westerners to understand. Many made little attempt to do so and would have wholeheartedly agreed with Winston Churchill's dismissal of him as a 'naked fakir'.

But only a man who was so deeply rooted in indigenous Indian traditions could have spoken to the heart of the Indian masses as Gandhi did. Much that looked most strange to English eyes was immediately comprehensible to his fellow countrymen. At one level Gandhi was the conventional Indian holy man. His renunciation of wealth and comfort, his adoption of the simplest dress—eventually a mere loin cloth—and of the simplest form of foods, and his daily toil with a hand spinning-wheel, were the marks of a holy man and a symbol of complete political identification with the peasant masses. His prolonged fasts to secure political objectives—which looked unpleasantly like emotional blackmail to an Englishman reared in a very different tradition—were immediately comprehensible to the Hindu who was used to the tradition that you shamed an opponent into giving you justice by the threat of a fast unto death.[13] On some matters Gandhi departed from current Hindu practice, most notably in his concern for the depressed status of the Untouchables who performed all the most menial functions. Significantly he argued not that the Hindu scriptures were wrong but that they had been misinterpreted. Once again, however, Gandhi showed himself aware that the grand gesture achieved more than any amount of intellectual argument and his willingness, as a caste Hindu, to perform ritually polluting tasks like the cleaning of latrines startled Indian opinion more than words could have done.[14] Gandhi, like Tilak before him, could always touch the irrational (the word is not necessarily pejorative) springs of human conduct in a way in which Gokhale and Nehru, great though their contributions may have been in other ways, could not.

Gandhi, however, was never wholesale in his rejection of the West and of western values as Tilak had been. His decision at the age of nineteen to go to London to study law at the Inner Temple distressed his orthodox relatives because it involved crossing the sea. He arrived in London, an open-minded young man, anxious as far as possible to conform to English fashions and practices. His determination to keep his promise to his mother that he would not eat meat led him to seek out vegetarian restaurants and so brought him into contact with various idealistic reforming groups, usually with socialist leanings. One man who influenced him—scarcely remembered in any other context—was H. S. Salt, a friend of George Bernard Shaw and the author of *A Plea for Vegetarianism*. Gandhi's first, not very successful venture into public life was to support a movement for the spread of vegetarianism.[15]

During his early formative years Gandhi was deeply impressed by certain western classics, above all by Tolstoy's *The Kingdom of God is within You* and *The Gospels in Brief, What to do?* and by John Ruskin's *Unto this Last*. He also made a serious study of Christianity and although, unlike Ram Mohan Roy, he never attempted an intellectual synthesis of eastern and western faiths, the influence of the Sermon on the Mount remained with him. Of equal importance was the fact that, through the Theosophists, he was led to the study of the Hindu scriptures, and the *Bhagavad Gita*, which he translated from Sanskrit into his own mother tongue, Gujerati, became increasingly the foundation of his thinking.[16]

Gandhi formulated his views slowly during the four years he was in England and the twenty years he was in South Africa, with only brief returns to India, between 1888 and 1915. He began with no dislike of the British empire. Indeed, like many westernised Indians of the period, he identified with it.[17] During the Boer War of 1899 to 1901 and the Zulu rising of 1906 he formed an ambulance corps to assist the British cause. He tried to raise a similar corps from Indian students in London in 1914–15. But in South Africa he saw his fellow Indians suffering disabilities unknown in Britain or India and he began to fashion those political weapons with which he later fought the British in India. He used conventional methods, fighting cases in the courts and founding his first newspaper, *Indian Opinion*, in 1904, but he also began the *satyagraha* movement and it was this which was to prove the revolutionary development.[18]

To the outside world it looked like a passive resistance or civil disobedience movement but Gandhi always insisted that it must be much more than that. The name he adopted for it, 'satyagraha', meant 'truth-force' and Gandhi wished it to be a spiritual as well as a political movement. By its very nature it must rule out violence. The vindication of truth must be achieved by self-suffering. Gandhi was still haunted by the phrase from the Sermon on the Mount: 'But I say unto you, that ye resist not evil.'[19] But Gandhi was also a shrewd enough politician to see that a civil disobedience campaign, if on a sufficiently wide scale, could be extremely embarrassing to any government, especially one that was in any way responsive to public opinion. It is highly unlikely that *satyagraha* would have worked against a totalitarian state, although Gandhi commended it in all earnestness to the Jews faced with Hitlerian persecution.[20] But Gandhi knew that in Britain he was not dealing with a monolithic regime. He was dealing with an open and democratic society where, whatever its defects, freedom of speech and argument was still respected even in the dangerous days of the 1930s. Even in his own experience of discrimination in South Africa he had frequently found a Briton to stand by him—an Englishman who would not let him be put out of a first-class carriage for which he had a ticket or the wife of the Durban police chief who kept a hostile crowd at bay for him with her umbrella.[21] Unlike some of his fellow agitators, Gandhi never ceased to believe that, in the last resort, if you could persuade an Englishman that he was wrong he would change his policy. When he finally returned to India in 1915, however, Gandhi had no immediate thought of challenging the British. It was events after World War I which took both Gandhi and the man who was to be his disciple and heir apparent, Jawarharlal Nehru, into the opposition camp.

Nehru was a contrast to Gandhi in almost every way.[22] He came from a very anglicised family. As a Kashmiri Brahman he was an aristocrat to his fingertips. His father, Motilal Nehru, was a wealthy and successful lawyer and the younger Nehru was educated at Harrow and Cambridge—where he read science. In 1900 Nehru, like Gandhi before him, went to read for the bar at the Inner Temple. But where Gandhi was devout, Nehru was an agnostic; where Gandhi was an ascetic, Nehru cared passionately about the material progress of his people; where Gandhi had an instinctive understanding of the poverty-stricken masses of India and attracted from them the veneration due to a recognisable type of holy man, Nehru, whose early life had been sheltered from such harsh realities, came to have an intellectual understanding of the problems of poverty in the course of his political work in the 1920s. Yet Nehru and Gandhi were able to work closely together and Nehru always acknowledged Gandhi as his mentor —even when he disagreed with him most strongly.

The years immediately after World War I were critical in the development of the Indian nationalist movement. The economic dislocation inseparable from the end of a great war and the demobilisation of a substantial number of men was compounded by the failure of the monsoon and the great influenza epidemic which reached particularly severe proportions in India. Epidemics and food shortages in themselves lead to public excitement and do not provide a tranquil background for major political changes. Even the well disposed began to doubt British sincerity when the government insisted on retaining wartime emergency legislation, including the right to detain without trial in certain cases, in the notorious Rowlatt Acts. Although the most-resented clauses were never enforced, the effect was much the same as if they had been.

Late in February 1919 Gandhi launched a civil disobedience campaign against the Acts which were on the point of becoming law. He presided over a meeting in Bombay on 1 March and attended a meeting at Delhi a week later. He called for a *hartal*, a kind of general strike, throughout India on 6 April but, through a misunderstanding, it was observed in many places, including Delhi, on 30 March. Some disorders followed—initially connected with the refusal of some traders to observe the *hartal*. In Delhi a detachment of troops and police was stoned and fired back. Eight civilians were killed. Gandhi wished to visit Delhi and the Punjab to exert his personal influence but he was refused permission by the British authorities.

By early April sporadic disorders had spread throughout the Punjab. European opinion was badly frightened and memories of 1857 had suddenly become extremely vivid. The *hartal* passed off quietly in Amritsar on 30 March but during the next few days several Europeans were murdered. They included three bank officials—in 1857 banks were particular targets for popular feeling. The most notorious event, however, was the attack upon an English woman teacher, a Miss Sherwood. A mob left her for dead after she had been refused admittance at a house to which she had run for shelter—she was subsequently rescued by the father of one of her Hindu pupils. By 11 April Amritsar was in the hands of the mob. Since all communications were cut, as the Lahore Commissioner, A. J. W. Kitchin, who was in Amritsar, remarked later, 'For all we knew, we were the only white men left in India.'[23] It was later that day that a relief force under General Dyer arrived. Dyer's force, however, was small. He had only 400 British and 700 Indian troops to control a city of 160,000 people. Almost his first act was to forbid all public meetings. Despite this, on 13 April, a large crowd assembled on some waste ground known as the Jallianwala Bagh. Although the purpose of the meeting was undoubtedly political, many of the crowd had come in from the countryside for the annual horse fair, knowing nothing of the prohibition on public meetings. Dyer marched his men to the Jallianwala Bagh and, without the customary preliminary warnings, ordered them to open fire. Some 379 people died and a large number of others were wounded. Dyer was apparently unaware that the crowd was unable to disperse quickly because his soldiers were blocking the main exit.

Dyer subsequently justified his action on the ground that it was a 'merciful severity' which prevented an even greater loss of life throughout the Punjab. He was called to account before a committee of inquiry presided over by a Scottish judge, Lord Hunter, and consisting of four Europeans and three Indians. The Hunter committee reported against Dyer and he was retired from the active list. The matter, however, continued to be hotly debated in England and in India. The House of Lords voted in his favour. The *Morning Post* got up a subscription which attracted donations from an extraordinary cross-section of the British public, clergymen, schoolgirls and former army officers. In India the National Congress had ignored the official Hunter committee and set up an inquiry of its own under the chairmanship of Gandhi. This reported that the Jallianwala Bagh massacre was 'a calculated piece of inhumanity towards utterly innocent and unarmed men, including children, and unparalleled for its ferocity in the history of modern British administration'. The Amritsar massacre was a traumatic event for both British and Indian opinion. Many Indian moderates dated their conversion to the anti-British cause from it although perhaps it only crystallised doubts and antagonisms which were already present in their minds.

At Nagpur in December 1920 Congress began to organise itself as a fighting body rather than a debating society. The 1920

session attracted over 14,000 delegates and contemporary observers noted a marked change in its social composition. One
alarmed official wrote that it had been swamped by a 'mass of
semi-educated persons swept up from all parts of India'.[24] It was
not at first certain that Congress would back Gandhi and his
non-co-operation policies but gradually he won the day. The
whole organisation of Congress was overhauled. Major policy
decisions were still to be taken at the annual sessions but there
were to be twenty-one provinces, based on linguistic groupings,
each headed by a provincial congress committee. The provinces
were sub-divided into rural and municipal districts. In theory
power came from below with the local bodies electing delegates
to the provincial committees and the provincial committees in
turn electing the 300 members of the All-India Congress Committee. This was constitutionally the highest executive body but,
in practice, it chose a 'working committee' which was the real
steering committee of the whole movement.

The Nagpur Conference adopted Gandhi's resolution, 'The
object of the Indian National Congress is the attainment of
Swarajya by the people of India by all legitimate and peaceful
means.' *Swaraj* ('self-government') could mean different things
to different men. Some still understood it to mean that the goal
was dominion status, others that there could be no stopping-place
short of total independence outside the empire. Gandhi himself
was content to leave it vague, not only to avoid divisions but
because he wished to be able to make a flexible response to
British actions.[25]

Gandhi's first civil disobedience campaign lasted until 1922.
It involved both Hindus and Moslems. Gandhi had worked
closely with Moslem groups in South Africa, indeed they had
been his chief supporters, and he was determined to carry on this
fruitful co-operation in India. The auguries were favourable.
Hindus and Moslems had reached a compromise in the so-called
Lucknow Pact in 1916. British fears that the Indian Moslems
would declare against them when Turkey entered World War I
on Germany's side in 1914 had not been realised but Moslem

feeling was aroused by the dismemberment of the Ottoman empire after the war. The Khalifat movement began a vigorous protest campaign and Gandhi gave it his public support.[26]

In many ways Gandhi's first Indian campaign was a remarkable success but the line between violent and non-violent protest is always a thin one. Disorders in Bombay gave the authorities an excuse to arrest large numbers of leading Congressmen. The worst outbreak of violence, which degenerated into communal strife between Moslems and Hindus, took place among the Moplahs of the Malabar coast and caused in the region of a thousand deaths. But the atrocity which received most publicity was the killing of twenty-two Indian policemen at Chauri Chaura in the United Provinces. This so shocked Gandhi himself that he called off the whole campaign. His action was endorsed by the Congress working committee in February 1922 despite the retrospective conviction of some nationalists that Gandhi's action had been a political blunder because the campaign was nearing success.[27]

Gandhi himself was arrested and sentenced to six years' imprisonment. He was allowed to make a long political statement in court and the judge, C. N. Broomfield, made in turn what must be one of the most remarkable statements ever made by a judge to the prisoner in the dock.[28] He acknowledged that Gandhi was in a different category from any man he had ever tried or was likely to try again. He did not question that Gandhi was regarded by his own people, not only as a great patriot and leader but also as a saint.[29] But he, Broomfield, had to deal with him only as a law-breaker and he thanked Gandhi for making his task easier by pleading guilty. In sentencing him he dropped a broad hint that the government should release him as soon as the situation became more normal and Gandhi was in fact released in 1924. Nehru had been drawn into the campaign and he too had been arrested and sent to jail in 1921. Nehru was to spend nine and Gandhi six of the next twenty-five years in jail. Both men made the best of their enforced leisure, Gandhi by meditation, Nehru by studying and writing.

Nehru visited Europe in 1926–7. The immediate purpose of his visit was to seek treatment in Switzerland for his wife who had developed tuberculosis. But the visit was important in the formation of Nehru's thought. He attended an anti-imperialist conference in Brussels in 1927 where he met nationalist leaders from other parts of Asia and Africa. The veteran British Labour leader, George Lansbury, was elected president and a permanent body, the League against Imperialism, set up. A few months later Nehru visited Moscow for the first time. Although he had had some slight contact with Fabian circles during his undergraduate days in Cambridge, it was during the 1920s that he was really formulating his political ideas. He was impressed both by the communists he met in Brussels and by his first experience of Soviet society. Two permanent impressions remained upon his mind from Brussels and Moscow. First, he saw a vision of an Afro-Asian group influencing world affairs and, secondly, he became convinced that Russia had no ambitions in India and consequently British defence policy in Asia was based upon a mistake. Both these ideas were to bear fruit when he was prime minister of an independent India. His feelings about communism were more divided. He acknowledged the remarkable improvements which it seemed to be achieving in Russia and he was prepared to accept some of its economic teachings but, from an early date, he was conscious of a conflict between Marxism and the nationalist ideas which he was clear-sighted enough to realise meant much more to him emotionally. For Nehru communism always remained a quarry from which he could take certain concepts; it was never a creed to which he gave allegiance.[30]

The Government of India Act of 1919 was due to be reviewed at the end of ten years and, in 1927, a parliamentary commission was appointed under an eminent lawyer, Sir John Simon, to report how far the aim of the 1919 Preamble to provide for 'the gradual development of self-governing institutions, with a view to the progressive realisation of responsible government in British India as an integral part of the empire' was being carried out. Simon was a leading Liberal who had a wide experience of handling cases involving the dominions before the judicial committee of the Privy Council. He was assisted by four Conservative and two Labour members of parliament, including the future Labour prime minister, Clement Attlee, but the commission included no Indians—an extraordinary example of obtuseness on the part of the British government, even granted the difficulty of finding Indians who could reasonably be regarded as 'impartial'.[31] Simon was met by demonstrations when he arrived in India and many Indians refused to give evidence to the commission. Nevertheless, at the end of two years' labour the commission produced a massive report. The first part was taken up with a detailed survey of Indian affairs. The second part recommended a slow but steady advance. In the provinces the system of dyarchy should be ended and all departments transferred to Indian ministers although the governors were to retain certain emergency powers. The provincial franchise was to be widened to include, among others, a large number of women voters. Communal electorates were to continue 'until agreement can be reached upon a better method' and the depressed classes (the Untouchables) 'will get representation by reservation of seats'. So far as the centre was concerned the Legislative Assembly should become the 'Federal Assembly' with representatives from the provinces and other parts of British India on the basis of population. Proportional representation was to be used to ensure that minority communities received due representation. The Council of State would continue but the commission also envisaged setting up a Council for Greater India which would include representatives of both British India and the princely states. The report was working cautiously towards a federal solution and it envisaged a system which would bring British India and the princely states together.[32]

The report had, however, been overtaken by events even before it was published. In 1926 Viscount Irwin (later Lord Halifax) had replaced the distant and formal Lord Reading as viceroy. Irwin was the grandson of that Charles Wood who had been a reforming president of the Board of Control and, subsequently,

secretary of state in the 1850s and 1860s. He was an Anglo-
Catholic and there was an anecdote long current about him that
he had first landed in India as viceroy on Good Friday and had
refused to transact any business until he had attended to his
religious duties. Although the story was inaccurate in detail—
Irwin had arrived on the Thursday—like many anecdotes, it
caught the flavour of the man. Irwin was a deeply, even occasionally fanatically, religious man—for example, he would not sit
down to dinner with the divorced. Whether his own religious
and scrupulous attitude to life had anything to do with it or not,
Irwin does seem to have been better able to understand Gandhi's
thought processes than were most Englishmen of the time and in
turn to command some liking and respect from the Indian leader.[33]
To be able to establish relations with Gandhi was rapidly becoming essential.

After his release from prison in 1924 Gandhi had retired to his
ashram near Ahmedabad but he was still the most influential
single figure in Indian politics. He continued to publish his
weekly newspaper, *Young India*, and to argue vehemently for
swadeshi and *khadi*, the symbolic campaign to persuade every
Indian to wear home-spun cloth. Even more importantly, he
campaigned for the Untouchables, whom he had renamed
Harijans, children of God. Despite his own disclaimers, he was
already venerated as a saint, almost a god, by the people. After
a public appearance his feet and shins would be covered by
scratches from devotees who had insisted on touching him.
Outside Gandhi's *ashram*, however, many of the omens were
bleak. The *entente* reached between the Hindus and the Moslems
in 1916 had broken down. There had been serious communal
riots, notably in Calcutta. On the political plane, a committee
under the chairmanship of Motilal Nehru had reported against
the continuation of communal electorates. Although other
recommendations of the committee, such as the immediate grant
of dominion status, had the support of some Moslems, a powerful
force emerged in the Moslem League, led by M. A. Jinnah,[34]
which began to insist that a federal system would be necessary

to protect Moslem interests and that, at least in the short run, separate electorates and guaranteed representation were essential.

Meanwhile a major change had taken place in England itself. The Conservatives had held office from 1924 to 1929. From 1924 until 1928 the Secretary of State for India had been Lord Birkenhead (F. E. Smith). Birkenhead's attitude to India had been rigidly Conservative. Like Curzon he saw the nationalist politicians of the Congress as a small and self-seeking group and held a (possibly archaic) view of Britain's responsibility for the whole of India. He was certainly not above some resort to the 'divide and rule' principle,[35] entangled with a genuine belief that Britain had a duty to protect the minorities against self-appointed spokesmen. But, as a result of the 1929 general election, Labour emerged as the strongest single party—although without an overall majority in the Commons—and Ramsay Macdonald formed a minority government with Wedgwood Benn as Secretary of State for India. The Labour party had expressed their sympathy for Indian nationalist aspirations for a generation and Birkenhead's paternalism was distasteful to them. Those Indians who still had confidence in British goodwill—a majority even among the politically active—looked for a gesture.

It came in the viceroy's statement of 31 October 1929, affirming that the 'natural issue' of Indian's constitutional progress was the attainment of dominion status. The statement also promised what became known as a 'round table conference' between the British and representatives of both British India and the princely states. Irwin's declaration was issued after a visit to London and long consultations with the government and it could, therefore, be regarded as an authoritative statement of London policy. Simon was angered by having the ground cut from under the feet of his painstaking inquiry. Birkenhead was highly critical.[36]

On the other side Indian opinion was still far from conciliated. Dominion status was still a future goal, not an immediate possibility, and a substantial party in Congress was now demanding, not dominion status at all, but complete independence. It was at this point that Gandhi returned to active politics with a grand and very effective gesture. There had been tentative movements in some parts of India, notably in the Bardoli area of Gujerat, to withhold the payment of taxes until grievances were redressed. Gandhi decided to unite the whole of Indian opinion in a gesture against the salt tax. It has been suggested that he was moved to do this by a fear that Congress would fall into the hands of extremists who would plunge the country into violence.[37] Salt was an evocative subject, just as it had been in the France of the *ancien régime*. It was a necessity of life and it was government monopoly. Although the tax on it was not excessive, its symbolic value was immense. Gandhi's stage management was impeccable. He set out from his *ashram* with a small following to march 240 miles to the sea to pick up untaxed, and therefore illegal, salt from the shore. Before he reached Dandi on the coast, nearly a month later on 6 April 1930, the whole of India was watching. Even though Gandhi picked up his ritual pinch of salt, Irwin tried very hard to avoid exacerbating feeling by arresting him, but when Gandhi and his followers planned a raid on the government salt depot at Dharsana, Irwin felt he had no alternative. Gandhi was arrested on 4 May. Although Gandhi himself had insisted that his campaign must be completely non-violent, there had been outbreaks of violence in various parts of India, notably in Chittagong where a Hindu revolutionary group had raided the arsenal and killed six people. British opinion was further alarmed by the Meerut conspiracy case where thirty Indians and British sympathisers were convicted of working at various places throughout India, under the orders of the Communist International, 'to deprive the King Emperor of the sovereignty of British India'. Their methods were alleged to have included 'the incitement of antagonism between Capital and Labour', the infiltration of existing trade unions and similar bodies, the creation of workers' and peasants' parties to work for revolution, and the encouragement of strikes and *hartals*. Both Gandhi and Nehru expressed their sympathy with the accused.[38]

Despite these inauspicious omens the first Round Table Conference was opened by the King in person in November 1930. Gandhi was in jail and Congress boycotted the meetings. Unless Gandhi could be brought to the conference table, no progress could be expected. Irwin made possibly his most important contribution as viceroy by negotiating directly with Gandhi. His action caused disgust in some places in England where critics complained that the so-called Gandhi-Irwin pact read more like a treaty between equals than an agreement between the Viceroy of India and a rebel, who had no official status at all. On his side Gandhi promised to call off his civil disobedience campaign and, in particular, to end the intimidation of traders who sold British goods. Congress would be represented at the Round Table Conference and would accept as the basis of the negotiations the goal of an All-India federation with certain safeguards, including those for minorities. In return the British would withdraw legislation designed to deal with the civil disobedience emergency and release from prison all campaigners who had not been convicted of violence. Nehru was shocked by the magnitude of the concessions Gandhi had made and only reluctantly accepted the agreement.[39]

Nevertheless the second session of the Round Table Conference looked more hopeful than anything that had gone before. The leading Indian figures were there. Gandhi represented Congress. M. A. Jinnah represented the Moslems. The political situation in Britain had changed again. In August 1931, a few days before the second session assembled, Ramsay Macdonald had, in the midst of economic crisis, formed his 'national government'. The new secretary of state for India was a Conservative, Sir Samuel Hoare. Hoare, however, was a man of a different stamp from Birkenhead. Although he found Gandhi a very difficult official guest—Gandhi, for example, insisted on staying with his East End friends instead of in the hotel officially provided and, throughout the conference, observed his 'day of silence' on Wednesday when he would communicate with people only in writing, Hoare was convinced that he 'held one of the master

H

keys to the book of the Constitution that we were trying to write'
and did his best to maintain good personal relations.[40]

The difficulties in the way of a settlement were formidable.
One problem was fundamental. Gandhi insisted that Congress
represented the whole of India. This claim was challenged both
by Jinnah for the Moslems and by Dr Ambedkar for the Untouchables. Both insisted that Congress represented only the
caste Hindus. They demanded separate electorates and other
safeguards. In pleading for special safeguards for the Untouchables Ambedkar used the famous metaphor that while all the
minorities might in some sense be 'in the same boat', yet the
others were travelling in Class A, B, or C, while the Untouchables
were 'in the hold' with no rights at all.[41] Unlike Birkenhead, who
had been attracted by the possibilities of 'divide and rule', Hoare
and Ramsay Macdonald seem to have accepted as reluctantly as
John Morley before them, that a communal solution was the only
possible one. The outcome was the 'Communal Award' by which
seats in the provincial assemblies were allocated in fixed proportions to different communities. The intended arrangements
between the Untouchables and the caste Hindus were, however,
modified by the Poona Pact between Gandhi and Ambedkar
when the Untouchables abandoned their claims to completely
separate electorates in the face of a threat by Gandhi to 'fast unto
death'.

At the end of the second session in November 1931 Gandhi
returned to India by way of Italy where he was unfortunately
reported to have said that he was going back to India to restart his
campaign against the British, particularly the boycott of British
goods which would 'prove a powerful means of rendering more
acute the British crisis already difficult through the devaluation
of the currency and unemployment'. Whether or not Gandhi
had expressed such sentiments—he denied it to Hoare[42]—he
returned to an India where terrorism was becoming endemic
and became involved in a civil disobedience campaign. Irwin
had been replaced as viceroy by Lord Willingdon. Willingdon was
a law and order man. He did not hesitate to arrest Gandhi and,

with strong backing from the National Government in London, claimed to have suppressed terrorism and restored normal conditions by 1934.

The Round Table Conference met for its third and last session in 1932 but without Gandhi and other prominent men it was of little significance. The initiative had now passed back to the India Office where Hoare, with the help of a team which included R. A. Butler, was trying to draft a new Government of India Act which would satisfy the more reasonable demands put forward in 1931. Even the British government, however, was deeply divided about the form the Act should take. Its most formidable opponents were Lord Salisbury and Winston Churchill. Churchill's opposition was so violent that it alienated him from his own party and made the acceptance of any office in the National Government impossible. It was India that ensured that Churchill was in the political wilderness during the critical days of German re-armament. Whether this political isolation left him free to warn his fellow countrymen of the dangers ahead or merely deprived him of all influence on government can only be a matter of opinion.

The influence of Salisbury and Churchill certainly delayed the passage of the Government of India Act of 1935. A select committee of both Houses of Parliament sat from April 1933 to November 1934. Lord Salisbury was persuaded to become a member of it while its chairman was the future viceroy, Lord Linlithgow, who had previously presided over a Royal Commission on Indian agriculture, but who was in fact a last-minute replacement for Lord Peel who had, briefly, been secretary of state in 1928–9. The committee was assisted by Indian 'assessors', twenty from British India and seven from the princely states. Salisbury drew the proceedings out for as long as possible, insisting on a minute examination of every aspect of what he regarded as a quite impracticable scheme for Indian federation. It was, however, Churchill who delayed the committee's work for two months in the spring of 1934 by arraigning Hoare before the committee of privileges for improperly influencing the evi-

dence of the Manchester Chamber of Commerce. Although
Hoare admitted discussions with representatives of the chamber,
and although he was probably not so innocent as he insisted of
bringing pressure to bear to stop the Manchester men from
'rocking the boat' in the defence of their own interests—they
wanted the resumption of more British control over Indian tariff
policy, the charges of breach of privilege were flimsy ones and
did not stand up. Nevertheless the tactic did cause further delay.
Hoare subsequently bitterly accused Churchill and his allies of
having delayed the passage of the measure so long that it had no
chance to begin to work properly before the outbreak of World
War II destroyed all chance of a deliberate and orderly progress to
independence.[43]

British opinion, however, was deeply divided in 1934 and
could have had no foreknowledge of the events of the 1940s.
The select committee itself only carried its report by nineteen
votes to nine and the minority was divided between five who
thought it went too far and four Labour members who thought it
much too timid. Nevertheless its recommendations were embodied
in the 1935 Act. The Act, a long and complicated one, provided
for a federation of British India and the princely states. There
was to be some measure of responsible government at the centre
although foreign affairs and defence were not transferred to
Indian control. The eleven provinces were to have autonomous
governments with ministries wholly responsible to elected legislatures. Although the provincial governors still had reserve
powers it was made clear that these were now intended for emergency use only. The franchise was widened but, in accordance
with the Communal Award, separate electorates were retained
for the Moslems and other minorities. Churchill opposed the
Act to the bitter end, maintaining that the British had as good a
right to be in India as anybody except perhaps the Untouchables
'who are the original stock'. The British government, he maintained, 'is incomparably the best Government that India has
ever seen or ever will see'. He did not disguise his belief that, if
they were left to themselves, the Indians of one creed would

simply persecute those of another. Clement Attlee, in a more sober speech, criticised the Act from the other side. He feared that it would fail because it would never command the real support of the Congress party.[44]

The first great stumbling block, however, proved to be the attitude of the princes. The idea of the federation of the whole of India was a noble one. There was also, plainly, the political hope that the conservative attitude of most of the princes would act as a useful check on the more radical Congress politicians. In 1935 there were over six hundred princely states with a total population of over 90 million people. Some, like Hyderabad, were bigger than many European countries. Others were little more than private estates of a few square miles. The princes varied as much as their estates did. Some were reforming landlords, who employed able ministers, and interested themselves in the welfare of their people much as the best type of English Whig had done. Others were pathological specimens like the elderly Nizam of Hyderabad who had 'a treasure of jewels in the vaults of his palace too great even to be valued' but refused to spend a rupee on his people, or the sadistic Maharaja of Alwar 'whose continued presence on his throne was thought by many to be an affront to public decency and a reproach to the Government of India'.[45] It had been laid down that the provisions of the 1935 Act concerning the central government should not become operative until 50 per cent of the princes had accepted it. Hoare had believed that the princes would favour a federation. Willingdon had always been doubtful. In fact the princes became more and more distrustful of the intentions of the Congress party and their suspicions were fully reciprocated. Negotiations were long and protracted and were actually broken off in 1939. As a result the 1935 Act, so far as it concerned the central government, never became operative and India entered World War II under the obsolete constitution of 1919.

The new constitution was brought into effect in the provinces and elections were held in 1937. Nehru led the Congress campaign, travelling all over India and addressing meetings that sometimes numbered 100,000 people. These were the ordinary people of India and one biographer, Michael Brecher, believes 'from this experience dates his genuine discovery of India . . . from that time onwards he possessed, in only slightly less measure than Gandhi, a capacity to feel the pulse of the Indian masses'.[46] Congress won a spectacular victory in the 1937 elections. Despite the existence of 'separate electorates', they gained 711 of the 1,585 seats at stake. They had absolute majorities in the Central Provinces, the United Provinces, Bihar, Orissa, Bombay and Madras and were the strongest single party in the North-West Frontier Province and Assam. The only states they failed to carry were Bengal, the Punjab and Sind where there were large Moslem communities. In general, the Congress did even better than its supporters had expected while the Moslem League made a very disappointing showing. A good deal was attributable to the superior Congress organisation but the results had an important influence on Congress thinking. They seemed to have confirmed the Congress view that they were the party of All-India and that the Moslem League or any other organisation which claimed to represent important rival interests was a disruptive and self-seeking body.

The size of their victory presented the Congress party with a dilemma. They had been willing to fight the election to show their strength but many of their members, including initially Nehru himself, had been against taking office and so helping the British to govern. Others, however, felt that they should take advantage of their first real chance of power to bring in reforms which they had been pressing for years. After talks with the new Viceroy, Lord Linlithgow, they agreed to form ministries in seven of the eleven provinces.[47]

Relations between the Congress and the Moslem League continued to deteriorate. Jinnah and the Moslem League refused to concede that the 1937 elections had invalidated their position. On their side the Congress was no longer interested in reaching compromises. In October 1937 Jinnah abandoned any hope of co-operation with the Congress in favour of building up the

Moslem League in opposition to Congress. For the first time the creation of a separate Moslem state became a serious political proposition. In 1933 a group of not very influential pamphleteers had put forward the proposition that Moslems too were entitled to self-determination in a state of their own. They had even invented a name for it—Pakistan, formed from the names of the states they regarded as essentially Moslem, the Punjab, the North-West Frontier Province (Afghanistan), Kashmir, Sind and Baluchistan. No one had taken it very seriously and Hoare commented on the fact that, during all the long questioning to which Salisbury had subjected him before the select committee to prove that federation was not practicable, the issue of a separate Moslem state had not been raised. From this point of view it can be said, as some commentators have said, that Pakistan was the product of the developments of a very few years, that it was brought into existence by conscious decisions by quite a small group of men and that they could have chosen to act differently.[48]

Although this is part of the truth, it is also true that Pakistan was the end-product of a very long historical development.[49] Leaving aside the original Moslem position as conquerors, the basic differences in political and social outlook between the two religions and any British 'divide-and-rule' policy, Professor Bagchi has drawn attention to the growing economic and social disparities between the two communities which underlay the separatist movement. From about 1881 the Moslem proportion of the population increased steadily and substantially. Whereas the 1881 census only recorded 1,974 Moslems per 10,000 of the population, that of 1941 recorded 2,384. 'Thus the population of provinces or districts with Muslim majorities increased in relation to the population of the rest of the country throughout the period under consideration.' But the Moslem regions also tended to be the backward ones and the Moslem community was still suffering from its earlier refusal to accept western education. It was almost entirely Hindu entrepreneurial and professional groups who dominated commerce, industry and the professions and found themselves in conflict with the old Moslem upper classes.

Particular provinces had particular problems. In East Bengal, in the jute-growing region, most landlords were Hindus, most cultivators Moslems. In the Punjab and the North-West, most of the population were Moslem but the traders and, more unpopular still, the money-lenders, were Hindus. Nehru was not unaware of the problem and even admitted that the Hindus had sometimes used their political and commercial strength to deny redress to Moslems but, in Professor Bagchi's view, Nehru was not prepared to contemplate the marked 'positive discrimination' in their favour which would have been necessary to bring the Moslem community on to the same level as the Hindu. The most he would promise was that there should be no discrimination against them. This was quite insufficient to reverse the fact that 'the economic, social and demographic bases for a separatist movement along communal lines among the Muslims grew stronger as the twentieth century wore on'.[50]

In 1939 the outbreak of World War II fundamentally altered the situation. The Indian nationalist leaders were under no illusion about the evils of fascism or the racial policies of Nazi Germany. Nehru had snubbed Mussolini in 1936 by refusing a pressing invitation to visit Rome. Even in 1938 Gandhi had been aware of the enormity of the German persecution of the Jews. He wrote in his weekly paper, *Harijan*, 'But the German persecution of the Jews seems to have no parallel in history. The tyrants of old never went so mad as Hitler seems to have gone ... If there ever could be a justifiable war in the name of and for humanity, a war against Germany to prevent the wanton persecution of a whole race would be completely justified. But I do not believe in any war.'[51] Not all Gandhi's allies were pacifists but most Indian nationalist leaders were bound to be divided in their minds about the war in Europe. They did not want the fascists to win. On the other hand, they could not avoid, like the Irish before them, seeing England's difficulty as their opportunity.

Indian leaders protested strongly that the British government in London had declared war on their behalf without consultation. Although in strict international law there was no alternative to this—when England was at war so were her dependencies—the matter could have been managed more tactfully. In October 1939 the Congress ministries in the provinces resigned *en bloc* and the provincial governors had to take over the administration. On 10 October the All-India Congress Committee passed a trenchant resolution: 'India must be declared an independent nation, and present application must be given to this status to the largest possible extent.' India's future constitution must be determined by an Indian constituent assembly.

The British at first only repeated that dominion status was the goal and that the position should be reviewed after the war in the light of Indian views. In short, the British thought that to raise the whole vast question of India's future in the midst of a life and death struggle in Europe was unrealistic, or treasonable, or both.[52] As the situation in Europe grew worse, as France fell and Britain herself endured the blitz and awaited invasion, the British grew at the same time more reluctant to take big decisions about the future and yet weaker to resist pressures. By a remarkable irony the prime minister in the new wartime coalition government was the Indian nationalists' old enemy, Winston Churchill, while the deputy prime minister was their old champion, Clement Attlee.

On 8 August 1940 the Viceroy, Linlithgow, invited a number of Indians to join his executive council (still functioning under the obsolete 1919 constitution) and promised the establishment of a constitution-making body after the war. He pleased nobody. The concessions were not enough to satisfy Congress which launched a new civil disobedience campaign. Five months earlier at Lahore the Moslem League had adopted as its official policy the setting up of 'independent states' in those north-western and north-eastern parts of India where there was a Moslem majority. Jinnah now demanded that the Moslems should be given an equal number of seats with the Hindus on the executive council. In 1941 the executive council was transformed so that it now consisted of eight Indian and three British members but the Indians on the council had little political backing and what might

once have been hailed as a great step forward now seemed almost
irrelevant.

The situation changed again with the entry of Japan into the
war on the side of Germany and Italy in December 1941 and the
long series of Japanese victories which culminated in the fall of
Singapore in February 1942—probably the most shattering blow
British prestige ever suffered in Asia—the overrunning of Burma
and the threat to India herself. One result of the loss of Burma
was the great Bengal famine of 1943, caused partly by the loss of
rice supplies from Burma but even more by speculation and fear.
The British seemed visibly to have lost one of their still remaining
claims to govern India—the provision of good administration and
the smooth working of a system which at least kept famine at bay.

The attitude of Indian leaders to Japan was more ambiguous
than their attitude to Hitler. Japan was a fellow Asiatic power and,
in their youth, many of them had admired the Japanese victory
over Russia and, still more, her transformation into an industrial
power who could speak on equal terms to the West. During
World War II Japan's treatment of conquered civilian populations was by no means bad, by the rough and ready standards of
war, and there was no Indian antagonism to Japan comparable
to the horror generated in Britain by the treatment of British
prisoners of war. On the other hand there was no serious movement in India actively to throw in their lot with the Japanese.
Japan's cause was not seen as a Pan-Asian one. What Indian
leaders wanted was Indian independence. The Japanese would
have been dubious allies in this ambition. The Indians saw them
rather as simply another source of pressure on the British.[53]

For the British it was above all necessary to keep the situation
in India in hand while they concentrated on their war effort. In
March 1942 a cabinet minister, Sir Stafford Cripps, was dispatched to India with a new offer.[54] Cripps was a man on the left
wing of the Labour party who professed Marxist principles. He
also had a reputation for unimpeachable integrity. It was hoped
that he would win the confidence of the Congress leaders and
of Gandhi in particular. Cripps, however, could only make a

limited advance on earlier offers. He suggested that there should be more Indian participation in government immediately with all the portfolios in the executive council, except defence, entrusted to Indians who should, this time, be chosen in consultation with the political parties. There should be an elected constituent assembly at the end of the war and the British government would undertake to accept its conclusions even if they included secession from the Commonwealth. But Cripps was compelled to insist on guarantees for racial and religious minorities and, more especially, on the provision that each province should be free to choose whether or not it would join the Indian union. Negotiations went on for seventeen days but in the end they broke down. The communal problem was still the great stumbling block. Congress leaders feared that the Moslems might carry the Punjab and even Bengal out of the Indian state, even though these provinces had large Hindu minorities. They put forward the counter-suggestion that control should be handed immediately to an Indian cabinet, nominated by the political parties. Cripps replied that such a body would be unrepresentative, responsible only to itself and unfair to the minorities. He could only reiterate that major changes must await the end of the war.

For the rest of the war the British government continued essentially to offer the Cripps proposals while the Congress continued to reject them. In 1942 Indian leaders even doubted the relevance of negotiating with the British any longer. It seemed more than likely that the whole British position in Asia would collapse before the Japanese. Whether or not Gandhi used the phrase that he was not interested in 'a post-dated cheque on a failing bank', it was a fair reflection of Indian opinion. On 8 August 1942 the All-India Congress Committee passed the famous 'Quit India' resolution. It demanded an immediate end to British rule, the handing of authority to the provincial governments and the summoning of a constituent assembly to decide the future form of the constitution. Congress promised that, if these points were conceded, they would continue the struggle against the Japanese and permit the stationing of allied troops in India.

If they were rejected, they warned, Congress would engage in a 'mass struggle'.[55] Other considerations apart, such an abrupt relinquishment of central authority would have been an unprecedented gamble. Gandhi was well aware of the risks and expressed his views in characteristic terms, 'Leave India in God's hands, in modern parlance, to anarchy, and that anarchy may lead to internecine war for a time or to unrestrained dacoities [brigandage]. From there a true India will rise in place of the false one we see.' It was not a gamble that appealed to the British. The following day, 9 August, the most prominent Congress leaders were arrested. The All-India Congress Committee and the provincial committees were disbanded. Some sporadic rebellion and some sabotage of communications resulted, although it fell short of the mass struggle promised on 8 August.

By contrast, in British eyes, the Moslems seemed almost reasonable. They were quite ready to continue to promise support so long as their pleas for self-determination were listened to. The absence of so many Congress leaders from the political stage gave the Moslem League the opportunity to consolidate its position in the predominantly Moslem areas. Moslem ministries were formed in Assam, Sind, Bengal and the North-West Frontier Province. In September 1944 Gandhi and Jinnah entered into direct negotiations in an attempt to resolve their differences. Gandhi still insisted that India was one and indivisible but he was prepared to offer considerable concessions. Plebiscites should be held in Moslem districts in the north-west and north-east. If the vote went in favour of separation they should become autonomous, although still linked to India for certain purposes of defence, foreign policy and commerce. Jinnah was not prepared to settle for anything less than the total independence of the six provinces, including Bengal, which he regarded as Moslem.

The war in Europe ended in May 1945. In Asia it continued until the dropping of the two atomic bombs on Hiroshima and Nagasaki in August. But the end of the war in Europe brought the promised general election in Britain and the landslide victory for the Labour party, led by Clement Attlee. Negotiations were resumed at a conference held at Simla in June 1945, presided over by Field-Marshal Wavell, who had succeeded Linlithgow as viceroy in October 1943. Invitations were issued to Gandhi, Jinnah, the premiers or ex-premiers of the provinces, various party leaders and representatives of the Untouchables, now officially called the 'Scheduled Castes'. The Congress leaders who were still in prison were released for the occasion.

On the face of it the British negotiating position was very much stronger than it had been in 1940–2. Britain had then appeared to be on the verge of defeat and even annihilation. The question had been whether the British could save themselves, never mind retain a great empire. They were now one of the victorious allied powers, facing no major foreign challenge. They had a great army in being. The strength was, however, illusory and both the British and the Indians knew it. The British economy had been almost destroyed by the war. During the next few years Britain was to be heavily dependent on American aid and no one in an official position in Britain deceived himself that America would help to bolster up a British regime in India. American attitudes to India at this time were ambiguous and ill-defined. Dr Norman Brown makes the point that the American 'image' of India was not particularly flattering but there was a long emotional tradition of anti-colonialism in the United States. Richard Law, the Parliamentary Under Secretary at the Foreign Office, recorded after a visit to America in 1942 that he was constantly being asked about the future of the British empire and about India in particular. American opinion tended to disapprove of the failure of the Cripps mission which they attributed to British unwillingness to grant Indian self-government.[56] Roosevelt above all constituted himself the leader of a campaign for worldwide democracy. After Roosevelt's death in April 1945 some of the fire went out of it and by 1946–7 the predominant American government attitude was a hope that Britain would settle her Indian dilemma quickly.

Expediency suggested that Britain should free herself from what was rapidly becoming the unmanageable burden of India as fast as possible. Ideologically the new Labour government was committed to expediting Indian independence. But the practical difficulties in the way of the liquidation of empire were still great. In August 1945 the British government announced that elections would take place immediately for both the central and the provincial legislatures. As they deemed that it would delay matters too long to bring a new franchise into operation, the elections were to be held on the old, still restrictive, 1935 franchise. Throughout this period the overwhelming desire for a speedy settlement was frequently allowed to override all other considerations. The Moslem League did much better than in the 1937 elections and the election only brought the conflict between the Congress and the Moslem League into sharper focus.

In the spring of 1946 the cabinet mission of Lord Pethick Lawrence, Sir Stafford Cripps and A. V. Alexander went out to seek an agreed basis for negotiations with the Indian leaders.[57] Part of their task was to convince the Indian leaders that the British withdrawal was imminent and that they must come to an accommodation between themselves. Briefly it seemed that an acceptable formula had been found. There should be a federal form of government but the powers of the central government should be severely restricted. Moreover, the provinces should be allowed, if they wished, to merge into groups roughly equivalent to the later India, West Pakistan and East Pakistan. The Moslems were considerably reassured by the proposal but Nehru and the Congress party quickly saw the implications of the 'group' idea and rejected it. Jinnah then withdrew his support from the proposals.

Wavell managed to form an interim government with ministers from both the main communities but Nehru's repudiation of the cabinet mission plan and what the Moslems regarded as unscrupulous Congress manoeuvres connected with the establishment of the interim government convinced Jinnah that the League must show its strength. He declared 16 August 1946 'Direct Action Day'. He later insisted that by direct action he meant no more than rallies and demonstrations but, as Gandhi had discovered in the 1920s, the line between demonstrations and violence is a thin one. The Bengal government, with its Moslem majority, made 16 August a public holiday. Serious disorders resulted, particularly in Calcutta, and at the end of Direct Action Day 4,000 people lay dead. When the constituent assembly finally met in December 1946, the Moslems refused to take their seats. All through the autumn and winter communal violence grew, especially in Bengal, and in February 1947 Nehru insisted that Congress would withdraw from the central government unless the Moslem League ministers were dismissed.

Wavell bluntly told Attlee that Britain had only two alternatives. She must either abandon her attempt to find an immediate solution and resign herself to staying in India for at least another ten years, or she must fix a date for withdrawal and, if necessary, hand over power to the only viable authorities, the provincial governments. Attlee at first rejected both alternatives and replaced Wavell by Lord Mountbatten who enjoyed all the prestige of the successful commander-in-chief of the last stages of the war in South-East Asia. The hard facts, however, remained the same. Britain had neither the will nor the resources to take up the Indian burden again. In any case the process of Indianisation had already gone too far. Almost no recruits had gone out to the Indian Civil Service since 1939 and the administration of India was already *de facto* largely in Indian hands. The alternative of setting a date remained. On 20 February 1947 Attlee announced that the British would leave India in June 1948. In setting such an early date for the British withdrawal Attlee hoped to shock the Indian leaders into a realisation that they must solve their own problems—but that was not the whole of the story.

Britain herself had undergone traumatic experiences in the winter of 1946–7. It had been the worst winter of the century and fuel supplies had almost totally broken down. Food rations, low enough during the war, had had to be further reduced. By the autumn of 1947 the butter ration was down to two ounces a week, the bacon ration to two ounces a fortnight. Even bread and potatoes which had been unrationed during the war were now on ration. It is hardly surprising that when a former member of Attlee's cabinet, Emmanuel Shinwell, was interviewed almost twenty-five years later at the time of the Indo-Pakistan War of 1971 and asked whether the British government had foreseen all the consequences of their decisions concerning India, he replied:

> If I'm asked the question was I intensely interested in self-government, no. I was intensely interested in what was going to happen in the mining industry, whether I was going to get enough coal, what was happening in my constituency because there was too much unemployment and low wages, these were the things . . . this I think to a very large extent affected members of the Labour Party. Very few people took part in the debates on foreign affairs.[58]

In this lay the essential explanation of Britain's precipitous retirement from her Indian responsibilities. Attlee was deeply committed to bringing about Indian self-government but, in the last resort, Britain was too concerned with her own internal problems to care much what the solution was so long as it was a quick one.

A speedy solution meant partition. Jinnah and the Moslem League would no longer consider anything else. Such a decision was most distasteful to the Congress leaders, including Gandhi and Nehru, who still insisted that they and not the League spoke for the majority of the Indian Moslems but they were persuaded to accept it on the grounds that the parts destined to become Pakistan were outlying areas, scarcely more Indian than Burma which was to become a sovereign state in 1948.

A year would certainly not have been too long a time in which to solve the grave problems connected with the partition of a sub-continent which had been governed as a political and economic unit for a century but in June 1947 Mountbatten announced, on behalf of the British government, that the transfer of power would now take place in August 1947, barely two months ahead. Even the selection of the exact date had a bizarre note in it. Mountbatten favoured the 15th because that would be the second anniversary of the Japanese surrender and he felt that it would be a subtle compliment to the million Indian soldiers who had fought under him, but the Indian astrologers gave their opinion that the 15th was an inauspicious day. It was therefore arranged that the formal transfer of power should take place at one minute to midnight on the previous day and the formal celebrations be held on the 15th.[59] The day was greeted with great rejoicings in Delhi but many problems remained unsolved.

There were to be two successor states to British India but how were the boundaries to be drawn? What was to be the relationship of the princely states to the new India and Pakistan? In most cases the boundaries of the new states were to be those of existing provinces but this was not satisfactory in the case of Bengal and the Punjab which did not clearly belong to either India or Pakistan. The decision was left to the legislatures of those provinces which both voted for the partition of their provinces. The actual demarcation into Moslem and Hindu areas there was carried out in great haste by a boundary commission headed by Sir Cyril Radcliffe. Most of the princely states agreed to join either India or Pakistan. The real problem concerned Hyderabad and Kashmir. Hyderabad, where there was a Moslem ruler but a Hindu majority among his subjects, was incorporated into India, virtually by force, in 1948. Kashmir, where there was a Hindu ruler but a large majority of Moslems, is still an unsolved problem, a quarter of a century and three Indo-Pakistan Wars later. To draw boundary lines was hard enough but this was only the beginning. Partition made no kind of economic sense. Pakistan consisted of two distinct areas, West Pakistan and East Pakistan (the latter essentially East Bengal), separated by over a thousand miles of Indian territory. Pakistan suggestions of a 'corridor' between the two met with no response from the Indian side. West Pakistan was not rich but East Pakistan was scarcely viable. It was essentially an agricultural hinterland, producing cotton, tea and above all jute, which was now cut off from its processing plant and its export ports which were all in India, in West Bengal. The division that left the jute-producing areas in Pakistan and the jute mills in India could be paralleled all along the border. The railways and irrigation systems had been laid down on the

assumption that the sub-continent would always remain one unit.
Sir Cyril Radcliffe, despairing of a fair division of the Punjab canal
system, could only recommend, '. . . where the drawing of a
boundary line cannot avoid disrupting such unitary services as
canal irrigation, railways, and electric power transmission, a
solution may be found by agreement between the two States for
some joint control of what has hitherto been a valuable common
service'.[60]

It seemed that partition would only be tolerable if there was a
high degree of co-operation between the severed parts and for a
time the British at least hoped that India and Pakistan might
continue to function as a kind of tacit federation. As a sign of
this it was suggested that Mountbatten might continue as governor-general of both countries. Such hopes perished in the
communal violence of the autumn and winter of 1947. The
violence did not spread all over India. Most of it was confined to
the two partitioned states of Bengal and the Punjab but there it
reached appalling proportions. Sober estimates have put the
dead at half a million. In addition perhaps some 12 million were
made homeless. Some 5 million Moslems fled to Pakistan, about
the same number of Hindus to India. Many of this vast dis-
placed population had to be accommodated in refugee camps, only
to be overtaken by natural disasters, floods and cholera epidemics.
For those British members of the ICS still remaining in India it
seemed like a negation of their life's work.[61] Gandhi, the apostle
of non-violence, was equally appalled and managed by his
presence and example to stem the worst excesses in Bengal. But
Gandhi himself was to be assassinated by a Hindu fanatic in
January 1948. It seemed that the sub-continent had not merely
been partitioned but two irreconcilably hostile nations had
emerged.

Notes to Chapter 7 will be found on pages 248–51.

Conclusion

THOMAS MUNRO had written on the last day of 1824, 'It ought undoubtedly to be our aim to raise the minds of the Indian people, and to take care that, whenever our connexion with India might cease, it did not appear that the only fruit of our dominion there had been to leave the people more abject and less able to govern themselves than we found them.' Had the British, when they finally quit India, left the Indians 'more abject and less able able to govern themselves' than when they assumed power in the eighteenth century?

The British left precipitously under the stress of enormous domestic problems and a greatly weakened world position but the traditions of 'devolution' and the development of self-government and local autonomy were so strong within the British empire that India was well prepared for an independent role in the modern world in a way in which, say, the Belgian Congo was not. There was a comparatively large educated class. Indians already controlled much of the administration and the legal system and had experience of representative government and ministerial responsibility.

Indian development had been lop-sided in some respects and the British were not blameless in this regard. The Indian middle classes included an unduly high proportion of 'intellectuals', of civil servants, lawyers, teachers and doctors, and an unduly low proportion of merchants and entrepreneurs.[1] In part this was due to social factors. To be a lawyer carried greater prestige than to be, say, a small factory owner but the subtle factors that held back Indian investment, and with it the creation of an entrepreneur class, have recently been analysed by Professor Bagchi.[2] Although the experience of different parts of India varied widely

the entrenched position of British banks and of British business-
men may well have been even more important than social factors
in holding back such developments. Nevertheless India did
have a very considerable industrial base on which to build in
1947, particularly in cotton and iron and steel but also in a wide
variety of other products such as aluminium. Dr Misra suggests
that opposition to British rule had welded the intellectual and
entrepreneurial classes together in India to an unusual degree.

Ignoring for the moment the loss of Pakistan, India was able
to function as one political and administrative unit in a way in
which she had never done even in the greatest days of the Mogul
empire. She proved to have an administration adequate for the
needs of, ultimately, over 500 million people. Many difficulties
have appeared. The state boundaries had to be re-drawn in 1956
and regionalism, usually connected with language questions,
became strong again in the late 1960s. For twenty years the
dominance of Congress was so great that India in many ways
appeared to be a one-party state. Yet this was not the case. India
remained a democratic country. It is one of the very few ex-
colonies to have retained genuine parliamentary government and
it is the more remarkable in that it is by far the largest democratic
state in the world with an electorate of over 250 millions. In
1967 the Congress party retained only a small majority in the
Lok Sabha, the lower house of parliament and it lost control of
nine state governments. Two years later, ironically in the midst
of the celebrations of the centenary of Gandhi's birth, the
Congress party split. Serious violence followed in various parts
of India. There were Hindu-Moslem clashes in Gujerat and
Maharashtra and outbreaks by extreme communist groups
(Naxilites) in areas as far apart as West Bengal and Kerala.
Democracy hung in the balance. But in the elections of March
1971, Nehru's daughter, Mrs Indira Gandhi, was able to lead
part of the Congress party to a landslide victory, winning 350
seats out of 523 in the Lok Sabha. The internal political history
of India since 1947 may perhaps demonstrate two things. First,
Hindu India with its great capacity for absorbing alien ideas,

has genuinely absorbed into itself the British parliamentary model. Secondly, many of the tensions within India, regional, linguistic, religious and social, for which Indian nationalists understandably blamed the British, have proved during the ensuing quarter century to be deeply woven into the fabric of India. The British effect upon most of them was probably superficial.

The question naturally arises—did independent India prove to have anything very distinctive to contribute to the world in political philosophy or international relations? Much of the political thinking which evolved in India in the pre-1914 period was a direct reply to the damage which Indian nationalists felt that the British connection was doing to their country. The *khadi* movement, for example, arose from the belief that the British had ruined the native industries of India. Gandhi raised it to the spiritual plane as a rejection of materialism. Yet was India in any meaningful way, more 'spiritual' and less materialistic than the West? There were many elements in Indian life which certainly were not. The Indian princes had often shown a rapacity not normally associated with asceticism. The Parsis had proved to be a very successful and hard-headed business community. The Indian traders who had gone to East and South Africa had certainly not shown themselves to be unworldly. Eastern 'spirituality' existed mainly in western myths. A similar contradiction may be found in the contrast between the picture of 'the mild Hindu' and the acknowledged fighting qualities of the Indian army in many theatres of war. Something may perhaps be explained by the great diversity of India. It would be as absurd, or more absurd, to expect the same qualities and characteristics in a Pathan and a Bengali as in an Italian and a German. 'National characteristics' applied to an area as large as India can only be an unrealistic stereotype. Yet the West did associate India with the emergence of one particular type of political protest, Gandhi's *satyagraha* movement, or non-violent civil disobedience. It is the one Indian political development which has assumed importance in the West in recent years, particularly when racial or anti-war issues have been at stake.

Gandhi's death in 1948 has been seen as fitting, even fortunate, by some of his greatest admirers. His life's work was accomplished. He had roused the Indian masses to a sense of Indian national identity. But he had already, during the critical decisions on partition, begun to be pushed out of decision-making. After his death, the new India paid lip-service to his ideals. The spinning-wheel was placed on the Indian flag. But, in tackling the enormous problems of Indian development and Indian poverty after 1947 Nehru turned not to Indian models but to western and Russian ones of state socialism and five-year plans. The first five-year plan was concerned mainly with agriculture, irrigation and power, later ones more with industry. Some British commentators, such as Reginald Coupland, admitted just before independence that only an Indian government could hope to force through the radical changes, including population limitation, which would be essential for real economic progress.[3] In the economic field, however, as in the political, a quarter of a century of independence has revealed how far the problems lay in the magnitude and difficulties of the task itself rather than in British maladroitness or ill-will. By 1971 India had achieved a growth rate of 5 per cent in national income but $2\frac{1}{2}$ per cent of this was absorbed by the demands of the increased population. Throughout the 1960s India was compelled to accept foreign aid and to raise substantial loans from Britain, Russia and West Germany. Both the foreign and the domestic policies of Nehru and his successors were never entirely free from the need to avoid giving too much offence to foreign banking interests.

It was in the field of foreign affairs that, at first, it seemed that India's, or more specifically, Nehru's contribution might be most distinctive. Here again old belief about British 'crimes' played a part. Too much money, the nationalists had always said, had been spent on defence. Nehru was reinforced in this view by his belief that the Soviet Union had no aggressive intentions against India. 'Non-alignment' was a distinctive policy in the days of the cold war and enabled Nehru to assume a leading position among the statesmen of the Afro-Asian *bloc* and to offer guidance to other newly independent nations. But in the field of policy which most immediately concerns her, in her relations with her neighbours, Pakistan and China, India has pursued policies of a nineteenth-century great power pattern. Relations with China reached their lowest point in the war of 1962. The boundary disputes between the two powers are themselves the legacy of the British period, since the Chinese maintain that the boundaries were drawn to their disadvantage when China was weak and the British empire at its height in India; but India has defended them to the limits of her physical capacity.[4] With Pakistan, Indian policy has been even more tinged with *realpolitik*. In 1948, immediately after partition, she established a military presence in part of the disputed state of Kashmir, which was consolidated in the undeclared war of 1965. She has been deaf to United Nations suggestions for a settlement by plebiscite.

Pakistan's history after independence has been much bleaker than that of India. Jinnah, the real architect of Pakistan, died in 1948. The first prime minister of the new state, Liaquat Ali Khan, was assassinated in October 1951. Pakistan first succumbed to military rule in 1959 when General Ayub Khan combined the offices of president and prime minister, although the outward apparatus of a constitutional state was preserved. For ten years some kind of equilibrium was maintained but in the last resort Pakistan, split into the eastern and western wings by a thousand miles of Indian territory, was probably neither geographically nor economically viable. A further complication was that, although the west, the former Sind, Baluchistan and North-West Frontier Province and part of the Punjab, was almost entirely Moslem— the Hindus having fled during the violence of 1947—the east (East Bengal) still included many Hindus. Ironically, they had been persuaded not to leave by Gandhi himself in his attempts to restore peace there in 1947. In March 1969 serious disorders forced General Ayub Khan to give place to General Yahya Khan, who promised to end presidential government and hold elections

for a constituent assembly. The elections were delayed in East
Pakistan by a series of natural disasters, a coincidence of political
and natural troubles which the British had known only too well.
First there were the serious floods of the summer of 1970 and
then, on the night of 12/13 November the great cyclone. The
elections were finally held in December and gave a sweeping
victory in the east to Sheikh Mujib-Ur-Rahman's Awami League
and in the west to Dr Bhutto's Pakistan People's Party. By March
1971 the Awami League was virtually governing what was beginning to be called Bangla Desh. The Indian government was
sympathetic but anxious not to be directly involved. But the
intervention of the Pakistan army, the wholesale killings, often
of Hindus, in the east, and the flight of several million refugees
to Indian soil brought India to the point of action. By November
there was border fighting in the east. In the first week of December a full-scale, although undeclared war was launched by both
sides on their western frontier. On 20 December General Yahya
Khan resigned in favour of Bhutto. Already, on 6 December, the
Indian government had recognised an independent Bangla Desh.
In January 1972 Britain, Australia and New Zealand recognised
Bangla Desh and Pakistan left the Commonwealth. In April 1972
Bangla Desh was admitted to the Commonwealth.

Britain has played no crucial role in recent events in the sub-
continent. Immediately after independence the future of the
Commonwealth still looked bright. India and Pakistan, to
Britain's pleasure and to some extent surprise, elected to remain
within it. A formula was found to allow them to retain membership even when they became republics—an awkward legal point
because the British Crown had come to be regarded as the symbolic link between member nations. The first generation of African
nationalists also seemed anxious to see the Commonwealth
continue.[5] The 1949 Commonwealth Conference was an
optimistic gathering which saw a future for the Commonwealth
as a genuinely multi-racial body which would unite a quarter of
the population of the world in common traditions and a mutual
desire for peace. It was not to be. The old material ties had dis-

appeared, or at least greatly diminished. The successor states in the Indian sub-continent were drawn into new groupings. While India led the non-aligned nations, Pakistan was a member during the cold war of both the Baghdad Pact and SEATO. More recently India has developed links with Russia, Pakistan with China. To an older generation of Englishmen perhaps the most startling confirmation of Britain's changed role in the world came in 1965 when it was Russia which mediated in the Indo-Pakistan War of that year.

Politically and economically Britain and India plainly interacted in many ways. Culturally, there was surprisingly little influence—leaving aside those obvious British effects in India which may more properly be called political. Both societies had strongly entrenched civilisations when they encountered one another. Historically, great religions have seldom yielded one to another. Christian missions made considerable progress in those parts of Africa where they found only animist and local religions. In India they made little headway against either Islam or Hinduism. In turn eastern religions, including Buddhism, affected only a tiny minority of the westerners who came into contact with them. Similarly India had little impact on English literature. The country inspired some masterpieces, the short stories of Rudyard Kipling, for example, or E. M. Forster's *A Passage to India* but the translation of the Hindu classics, like the *Bhagavad Gita*, although they roused some interest in scholarly circles in England, had little influence on the mainstream development of English literature. Some Indian words, such as bungalow,[6] passed into normal English usage but there was no significant effect on the English language. In the opposite direction the influence was, of course, greater. The mere existence of English as a *lingua franca*—a position which post-independence governments have been unable to eliminate—was bound to have an effect, not only in providing a common means of communication for educated men across the continent, but also in the literature the educated studied and the general formulation of their ideas.[7] But the English impact was probably at least as, or more, important in sending the Indians back to study the origins of their own thought and philosophy and in the resulting renaissance of vernacular literature, particularly in Bengali.

It is impossible to study Indian history without taking account of the British influence. Strangely it is often possible to study British history, even nineteenth-century British history, without taking account of India. A brief mention of the Mutiny and of the proclamation of the Queen as Empress of India and the story is told. Brief reflection should show how superficial such a view is. For a few generations, Britain was not simply a middle-ranking European power as she had been before and as she has become again. She was also the centre of an empire which brought people of many races into close contact. The effect on her foreign policy hardly needs labouring. For generations, events 'east of Suez' were an important element in British policy. The effects on her domestic policy were more subtle. She did not, as men like Hobson feared, become a despot to make the rule of a great empire easier. It is questionable whether ruling an empire drained Britain of talents and enterprise which would have been better employed at home. Proportionately as many men sought their fortunes in India in the eighteenth century when Britain was pioneering the industrial revolution as did so in the late nineteenth century was she was beginning to fall behind Germany and the United States. Only occasionally did India have a direct effect on the British Parliament, conspicuously in the late eighteenth century when Burke feared that the 'delinquents of India' might become the Commons of Britain; more marginally when groups in Parliament, the Irish or John Bright and his friends, took up Indian causes; when Disraeli's flamboyant policies brought thunderous denunciations from Gladstone; or when Keir Hardie and Ramsay Macdonald began to see a common cause of the underprivileged in India and in Britain. Nevertheless, the possession of India compelled Britons to evolve a whole philosophy of empire, from Burke's doctrines of trusteeship, through the application of Utilitarian principles to India, the 'imperialist' doctrines of the late nineteenth century and twentieth-century ideas of racial equality. The British had an exceptionally strong constitutional tradition of their own, reinforced by their dealings with their colonies of settlement. The accidents of history that determined that India passed under British rule, rather than French or, perhaps, Russian rule, at a time when it was extremely unlikely that India would have been able to maintain her independence against the superior technology and organisation of the European powers also meant that India's emergence as a twentieth-century power bore a particular stamp and that her transition from a semi-developed to a developed country (a transition not yet complete) has provided a different model from that of Russia, China or Japan.

Notes to Conclusion will be found on page 251.

Notes and References

Chapter 1 DID THE BRITISH INTEND TO CONQUER INDIA?
(pages 13–51)

1 For the story of Thomas Stephens (or Stevens) see Rawlinson, H. G., *British Beginnings in Western India 1579–1657* (Oxford 1920), 23–7, 34 and *Dictionary of National Biography*, Supplement, iii, 355.

2 Pannikar, K. M., *Asia and Western Dominance* (1953), 11, 27–57.

3 There is a useful summary of modern views on Indian ethnology in Spate, O. H. K. and Learmouth, A. T. A., *India and Pakistan* (3rd ed 1972), 151–3. For an interesting discussion of the development of colour-consciousness see Cromer, Lord, *Ancient and Modern Imperialism* (1910), 128–43.

4 For the old view see Cromer, 119–27; for the new view Spate and Learmouth, 153–8.

5 Zinkin, Taya, *Caste To-day* (1962), 2; for a full modern discussion see Hutton, J. H., *Caste in India* (1946).

6 Moloney, J. C., *A Book of South India* (1926), 106, quoted Spate and Learmouth, 165.

7 Wint, Guy, *The British in Asia* (1947), 41.

8 Basham, A. L., *The Wonder That Was India* (3rd ed 1967), 258–9; Thapar, Romila, *A History of India*, 1 (1966), 68.

9 Quoted Pannikar, 23–4.

10 Hunter, W. W., *The Indian Empire* (2nd ed 1886), 104–9; Basham, 497–8, 500–2, 491–3.

11 Basham, A. L., 'Modern Historians of Ancient India' in Philips, C. H. (ed), *Historians of India, Pakistan and Ceylon* (1961), 269. Dr Thapar goes so far as to say that the Greek campaign 'made no impression historically or politically on India, and not even a mention of Alexander is to be found in any older Indian sources', Thapar, 59.

12 For a new study of the Mogul emperors see Gascoigne, Bamber, *The Great Moguls* (1971).

13 Spear, P., *A History of India*, 2 (1965), 70. This is not the view of some Indian authorities, see p 99.

14 Pannikar, 27–57, 380–5; Boxer, C. R., *The Portuguese Seaborne Empire, 1415–1825* (1969), 41–7, 65–83, 302–3.

15 For the adventures of this quartet see Rawlinson, 27–34; Foster, W., *England's Quest for Eastern Trade* (1933), 79–109; Ryley, J. Horton, *Ralph Fitch, England's Pioneer to India and Burma* (1899).

16 The most accessible edition of Sir Thomas Roe's journal is that edited by William Foster, *The Embassy of Sir Thomas Roe to the Court of the Great Mogul, 1615–1619* (2 vols in one, reprinted Nendeln, Liechtenstein, 1967, from Hakluyt Society ed of 1899).

17 Roe, 110–14, 120–4.

18 See discussion of this in Rawlinson, H. G., 'Indian Influence on the West', in O'Malley, L. S. S. (ed), *Modern India and the West* (1941), 542–3. The probability that Milton knew Roe personally, and had not merely read his writings, springs from the evidence of his poems that he was familiar with the correct pronunciation of Indian proper names.

19 Roe, 110.

20 This was particularly true of François Bernier, who influenced Montesquieu. His work was published in English (trans A. Constable) as *Travels in the Mogul Empire, 1656–1668* (1891).

21 Sutherland, Lucy, *The East India Company in Eighteenth-Century Politics* (Oxford 1952), 9.

22 Quoted Hunter, 365.

23 Sutherland, 6.

24 Furber, Holden, *John Company at Work* (Cambridge, Mass. 1951), 227ff.

25 For details of the 'country trade' see Furber, esp ch 5.

26 For general discussion of this see Pannikar.

27 Harlow, vol 2 (1964), 7.

28 Roe, 344–5.

29 These descriptions of Madras, Bombay and Calcutta are taken respectively from Lockyer, Charles, *An Account of the Trade in India* (1711), 4; Ovington, T., *A Voyage to Surat* (1689), 89–90; and Hamilton, A., *A New Account of the East Indies*, 2, 7–14, all quoted Spear, F. G. P., *The Nabobs, A Study of the Social Life of the English in Eighteenth-Century India* (1932), 3–5.

30 Harlow, vol 2, 10.

31 Macaulay, T. B., 'Warren Hastings' (*Edinburgh Review* 1841), reprinted *Critical and Historical Essays*, 2 (1876), 598; Muir, Ramsay, *The Making of British India 1756–1858* (1923), 2.

32 Nehru, J., *The Discovery of India* (1946), 229.

33 Masani, R. P., *Britain in India* (1960), 7–9; see too F. S. Bajwa's introduction to the 1971 edition of *The Making of British India*, viii–xii.

34 Sutherland, 2; Griffiths, P., *The British Impact on India* (1952), 56.

35 Woodruff, P., *The Men Who Ruled India: The Founders* (1963 ed), 71–5.

36 Hobson, J. A., *Imperialism, A Study* (3rd ed 1938), 8–13.

37 Sutherland, 46.

38 On Dupleix see Martineau, A., *Dupleix et l'Inde Française* (4 vols Paris 1920–8) and Dodwell, H. H., *Dupleix and Clive* (1920).

39 Apart from Dodwell, mentioned above, G. R. Gleig's *The Life of Robert First Lord Clive* (1907) still contains interesting information.
40 Quoted Ramsay Muir, 40–1.
41 See further discussion of this pp 104–5.
42 Barber, Noël, *The Black Hole* (1965).
43 Pannikar, 99–100.
44 Ramsay Muir, 78–81, 92–5. For a more general discussion of the significance of the 'Investment', as the grant of the *diwani* came to be called, see pp 107–13.
45 Spear, *History of India*, 58–60.
46 Dighe, V. G., 'Modern Historical Writing in Marathi', in Philip, C. H. (ed), *Historians of India, Pakistan and Ceylon* (1961), 479.
47 Pannikar, 104–5 but see pp 95–100.
48 Hunter, 317.
49 Harlow, vol 1, 3–6.

Chapter 2 THE BRITISH REACTION TO INDIA
(pages 52–79)

1   There is a good modern study in Mukherjee, S. N., *Sir William Jones: A Study in Eighteenth Century British Attitudes to India* (1968). See also Bearce, G. D., *British Attitudes towards India, 1784–1858* (1961), 20–6.
2   See the discussion of this in Majumdar, R. C., 'Ideas of History in Sanskrit Literature' and 'Nationalist Historians', in *Historians of India, Pakistan and Ceylon* (ed C. H. Philips), 13–28, 416.
3   Gandhi, M. K., *An Autobiography: The Story of My Experiments with Truth* (1966 ed), 57; Woodcock, G., *Gandhi* (1972), 22.
4   For a useful summary see Basham, 5–8.
5   *Observations on the State of Society among the Asiatic Subjects of Great Britain, Particularly with Respect to Morals: and on the Means of Improving It, Written Chiefly in Year 1792* (privately printed 1797), 71. Cf Embree, A. T., *Charles Grant and British Rule in India* (1963).
6   Quoted Rawlinson, H. G., *British Beginnings in Western India, 1579–1657*, 130. Cf Spear, P., *The Nabobs*, 6–22.
7   Dr Fryer, *Travels* (1696), quoted Ramsay Muir, 24
8   For discussion see Sencourt, R., *India in English Literature* (1925), 206–14.
9   Macaulay, T. B., 'Lord Clive' (*Edinburgh Review* January 1840), reprinted *Critical and Historical Essays Contributed to the Edinburgh Review* (1876), 534.
10 Fawcett, C., *The First Century of British Justice in India* (Oxford 1934), 43.
11 For discussion see Cobban, A., *In Search of Humanity: The Role of the Enlightenment in Modern History* (1960), esp chs 14 and 19.
12 Stokes, E., *The English Utilitarians and India*, xiii.
13 Sutherland, L., *The East India Company in Eighteenth Century Politics, passim;* Gleig, G. R., *The Life of Robert First Lord Clive.*

14   For a good modern discussion of this see Marshall, P. J., *The Impeachment of Warren Hastings* (1965).

15   Marshall, 187–9.

16   Speech, 7 May 1789, *The Speeches of Edmund Burke on the Impeachment of Warren Hastings*, 1 (1895), 448–9.

17   Speech, 15 February 1788, ibid, 93–4.

18   Speech, 1 December 1783, *Works*, 4 (1826), 8.

19   Smith, Adam, *The Wealth of Nations*, 2 (Everyman ed 1910), 71–4

20   Cromer, Lord, *Modern Egypt* 2 (1908), ch 61.

21   Woodruff, P., vol 1 (1963 ed), 15–16; vol 2, 75–97. Vol 2 is called *The Guardians*. Woodruff was aware of the dangers of the Platonic concept which could become totalitarian, vol 2, 368.

22   This is controversial. On the one side P. Spear in *The Nabobs* and John Strachey in *End of Empire* (1959) contrasted the equality of the eighteenth century with later snobbery. Strachey recalled that two collateral ancestors of his own, Colonel Kirkpatrick and Edward Strachey, married what would later have been called 'native women' with no ill effects on their careers (55). But Woodruff thinks 'from the earliest days most of the English kept to themselves' (vol 2, 383).

23   Griffiths, P., *The British Impact on India* (1965 ed), 191–3.

24   Pannikar, *Asia and Western Dominance*, 156.

25   See MacDonagh, O., 'The Nineteenth Century Revolution in Government: A Reappraisal', *Historical Journal* 1 (1958), 52–67; Parris, H., 'The Nineteenth Century Revolution in Government: A Reappraisal Reappraised', *Historical Journal* 3 (1960) 17–37.

26   Speech, 1 December 1783, *Selections* (ed A. M. D. Hughes, Oxford 1921), 111.

27   Stokes, xvi.

28   Bearce, 27–33.

29   Ramsay Muir, 9.

30   Aspinall, A., *Cornwallis in Bengal* (1931); Gopal, S., *The Permanent Settlement in Bengal* (1949).

31   See the most important discussion of this in Stokes, E., *English Utilitarians and India*.

32   See Colebrooke, T. E., *Life of Hon. Mountstuart Elphinstone* (1884); Bearce, 128–49; Ballhatchet, K., *Social Policy and Social Change in Western India, 1817–30* (1957), *passim*.

33   Gleig, G. R., *Life of Sir Thomas Munro with Correspondence* (1830); Bradshaw, John, *Sir Thomas Munro and the British settlement of the Madras Presidency*; Stokes, 20–2, 141–8; Bearce, 121–7, 131–49.

34   Stokes, 44–7.

35   T. E. Colebrooke, ii, 72.

36   *Hansard*, 3rd ser, vol 19, 535–6 (10 July 1833).

37   Quoted Stokes, 46–7.

38   Stokes, 55–8; Bearce, 144–8, 282–6.

39   Quoted Ramsay Muir, 298–301.

40   Cromer, *Ancient and Modern Imperialism*, 97–107.

41 Govt of India Resolution, 30 June 1868, quoted Philips, C. H. (ed),
    The Evolution of India and Pakistan, 1858–1947: *Select Documents*
    (1962), 537–8.
42 *Hansard*, 3rd ser, vol 19, 533 (10 July 1833).
43 Pannikar, *Asia and Western Dominance*, 497.
44 Griffiths, 264–72; Wordsworth, W. C., 'The Press', in O'Malley (ed),
    188–220.
45 Menen, A., *Dead Men in the Silver Market*, quoted Bruce, M., *The
    Shaping of the Modern World* (1958), 554.
46 Kaye, John, *The Administration of the East India Company: A History
    of Indian Progress* (1853), 758.
47 Quoted Woodruff, ii, 326.
48 R. C. Dutt called the rani of Jhansi 'the Joan of Arc of modern Indian
    Romance', *Economic History of India in the Victorian Age* (2nd ed
    1906), 28.

Chapter 3 THE INDIAN REACTION TO THE BRITISH
           CONQUEST (pages 80–102)

 1 Taylor, P. Meadows, *Tippoo Sultaun*, *A Tale of the Mysore War*
    (1880), quoted Archer, M., *Tippoo's Tiger* (1959), 9–10.
 2 Sen, S. N., *Eighteen Fifty-Seven* (Calcutta 1957), 8–12, 46; Majum-
    dar, R. C., *The Sepoy Mutiny and the Revolt of 1857* (2nd ed Calcutta
    1963), 433–40.
 3 O'Malley, L. S. S., 'The Impact of European Civilisation', in *Modern
    India and the West* (ed O'Malley 1941), 68.
 4 Woodruff, P., *The Founders*, 327.
 5 There is no up-to-date biography of Ram Mohan Roy although there
    is a study of the Brahmo Samaj in Sen, K. P., *Biography of a New
    Faith* (2 vols Calcutta 1950).
 6 Quoted McLane, John R. (ed), *The Political Awakening of India*
    (Englewood Cliffs, N. J. 1970), 21.
 7 For discussion of this see Griffiths, P., 258–9.
 8 McLane, 1.
 9 Cumpston, M., 'Some early Indian Nationalists and their allies in
    the British Parliament, 1851–1906', *English Historical Review*, 76
    (1961), 279–97.
10 For Bright's particular role see Sturgis, J. L., *John Bright and the
    Empire* (1969).
11 Sturgis, 16–39.
12 Masani, R. P., *Dadabhai Naoroji* (1939), 31–60.
13 Sturgis, 26–30.
14 This changing attitude was reflected in the titles of major studies.
    Sir John Kaye called his classic work *A History of the Sepoy War in
    India* (3 vols 1864–76). V. D. Savarkar called his *The Indian War of
    Independence, 1857* (1909). S. N. Sen contents himself with *Eighteen
    Fifty-Seven* (Calcutta 1957); Majumdar prefers *The Sepoy Mutiny*

and the Revolt of 1857 (Calcutta 1957); Chaudhuri limited his to *Civil Rebellion in the Indian Mutinies, 1857–59* (Calcutta 1957).

15 Palmer, J. A. B., *The Mutiny Outbreak at Meerut in 1857* (1966), 134–7.

16 Most British authorities, eg Roberts, Lord, *Forty-One Years in India* (1900), 241, have accepted that there was carelessness about the materials used but Palmer came to the conclusion (14) that it probably was mutton fat as the authorities said at the time.

17 Palmer, 6.

18 For discussion of earlier mutinies see Majumdar, 29–40.

19 Quoted Cotton, J. S., *Mountstuart Elphinstone and the Making of South-Western India* (Oxford 1896), 185–6.

20 Woodruff, *The Founders*, 346; Majumdar, 36. For a modern view see Cohen, A. P., *The Indian Army: Its Contribution to the Development of a Nation* (Berkeley 1971).

21 Palmer, 58–67. It is possible that, in practice although not in the drill manual, cartridges usually had been opened by hand, Palmer, 12–13, 16–19.

22 Palmer, 95, 104–5.

23 Majumdar discusses Sitaram's testimony at length, 341–50, 367–71, 376–7. For a short, clear statement of British suspicions see Roberts, Lord, 231–44.

24 Sen, 398–405.

25 Palmer, 120–1, 129–34.

26 The handful of European officers who chanced to be in the town made a strenuous attempt to hold the arsenal and blew it up rather than allow it to fall into rebel hands. Five of them received the Victoria Cross, Sen, 67–118.

27 Majumdar, 84–8, 250–69; Sen, 129–37.

28 Sen, 151.

29 Quoted Sen, 415.

30 For a balanced account of 'atrocities' on both sides see Majumdar, 192–222.

31 See for example Russell, W. H., *My Diary in India in the Year 1858–9* (2 vols 1860) 2, 380, quoted Majumdar, 397–8.

32 Sen, 406.

33 Sen, 406.

34 A. K. Azad, Introduction to Sen, xi–xii.

35 Sen, 177–9.

36 *Narrative of Events Attending the Outbreak of Disturbances* (1859), quoted Majumdar, 105; Chaudhuri, 19–20, 278.

37 Sen, 406–7; Palmer, 88–95.

38 Majumdar, 410, following the argument of Sir Syed Ahmed Khan's *An Essay on the Causes of the Indian Revolt* (1860).

39 Sen, 412; Chaudhuri, 273–4.

40 Raikes, C., *Notes on the Revolt in the North-Western Provinces of India* (1858), quoted Majumdar, 396–7.

I

41   Majumdar, 404–8.
42   Majumdar, 395–6.
43   Quoted Majumdar, 395.
44   Chaudhuri, 299; Sen, 411.
45   Azad, Introduction to Sen, xvii–xx.
46   Majumdar, 398–406, esp 400, 403; Chaudhuri, 281.
47   John Greenleaf Whittier was an American poet and a staunch anti-
     slavery campaigner. His Lucknow poem appeared in a number of
     Victorian anthologies.
48   Robinson, R. and Gallagher, J., *Africa and the Victorians* (1961), 8,
     10.
49   Quoted Philips, *Select Documents*, 57.

Chapter 4   DID THE BRITISH CONNECTION DISTORT THE
              INDIAN ECONOMY? (pages 103–32)
 1   Sturgis, 71.
 2   Philips, *Select Documents*, 58.
 3   Dilke, Charles, *Greater Britain*, 2 (1868), 394–5.
 4   Quoted Griffiths, 365.
 5   See Woodruff's chapter 'One of the Worst', vol 1, 104–10.
 6   Quoted Dutt, Romesh Chandar, *The Economic History of India: 1,
     Under Early British Rule* (1968 ed), 26.
 7   In particular Morris, M. D., 'Towards a Reinterpretation of Nine-
     teenth Century Indian Economic History', *Journal of Economic
     History* (1963). This is reprinted together with critical articles by
     Toru Matsui, Bipan Chandra and T. Raychaudhuri in *The Indian
     Economic and Social History Review*, 5 (1968), 1–100, 319–88.
 8   Quoted Dutt, 1, 262–3.
 9   Dutt, vol 1, vii–ix; Dutt, *The Economic History of India: 2, In the
     Victorian Age* (1968 ed), v–ix.
10   Dutt, Rajani Palme, *India Today* (1940), 106, 139.
11   Nehru, Jawaharlal, *The Discovery of India* (1946), 243, 262–3.
12   Griffiths, 360.
13   Dutt, R. C., vol 1, ix–x; Anstey, Vera, *The Economic Development of
     India* (3rd ed 1936), 5.
14   Dutt, R. P., 107.
15   Nehru, 237–8.
16   Misra, B. B., *The Indian Middle Classes* (1961), 7–11.
17   Anstey, Vera, *The Economic Development of India* (3rd ed 1936), 2–3.
18   Marx in *New York Daily Tribune*, quoted Strachey, John, *End of
     Empire* (1959), 48–9.
19   Morris, *Indian Economic and Social History Review*, vol 5, 5–7.
20   Adams, Brooks, *The Law of Civilization and Decay* (1895).
21   Nehru, 247–9; Dutt, R. P., 116–24.
22   Furber, Holden, *John Company at Work* (Cambridge, Mass. 1951),
     304–16. See discussion in Strachey, 61–8 and Marshall, P. J.,
     Problems of Empire; Britain and India 1757–1813 (1968), 92–4.

23 Williams, Eric, *Capitalism and Slavery* (2nd ed 1964). See critique by Anstey, Roger, 'Capitalism and Slavery: A Critique', *Economic History Review*, 2nd ser, 21 (1968), 307.

24 Quoted Griffiths, 397–8.

25 Morris, *Indian Economic and Social History Review*, vol 5, 378; cf Chaudhuri, ibid, 93–4.

26 Thorner, Daniel & Alice, *Land and Labour in India* (1962), 70–81.

27 Sutherland, 36; Furber, 193; Griffiths, 369–71, 391–3.

28 Coupland, *India: A Re-statement* (1945), 53–4; Anstey, 210; Ward B., *India and the West* (1961), 118–31.

29 The documents relating to this most important decision are printed in Keith, A. B., *Documents on British Colonial Policy, 1763–1917* (1953 ed) pt 2, 51–83.

30 Habakkuk, H. J., 'Free Trade and Commercial Expansion, 1853–1870', *Cambridge History of the British Empire*, 11 (1940), 753; Gallagher, J. and Robinson, R., 'The Imperialism of Free Trade', *Economic History Review*, 2nd ser, 6 (1953), 1–15; Harnetty, P., *Imperialism and Free Trade: Lancashire and India in the Mid-Nineteenth Century* (Manchester 1972).

31 Harnetty, 7–31.

32 Dutt, R. C., vol 2, 402–3.

33 India Office Library, *Northbrook Papers*, MSS Eur C. 144, 12. Salisbury to Northbrook, 27 January, 29 September, 5 November 1875.

34 Harnetty, 33; Gujiral, Dalit, 'Sir Louis Mallet's Mission to Lord Northbrook on the Question of the Cotton Duties', *Journal of Indian History*, 39 (1961), 473–87.

35 *Northbrook Papers*, MSS Eur C. 144, 11/12 esp Salisbury to Northbrook, 17 July 1874, 19 February, 25 March, 7, 15 September 1875, Northbrook to Salisbury, 9, 16 August 1875; Christ Church College, Oxford, *Salisbury Papers*, Series E. T. G. Baring, esp Northbrook to Salisbury, 2, 30 August, 12 September, 1875, 7 January, 3 March 1876; Series E, Disraeli, vol 1, Salisbury to Disraeli, Most Confidential, 10 October, Disraeli to Salisbury, 15 October 1875.

36 Harnetty, 33–4.

37 Dutt, R. C., vol 2, 538–40.

38 National Library of Scotland, Edinburgh, *Minto Papers*, Box 229, 'Secret' (ie Private) Correspondence with Morley, Morley to Minto, 3 September 1908, Minto to Morley, 23 September 1908.

39 See for example Greaves, R. L., *Persia and the Defence of India, 1884–92* (1959), *passim*; Harnetty, 59–81.

40 Quoted Strachey, 50.

41 Dutt, R. C., vol 1, viii.

42 Public Record Office, London, *Carnarvon Papers*, 30/6/15, Mallet to Carnarvon, 6 January 1877, Carnarvon to Mallet, 7 January 1877. This file contains a very frank discussion at government level of British attitudes to Indian famines.

43   Ibid, Frere to Carnarvon, 17 January 1877.

44   O'Malley, 271.

45   Griffiths, 405–14.

46   Dutt, R. C., *Open Letters to Lord Curzon on Famines and Land Assessments in India* (1900); Dilkes, David, *Curzon in India*, 1 (1969), 232–3; Woodruff, *The Guardians*, 157–9.

47   Dutt devoted many chapters of his *Economic History of India in the Victorian Age* to detailed analyses of land settlements in different areas. For the argument that taxes were not excessive at the *end* of the century see Coupland, 58–9; and Anstey, 374–7.

48   Quoted Strachey, 48–9.

49   Harnetty, 82ff; Silver, A. W., *Manchester Men and Indian Cotton, 1847–1872* (Manchester 1966)

50   Quoted Woodruff, *The Guardians*, 55.

51   Wingate, G., *Our Financial Relations with India* (1859). On the same theme see William Digby's ironic *Prosperous British India* (1901).

52   Dutt, R. C., vol 1, xiii-xiv.

53   Dutt, R. C., vol 2, 230.

54   In 1970–1 the total Indian expenditure was 3,152.18 crores of rupees: the defence budget took 1,017.84, civil administration 189.70, social and development services 319.85.

55   Dutt, R. C., vol 2, 219.

56   Dutt, R. P., 141–2; Anstey, 144–8.

57   Griffiths, 448–50.

58   Buchanan, D. H., *Development of Capitalist Enterprise in India* (1934); Harris, F., *Jamsetji Nusserwanji Tata* (Bombay 2nd ed 1958).

59   Harris, 219–41.

60   Griffiths, 360.

Chapter 5   DID INDIA DISTORT BRITISH FOREIGN POLICY?
(pages 133–53)

1   Quoted Cotton, J. S., 185.

2   Anderson, M. S., *The Eastern Question* (1966), 391.

3   Cecil, vol 2, 79.

4   Quoted Grenville, J. A. S., *Lord Salisbury and Foreign Policy* (1964), 26.

5   Zinkin, M. and T., *Britain and India; Requiem for Empire* (1964), 40–1.

6   Taylor, A. J. P., *The Struggle for the Mastery in Europe* (1954), 61.

7   Anderson, 390–2.

8   Grey of Falloden, *Twenty-Five Years*, 1 (1925), 6–7.

9   Robinson, R. and Gallagher, J., *Africa and the Victorians* (1961), 21.

10   For all these routes see Hoskins, H. L., *British Routes to India* (1928; repr 1968).

11   Quoted Mowat, R. B., *The Diplomacy of Napoleon* (1924), 57.

12   Quoted Bulwer, Henry, *Life of Viscount Palmerston*, vol 2 (1872), 145.

13 *Hansard*, 3rd ser, vol 132, 141 (31 March 1854).

14 Quoted Hoskins, 142.

15 Robinson, R. and Gallagher, J., *Africa and the Victorians*.

16 Temperley, H. W. V., *England and the Near East: The Crimea* (1936; repr 1964), 4.

17 For full discussion of this see Grenville, 24ff, 74ff.

18 Zinkin, 46.

19 For modern discussion see Fraser-Tytler, W. K., *Afghanistan; A Study of Political Developments in Central and Southern Asia* (2nd ed 1953), 1–14, 139, 299–300; and Alder, G. J., *British India's Northern Frontier, 1865–95* (1963).

20 Salisbury once wrote to Lytton, 'I could hardly speak charitably to Lord Lawrence [Viceroy 1864–9], whom it was my fate to sit next for two hours, when I thought of all the mischief his masterly inactivity had caused,' Christ Church College, Oxford, *Salisbury Papers*, Series E, Lytton, Salisbury to Lytton, 2 June 1876.

21 India Office Library, *Northbrook Papers*, MSS Eur G. 144, 12. Salisbury to Northbrook, 19 November 1875. Cf letter of 12 November saying the large English army needed to watch the Russians in Afghanistan would be a serious drain if troubles developed in the Near East.

22 Thornton, A. P., 'Afghanistan in Anglo-Russian Diplomacy, 1869–1873', *Cambridge Historical Journal*, 11 (1954), 204–18.

23 Hughenden Manor, *Disraeli Papers* (in charge of National Trust), B/XVIII/A. Memorandum by secretary of state for India, 9 December 1867.

24 *Salisbury Papers*, Series E, Disraeli, Disraeli to Salisbury, 24 November 1876, 26 November 1877.

25 *Salisbury Papers*, Series E, Lytton, Lytton to Salisbury, Sorrento, 14 March 1876; Disraeli Papers, B/XX/Ce, Salisbury to Disraeli, 31 October 1876.

26 *Northbrook Papers*, MSS Eur G. 144, 12. Salisbury to Northbrook, 30 April 1875.

27 The text of the agreements is in Gooch, G. P. and Temperley, H. W. V., *British Documents on the Origins of the War*, 4 (1929), 618–20.

28 Greaves, R., *Persia and the Defence of India 1884–1892* (1959).

29 Grey of Falloden, vol 1, 12–14; Gooch and Temperley, 2 (1927), 396–7.

30 Howard, C., *Splendid Isolation* (1967).

31 Grey of Falloden, vol 1, 4.

32 Spate and Learmouth, 182–4; Boxer, 44–5.

33 Mangat, J. S., *A History of Asians in East Africa* (Oxford 1969).

34 Mangat, 39.

35 For discussion of citizenship see Hancock, W. K., *Survey of British Commonwealth Affairs*, vol 1 (1937), 'Problems of Nationality, 1918–36', 591–5.

Chapter 6 THE IMPERIAL PERIOD
(page 154–85)

1 Quoted Philips, *The Evolution of India and Pakistan*, 151.
2 Quoted Dutt, vol 1, 425.
3 Quoted Cumpston, *E. H. R.*, 76 (1961), 280.
4 In a letter to Northbrook on 10 December 1875 he called the Commons 'ignorant and sentimental', India Office Library, *Northbrook Papers*, MSS Eur C. 144, 12.
5 Quoted Philips, 41.
6 Buckle, G. E., *Life of Disraeli*, 5 (1920), 409.
7 See discussion between Lord Cromer, Lord Bryce, J. B. Bury, John Buchan and others on Cromer's *Ancient and Modern Imperialism*, Public Record Office, *Cromer Papers*, F.O. 633/12.
8 Buckle, vol 5, 432; cf Buckle, G. E. (ed), *Letters of Queen Victoria*, 2nd ser, 2 (1926), 278–9, Northbrook to Victoria, 11 August 1873.
9 Quoted Gopal, S., *British Policy in India, 1858–1905* (1965), 121.
10 Moore, R. J., *Liberalism and Indian Politics, 1872–1922* (1966), 14; cf the discussion in Metcalf, T. R., *The Aftermath of Revolt; India, 1857–70* (Princeton, New Jersey 1965).
11 For a modern biography see Maclagan, M., *Clemency Canning* (1962).
12 Metcalf, 134–73.
13 Christ Church College, Oxford, *Salisbury Papers*, Series E, Lytton, Salisbury to Lytton, 9 June 1876.
14 For a discussion of Wood's reforms see Moore, R. J., *Sir Charles Wood's Indian Policy, 1853–1866* (1966).
15 Quoted Philips, 38.
16 See Cohen, Stephen P., *The Indian Army: Its Contribution to the Development of a Nation* (Berkeley, California 1971).
17 Public Record Office, *Granville Papers*, P.R.O. 30/29/132, Hartington to Granville, 11 March 1882.
18 Banerjea, S., *A Nation in Making: Being the Reminiscences of Fifty Years of Public Life* (1925 repr 1963), 9, 23.
19 Gopal, 64–5.
20 Blunt, W. S., *The Secret History of the English Occupation of Egypt* (1907 ed), 59–65; *My Diaries* (single vol ed 1932), *passim*, esp 632–5.
21 Gopal, 116.
22 *Salisbury Papers*, Series E, Lytton, Lytton to Salisbury, 24 March 1876; cf Blake, R., *Disraeli* (1966), 562–3.
23 *Salisbury Papers*, Series E, Lytton, Salisbury to Lytton, 9 June, 7 July 1876.
24 Cecil, vol 2, 68.
25 Wolf, Lucien, *Life of the First Marquess of Ripon* (1921).
26 Sir William Hunter to H. W. Primrose, 28 September 1882, quoted Gopal, 148. See too Gopal, S., *The Viceroyalty of Lord Ripon* (Oxford 1953).
27 Govt of India's Resolution on the Constitution of Local Boards, 18 May 1882, quoted Philips, 50.

28 Ripon's subsequent contention that he expected no trouble is not quite candid. He told Northbrook on 5 February that he had last week brought in a Bill on 'a rather delicate subject' but had so far encountered less opposition than he expected. India Office Library, *Northbrook Papers*, MSS Eur C. 144, 3. Ripon to Northbrook, 5 February 1883.

29 Ripon to Kimberley, 4 March 1883, copy in MSS Eur C. 144, 3.

30 MSS Eur C. 144, 3. Ripon to Northbrook, 20 February 1883.

31 MSS Eur C. 144, 3. Ripon to Northbrook, 5 March 1883.

32 MSS Eur C. 144, 3. John Beames to Secretary of Govt of Bengal, 7 May 1883.

33 The Rev Mr Finter, President of the Eurasian and Anglo-Indian Association provoked loud cheers by saying 'If he [an Englishman] went to Turkey, he found himself there in the arms of his Queen,' India Office Library, L/PJ/3/383, Proceedings of Public Meeting at Calcutta Town Hall, 28 February 1883.

34 L/PJ/3/383, S. H. Phillpots, District Judge, Ahmadabad, to Chief Secretary, Govt of Bombay, 24 June 1883; G. W. Borrodaile, District Magistrate, Broach, to Secretary, Govt of Bombay, 30 April 1883.

35 L/PJ/3/384, Petitions from Bengal Chamber of Commerce, 6 March, 'British-born subjects of Her Majesty the Queen-Empress and Employés of the East India Railway Company', nd, Assam Planters, 23 March 1883.

36 L/PJ/3/384, Joint Secretary, Howrah People's Association to Secretary of Govt of India, Legislative Dept, 26 August 1883.

37 Quoted Gopal, *British Policy*, 153; Dufferin later partially modified his view, ibid, 165–79.

38 Bonnerjee, W. C., *Indian Politics* (1898), quoted Philips, 138–9.

39 Quoted Majumdar, R. C. and others, *An Advanced History of India* (1961), 889–90.

40 There is a useful selection of these resolutions in Philips, 151–6.

41 Masani, 71–84, 96–118; Sturgis, 40–78.

42 Quoted Cumpston, *Economic History Review*, 76 (1961), 297.

43 Gopal, 161.

44 MSS Eur C. 144, 3. Northbrook to Ripon, 8 February, 29 March 1883.

45 Cumpston, 291–2.

46 Masani, 240–85.

47 For a good study of the two men see Wolpert, S. A., *Tilak and Gokhale: Revolution and Reform in the Making of Modern India* (Berkeley 1962).

48 On Tilak's rejection of social reform see Wolpert, 51–2.

49 Quoted *Advanced History of India*, 886.

50 See two recent biographies: Dilks, D., *Curzon in India* (2 vols 1969–70); Edwardes, M., *High Noon of Empire: India under Curzon* (1965).

51 Nicolson, H., *Curzon: The Last Phase* (1934), 12–16.
52 Dilks, vol 1, 95.
53 Quoted Gopal, 298.
54 Quoted Wasti, Syed Razi, *Lord Minto and the Indian Nationalist Movement, 1905 to 1910* (Oxford 1964), 2.
55 Wasti, 1–2.
56 Quoted Philips, 164.
57 Quoted Philips, 162.
58 Quoted Philips, 166–7.
59 Quoted Philips, 187–9.
60 Woodruff, *The Guardians*, 178–9.
61 Quoted Moore, 91.
62 Wasti, 12–13.
63 Wasti, 169ff.
64 Moore, 93–4, 99–101.
65 Wasti, 217–20.
66 Dua, R. P., *The Impact of the Russo-Japanese (1905) War on Indian Politics* (Delhi 1966), 23, 25, 26–7, 32–3, 87–8.
67 Quoted Griffiths, 296. Some terrorism was directly inspired by the Russo-Japanese War, Dua, 75–6.

Chapter 7 THE TWENTIETH CENTURY
(pages 186–226)

1 Quoted Keith, A. B., *Speeches and Documents on the British Dominions, 1918–1931* (1961 ed), 5; for India's role at pre-war conferences see Kendle, J. E., *The Colonial and Imperial Conferences, 1887–1911* (1967). For India's anomalous position in international affairs see The Government of India's Memorandum on the International Status of India, 1929, quoted Philips, 500–2.
2 Quoted Philips, *Select Documents*, 264–5.
3 Ibid, 266–7.
4 Hobson, 113–26, 145–52. For Lytton and Salisbury's exasperation with parliamentary procedures at the time of the Royal Titles Act see above pp 162–3.
5 For the most notorious exposé of the oppression of Indian women see Kathleen Mayo's *Mother India* (1927) which ran through 18 editions in 5 years. Dr W. Norman Brown says it did more to create ill-feeling between India and the USA than any other book, *The United States and India and Pakistan* (Harvard 1963 ed), 364.
6 Quoted Hughes, Emrys (ed), *Keir Hardie's Speeches and Writings* (Glasgow nd), 127–8, 130–1.
7 Hardie, K., *India, Impressions and Suggestions* (1909), 102.
8 Macdonald, J. Ramsay, *The Awakening of India* (1910), 297, 301–20.
9 Iman, Zafar, *Colonialism in East-West Relations: A Study of Soviet Policy towards India and Anglo-Soviet Relations, 1914–1947* (New Delhi 1969), 8–9, 39, 51–66, 145–7.
10 Ibid, 146–7, 436–8.

11 Gandhi, M. K. (trans Mahedev Desai), *An Autobiography* (1966 ed), 4.

12 Ibid, 17–20, 171–7.

13 For the development of Gandhi's thought on these subjects see ibid, 177–9, 267–9, 274–8, 285–7, 358–62, 407–14.

14 Ibid, 231–3. Cf Ronald Duncan's recollections of Gandhi's example at his *ashram*, when Gandhi himself cleared up the excreta round a village well, *Selected Writings of Mahatma Gandhi* (ed R. Duncan 1971), 17–8.

15 *Autobiography*, 34–50.

16 Ibid, 57–9, 101–4, 112–15, 132–4.

17 He wrote in his *Autobiography*, 'Hardly ever have I known anybody to cherish such loyalty as I did to the British Constitution,' 142, cf 179, 261.

18 Ibid, 121–31, 229–31, 238–56, 266–7; Brown, J., *Gandhi's Rise to Power* (1972), 1–15.

19 'The Practice of Satyagraha', extracts from *Young India*, quoted Duncan, *Selected Writings*, 65–76.

20 He wrote 'Let the Jews who claim to be the chosen race prove their title by choosing the way of non-violence for vindicating their position on earth,' *Harijan*, 26 November 1938, quoted Duncan, 82–6.

21 Gandhi, *Autobiography*, 92–8, 160–1.

22 The contrast stands out most clearly between Gandhi's discursive and philosophical *Autobiography* and Nehru's factual and western-style *Autobiography* (1936).

23 Quoted Furneaux, Rupert, *Massacre at Amritsar* (1963), 68. This is the fullest recent account of events.

24 Brown, 293.

25 Gandhi's speech moving the resolution, quoted Philips, 216–18.

26 Brown, 190–229.

27 For his critics see Brecher, Michael, *Nehru: A Political Biography* (1959), 77–9.

28 Philips, 222–4.

29 Six years earlier General Smuts had grimly acknowledged his claims to saintliness. 'The saint has left our shores,' he wrote, 'I sincerely hope for ever'; quoted Brown, 3.

30 Nehru, *Autobiography* (1942 ed), 161–5, 365–9; Brecher, 109–21.

31 The reasons for the decision are discussed in Birkenhead, Earl of, *The Life of Lord Halifax* (1965), 236–45. Simon also left his account of the Commission in *Retrospect: The Memoirs of the Rt Hon Viscount Simon* (1952), 144–56.

32 There are extracts of the Simon Commission recommendations in Philips, 290–2 and from various parts of the Report in Simon, 296–305.

33 Birkenhead, 11–16, 174, although Halifax too found Gandhi difficult to understand at first. He wrote of their first meeting, 'It was rather like talking to someone who had stepped off another planet,' 247.

34 Jinnah's character and motives have been variously assessed. For a
    recent interpretation see Khalid B. Sayeed, 'The Personality of
    Jinnah and his Political Strategy' in Philips, C. H. and Wainwright,
    M. D. (eds), *The Partition of India: Policies and Perspectives, 1935–
    1947* (1970), 276–93.

35 The one argument he had seen in favour of Indians on the Simon
    Commission was that the Hindus and Moslems would quarrel so
    much that they would justify a report that no further constitutional
    advance was possible at present, Birkenhead, 239.

36 Birkenhead, 268–76; Simon, 150–5.

37 Spear supports this view, *History of India*, vol 2, 202.

38 For the charges see Philips, 258–9; cf Iman, 230–1, 297–9, 337.

39 Birkenhead, 291–312; Nehru, 256–60.

40 Templewood, Viscount, *Nine Troubled Years* (1954), 54–60.

41 Quoted Philips, 294.

42 Templewood, 64–5.

43 Templewood, 88–103.

44 Philips, 315–35.

45 Birkenhead, 184–6.

46 Brecher, 227–8.

47 Brecher, 230–31; Glendevon, John, *The Viceroy at Bay* (1971), 49–
    68.

48 For discussion of the deterioration of relations between the Congress
    and the League see Mehretra, S. R., 'The Congress and the Partition
    of India' and Ispahani, M. A. H., 'Factors leading to the Partition
    of British India', Philips, C. H. and Wainwright, M. D. (eds), *The
    Partition of India*, 188–213, 341–5.

49 For an analysis see Hasan, Mumtaz, 'The Background of the Par-
    tition of the Indo-Pakistan Sub-Continent', ibid, 319–30.

50 Bagchi, A. K., *Private Investment in India 1900–1939* (1972), 428–33.

51 Quoted Duncan, 83.

52 Rather later in the war Churchill wrote to Attlee (7 January 1942),
    'I hope my colleagues will realise the dangers of raising constitutional
    issue, still more of making constitutional changes, in India at a
    moment when the enemy is upon the frontier,' Mansergh, N. (ed),
    India: The Transfer of Power, 1942–1947, I (1970), 14.

53 Nehru spoke out in favour of fighting the Japanese but some Indians
    were known to be making preparations in case the Japanese won, see
    for example Sir H. Twynan (Governor of Central Provinces and
    Bihar) to Linlithgow, 15 April 1942, ibid, 782–4.

54 The full story of the Cripps Mission is told in Mansergh, N. (ed),
    India: The Transfer of Power, 1942–1947, vol I (1970). Incredibly
    the British later maintained that they had not seen the possible
    absurdity of sending out the Cripps Mission at the very moment they
    were being 'defeated right and left by the Japanese', Amery to
    Linlithgow, 17 November 1942, 279.

55 Philips, 342.

56   Richard Law's report, nd, *The Transfer of Power*, 2 (1971), 252–6;
     President Roosevelt to H. L. Hopkins (Special Adviser), 12 April
     1942, ibid, 3 (1971), 759; cf Brown, W. N., *The United States and
     India and Pakistan* (1963 ed), 360–9.
57   For a first hand account see Menon, V. P., *The Transfer of Power in
     India* (1957). For the argument that the cabinet mission came very
     close to averting partition see Noerani, A. G., 'The Cabinet Mission
     and its Aftermath', *Partition of India*, 104–116.
58   'The World at One', 9 December 1971.
59   Earl Mountbatten of Burma, 'How Independence came to one fifth
     of humanity', *The Times*, 19 February 1973.
60   Quoted Philips, 680–1
61   For one bitter personal account see Moon, Penderel, *Divide and Quit*
     (1964); cf Woodruff, *The Guardians*, 338–47, 362.

CONCLUSION
(pages 227–35)

1   Misra, P. D., *The Indian Middle Classes: their growth in modern times*
     (1961), 12, 69–210, 307–40.
2   Bagchi, A. K., 'European and Indian Entrepreneurship in India,
     1900–1930', *Elites in South Asia* (ed Leach, E. and Mukherjee, S. E.
     1970), 223; more fully discussed Bagchi, A. K., *Private Investment
     in India 1900–1939* (1972).
3   Coupland, H., *India: A Re-statement*, 62–3, '. . . it lay beyond the
     power of an alien Government to grapple with the root causes of
     Indian poverty'.
4   For an interpretation see Maxwell, N., *India's China War* (1970).
5   See for example Awolowo, *The Path to Nigerian Freedom* (1947), 28–9.
6   A fascinating collection is given in Yule, H. and Burnell, A. G.,
     *Hobson-Jobson: A Glossary of Colloquial Anglo-Indian Words and
     Phrases* (1886; repr, ed Crook, W. 1968).
7   See pp 73–4.

Select Bibliography

Note: Generally speaking I have not listed the standard biographies of English statesmen but I have made a few exceptions to this rule when I have had particular reason to quote or discuss them extensively, eg Lady G. Cecil's *Life of Lord Salisbury* or Lord Birkenhead's *Lord Halifax*.

Adams, Brooks. *The Law of Civilization and Decay* (1895).
Alder, G. J. *British India's Northern Frontier, 1865–1895* (1963).
Anderson, M. S. *The Eastern Question* (1966).
Anstey, Vera. *The Economic Development of India* (3rd ed 1936).
Archer, M. *Tipoo's Tiger* (1959).
Aspinall, A. *Cornwallis in Bengal* (1931).
Bagchi, A. K. *Private Investment in India, 1900–1939* (1972).
——. 'European and Indian Entrepreneurship in India, 1900–1939', *Elites in South Asia* (eds Leach, E. and Mukherjee, S. N., 1970), 223.
Ballhatchet, K. *Social Policy and Social Change in Western India, 1817–1830* (1957).
Banerjea, Sir Surendranath. *A Nation in Making: Being the Reminiscences of Fifty Years of Public Life* (1925; repr 1963).
Barber, Noël. *The Black Hole of Calcutta* (1965).
Basham, A. L. *The Wonder That Was India: A Survey of the History and Culture of the Indian Sub-continent before the Coming of the Muslims* (1954; 3rd rev ed 1967).
Bearce, G. D. *British Attitudes towards India, 1784–1858* (1961).
Bennett, G. *The Concept of Empire: Burke to Attlee, 1774–1947* (1953).
Bernier, François. *Travels in the Mogul Empire, 1656–1668* (trans Constable, A., 1891).

Birkenhead, Earl of. *Halifax: The Life of Lord Halifax* (1965).

Boxer, C. R. *The Portuguese Seaborne Empire, 1415–1825* (1969).

Bradshaw, John. *Sir Thomas Munro and the British Settlement of the Madras Presidency* (1894).

Brecher, Michael. *Nehru: A Political Biography* (1959).

Brown, Judith. *Gandhi's Rise to Power* (1972).

Brown, W. Norman. *The United States and India and Pakistan* (1963 ed).

Buchanan, D. H. *The Development of Capitalist Enterprise in India* (1934).

Burke, Edmund. *The Speeches of Edmund Burke on the Impeachment of Warren Hastings*, 2 vols (1895).

Cambridge History of India (ed Dodwell, H. H.), vols 5 and 6, which also form vols 4 and 5 of the *Cambridge History of the British Empire* (1929, 1932).

Cecil, Lady Gwendolen. *Life of Robert, Marquis of Salisbury*, 4 vols (1921–32).

Chaudhuri, S. B. *Civil Disturbances during British Rule in India, 1765–1857* (1955).

——. *Civil Rebellion in the Indian Mutinies, 1857–1859* (1957).

Cobban, A. *In Search of Humanity: The Role of the Enlightenment in Modern History* (1960).

Cohen, Stephen P. *The Indian Army: Its contribution to the Development of a Nation* (1971).

Colebrook, T. E. *The Life of Mountstuart Elphinstone*, 2 vols (1884).

Cotton, J. S. *Mountstuart Elphinstone and the Making of South-Western India* (Oxford 1896).

Coupland, R. *India: A Re-statement* (1945).

Cromer, Lord. *Ancient and Modern Imperialism* (1910).

Cumpston, M. 'Some Early Indian Nationalists and Their Allies in the British Parliament, 1851–1906', *English Historical Review*, 76 (1961), 279–97.

Digby, William. *'Prosperous' British India* (1901).

Digges, Sir Dudley. *The Defence of Trade* (1615).

Dilke, Sir Charles. *Greater Britain*, 2 vols (1868).

Dilkes, David. *Curzon in India*, 2 vols (1969–70).

Dodwell, Henry. *Dupleix and Clive: The Beginning of Empire* (1920).

Dua, R. P. *The Impact of the Russo-Japanese (1905) War on Indian Politics* (Delhi 1966).

Duncan, R. *Selected Writings of Mahatma Gandhi* (1951; repr 1971).

Dutt, Rajani Palme. *India Today* (1940).

Dutt, Romesh Chandar. *The Economic History of India*: vol 1, *Early British Rule*; vol 2, *In the Victorian Age* (1902, 1904; 2nd ed of 1906 repr 1968).

——. *Open Letters to Lord Curzon on Famine and Land Assessments in India* (1900).

Edwardes, Michael. *British India* (1967).

——. *Bound to Exile* (1969).

——. *High Noon of Empire: India under Curzon* (1965).

Embree, A. T. *Charles Grant and British Rule in India* (1963).

Fawcett, C. *The First Century of British Justice in India* (1934).

Feiling, K. *Warren Hastings* (1954).

Fischer, Georges. *Le parti travailliste et la décolonisation de l'Inde* (Paris 1966).

Foster, W. *England's Quest for Eastern Trade* (1933).

Fraser-Tytler, W. K. *Afghanistan: A Study of Political Developments in Central and Southern Asia* (2nd ed 1953).

Furber, Holden. *John Company at Work* (1951).

Furneaux, Rupert. *Massacre at Amritsar* (1963).

Gandhi, Mohandas Karamchand. *An Autobiography: The Story of My Experiments with Truth* (trans Desai, Mahadev, 1949; repr 1966).

Gascoigne, Bamber. *The Great Moguls* (1971).

Gleig, G. R. *Life of Robert, First Lord Clive* (1848; 2nd ed 1907).

——. *Life of Sir Thomas Munro with Correspondence*, 3 vols (1830–49).

Glendevon, John. *The Viceroy at Bay: Lord Linlithgow in India 1936–1943* (1971).

Gopal, S. *The Permanent Settlement in Bengal* (1949).

——. *The Viceroyalty of Lord Ripon* (1953).

——. *The Viceroyalty of Lord Irwin* (1957).

——. *British Policy in India, 1858–1905* (1965).

——. *Modern India* (1967).

Greaves, R. *Persia and the Defence of India, 1884–1892* (1959).

Grey of Falloden. *Twenty Five Years*, 2 vols (1925).

Griffiths, Sir Percival. *The British Impact on India* (1953; repr 1965).

Grenville, J. A. S. *Lord Salisbury and Foreign Policy: the Close of the Nineteenth Century* (1964).

Gujral, Lalit. 'Sir Louis Mallet's Mission to Lord Northbrook on the Question of the Cotton Duties', *Journal of Indian History*, 39 (1961), 473–87.

Hancock, W. K. *Survey of British Commonwealth Affairs*, vol 1 (1937).

Hardie, Keir. *India, Impressions and Suggestions* (1909).

Harlow, Vincent T. *The Founding of the Second British Empire, 1763–1793*, 2 vols (1952, 1964).

Harnetty, Peter. *Imperialism and Free Trade: Lancashire and India in the Mid-Nineteenth century* (1972).

Harris, F. *Jamsetji Nusserwanji Tata* (2nd ed 1958).

Heber, George. *Narrative of a Journey through the Upper Provinces of India* (1828).

Hobson, J. A. *Imperialism: A Study* (1902; 3rd ed 1938).

Holzman, J. M. *The Nabobs in England: A Study of the Returned Anglo-Indian, 1760–1785* (1926).

Hoskins, H. L. *British Routes to India* (1928; repr 1968).

Howard, C. *Splendid Isolation* (1967).

Hunter, W. W. *The Indian Empire: Its People, History and Products* (2nd ed 1886).

——. *History of British India*, 2 vols (1899).

Hutton, J. H. *Caste in India* (1946).

Imam, Zafar. *Colonialism in East-West Relations: A Study of Soviet Policy towards India and Anglo-Soviet Relations* (1969).

Kaye, Sir John. *The Administration of the East India Company: A History of Indian Progress* (1853).

——. *A History of the Sepoy War in India*, 3 vols (1864–76).

Keynes, J. M. Review of Sir Theodore Morison's *The Economic Transition of India, Economic Journal* (1911), 430.

Khan, Sir Syed Ahmed. *An Essay on the Causes of the Indian Revolt* (1860).

Lewis, M. D. *The British in India: Imperialism or Trusteeship* (1962).

Macaulay, T. B. 'Warren Hastings' and 'Lord Clive', *Critical and Historical Essays Reprinted from the Edinburgh Review* (1876).

Macdonald, J. Ramsay. *The Awakening of India* (1910).

Maclagen, M. *Clemency Canning* (1962).

McLane, J. R. *The Political Awakening of India* (NJ 1970).

Majumdar, R. C., Raychaudhuri, H. C. & Datta, K. *An Advanced History of India* (1946; repr 1961).

——. *The Sepoy Mutiny and the Revolt of 1857* (1963).

Mangat, J. S. *A History of Asians in East Africa* (1969).

Mansergh, N. *Survey of British Commonwealth Affairs, 1931–1952*, 2 vols (1952, 1958).

Mansergh, N. (ed). *India: The Transfer of Power, 1942–1947*, 3 vols continuing (1970–).

Marshall, P. J. *The Impeachment of Warren Hastings* (1965).

——. *Problems of Empire: Britain and India, 1757–1813* (1968).

Martineau, A. *Dupleix et l'Inde Française*, 4 vols (Paris 1920–8).

Masani, R. P. *Dadabhai Naoroji* (1939).

——. *Britain in India* (1960).

Maxwell, N. *India's China War* (1970; new ed 1972).

Mayo, Kathleen. *Mother India* (1927).

Menon, V. P. *The Transfer of Power in India* (1957).

Metcalf, T. R. *The Aftermath of Revolt, 1857–70* (NJ 1965).

Misra, B. B. *The Indian Middle Classes: Their Growth in Modern Times* (1961).

Mitra, Dina Bandhu. *The Mirror of Indigo* (trans Long, James 1860).

Moon, Penderel. *Divide and Quit* (1964).

Moore, R. J. *Liberalism and Indian Politics, 1872–1922* (1966).

——. *Sir Charles Wood's Indian Policy, 1853–1866* (1966).

Moreland, W. E. *India at the Death of Akbar* (1920).

Morris, M. D. 'Towards a Reinterpretation of Nineteenth Century Indian Economic History' (first published *Journal of Economic History* 1963); repr with replies by Toru Matsui, Bipan Chandra and T. Raychaudhuri, *Indian Economic and Social History Review*, 5 (1968), 1–100, 319–88.

Mowat, R. B. *The Diplomacy of Napoleon* (1924).

Muir, Ramsay. *The Making of British India, 1756–1858* (1923; repr with introduction by F. S. Bajwa, Delhi 1971).

Mukherjee, S. N. *Sir William Jones: A Study in Eighteenth Century British Attitudes to India* (1968).

Mun, Thomas. *A Discourse of Trade from England into the East Indies* (1621).

Naoroji, Dadabhai. *The Poverty of India* (1878).

——. *Poverty and Un-British Rule in India* (1901).

Nehru, Jawaharlal. *Autobiography: Towards Freedom* (1936; rev ed 1942).

——. *The Discovery of India* (1946).

O'Malley, L. S. S. *The Indian Civil Service* (1931).

——. *Modern India and the West* (1941).

Palmer, J. A. B. *The Mutiny Outbreak at Meerut in 1857* (1966).

Pandey, B. N. *The Break Up of British India* (1969).

Pannikar, K. M. *Asia and European Dominance* (1953).

Philips, C. H. *The East India Company, 1784–1834* (1940; repr 1961).

——. *The Evolution of India and Pakistan, 1858–1947* (Select Documents on the History of India and Pakistan, vol 4, 1962).

Philips, C. H. (ed). *Historians of India, Pakistan and Ceylon* (1961).

Philips, C. H. and Wainwright, M. D. (eds). *The Partition of India: Policies and Perspectives, 1935–1947* (1970).

Piggott, Stuart. *Prehistoric India* (1950).

Raikes, C. *Notes on the Revolt in the North-Western Provinces of India* (1858).

Rawlinson, H. G. *British Beginnings in Western India, 1579–1657: An Account of the Early Days of the British Factory of Surat* (1920).

Roberts, Lord. *Forty-One Years in India: From Subaltern to Commander-in-Chief* (1900).

Robinson, R. and Gallagher, J. *Africa and the Victorians: The Official Mind of Imperialism* (1961).

Roe, Sir Thomas (ed Foster, William). *The Embassy of Sir Thomas Roe to the Court of the Great Mogul, 1615–1619* (2 vols in one, repr Nendeln, Liechtenstein, 1967, from the Hakluyt Society ed of 1899).

Russell, W. H. *My Diary in India in the Year 1858–9*, 2 vols (1860).

Ryley, J. Horton. *Ralph Fitch, England's Pioneer to India and Burma* (1899).

Savarkar, V. D. *The Indian War of Independence, 1857* (1909).

Scott, W. R. *The Constitution and Finance of English, Scottish and Irish Joint Stock Companies to 1720*, 2 vols (1910–12).

Sen, K. P. *Biography of a New Faith* (1950).

Sen, S. N. *Eighteen Fifty Seven* (1957).

Sencourt, R. *India in English Literature* (1925).

Silver, A. W. *Manchester Men and Indian Cotton, 1847–1872* (1966).

Simon, Viscount. *Retrospect: The Memoirs of the Rt Hon Viscount Simon* (1952).

Sittaramaya, B. P. *History of the Indian National Congress*, 2 vols (Madras 1935, 1947).

Spate, O. H. K. & Learmouth, A. T. A. *India and Pakistan: A General and Regional Geography* (1954; new ed 1972).

Spear, T. G. P. *The Nabobs, a Study of the Social Life of the English in Eighteenth-Century India* (1932).

——. *A History of India*, vol 2 (1965).

Stokes, Eric. *English Utilitarians and India* (Oxford 1959).

Strachey, John. *End of Empire* (1959).

Sturgis, J. L. *John Bright and the Empire* (1969).

Sutherland, L. S. *The East India Company in Eighteenth-Century Politics* (Oxford 1952).

Taylor, A. J. P. *The Struggle for the Mastery in Europe* (1954).

Taylor, P. Meadows. *Tipoo Sultaun: A Tale of the Mysore War* (1880).

Temperley, H. W. V. *England and the Near East: The Crimea* (1936; repr 1964).

Templewood, Viscount (Samuel Hoare). *Nine Troubled Years* (1954).

Thapar, Romila. *A History of India*, vol 2 (1966).

Thompson, E. & Garratt, G. T. *The Rise and Fulfilment of British Rule in India* (1935).

Thorner, Daniel and Alice. *Land and Labour in India* (Bombay 1962).

Thornton, A. P. 'Afghanistan in Anglo-Russian Diplomacy, 1869–1873', *Cambridge Historical Journal*, 11 (1954), 204–18.

Tinker, H. *India and Pakistan: A Short Political Guide.*

Ward, Barbara. *India and the West* (1961).

Wasti, S. R. *Lord Minto and the Indian Nationalist Movement, 1905 to 1910* (1964).

Williams, Eric. *Capitalism and Slavery* (2nd ed 1964).

Wingate, Sir George. *Our Financial Relations with India* (1859).

Wint, Guy. *The British in Asia* (1947).

Wolpert, S. A. *Tilak and Gokhale: Revolution and Reform in the Making of Modern India* (1962).

Woodcock, George. *Gandhi* (1972).

Woodruff, Philip (pseud of Mason, P.) *The Men Who Ruled India*, vol 1, *The Founders* (1953); vol 2, *The Guardians* (1954); new ed 1963.

Yule, H. & Burnell, A. G. *Hobson-Jobson: A Glossary of Colloquial Anglo-Indian Words and Phrases* (1886; repr ed Crook, W., 1968).

Zinkin, M. & T. *Britain and India: Requiem for Empire* (1964).

Zinkin, Taya. *Caste Today* (1962).

Index